BRITAIN'S ORCHIDS

A field guide to the orchids of Great Britain and Ireland

Sean Cole and Mike Waller

Artwork by Sarah Stribbling

WILDGuides

PRINCETON
press.princeton.edu

Published by Princeton University Press,
41 William Street, Princeton, New Jersey 08540
In the United Kingdom: Princeton University Press, 6 Oxford Street,
Woodstock, Oxfordshire OX20 1TR
press.princeton.edu

British Library Cataloging-in-Publication Data is available

Library of Congress Control Number 2020930979
ISBN 978-0-691-17761-8
Ebook ISBN 978-0-691-20647-9

Production and design by **WILD***Guides* Ltd., Old Basing, Hampshire UK.
Printed in Italy

10 9 8 7 6 5 4 3 2 1

Contents

Acknowledgements

This book is the sum of not just our own field experience, but also that of many others who have helped us since we became interested in orchids. Many people have freely shared their knowledge, time, research and opinions over this period and we are extremely grateful to all of them.

We would firstly like to thank our good friend James Lowen, without whom this book would never have got off the ground, and Robert Kirk at Princeton University Press, and both Rob Still and Andy Swash at **WILD***Guides*, for believing in us enough to commission the book. Rob has also been instrumental in ensuring the book fulfils our expectations and looks as fantastic as we had hoped. Sarah Stribbling has produced a set of truly stunning illustrations and we thank her for her resilience and patience throughout the process. Our thanks also to Sally MacGill for copy-editing the original text, Chris and Jude Gibson for their thorough review, technical edit and proofreading, and to Brian Clews and Gill Swash for proofreading and checking. Our respective partners, Trudy Cole and Sophie Binder, have likewise been extremely tolerant of our multiple lengthy field excursions and the subsequent screen time spent processing images, writing, and doing preparation work, as well as putting up with the project being a constant topic of conversation! Mike would like to also thank his mother, Jenny Waller, for her tireless support of his interest in the early years, selflessly driving him to far-flung locations in the pursuit of orchids.

Along the way, several other people were key to ensuring the accuracy and veracity of many topics, namely: Neil Barrett, Prof. Richard Bateman, Jean Claessens, Jacques Kleynen, Andy Byfield, Sophie Lake, Brian Laney, Les Lewis, Mark Lynes, Rich Mielcarek and Terry Swainbank. The text in the book is also so much better for the proofreading that Prof. Ian Howarth undertook so generously and professionally.

Kevin Walker and the Botanical Society of Britain & Ireland (BSBI) have been extremely generous in providing maps and other statistical data, along with a number of specific datasets from BSBI county recorders. The Hardy Orchid Society also gave us much useful information. Further advice and information was provided by: Roy Frost, Alan Gendle, Graham Giles, Uwe Grabner, Simon Harrap, Chris Hazell, Gareth Knass, Rainar Kurbel, Byron Machin and Steve Povey.

Excellent quality photographs for reference or use in the book were generously contributed by many people. A full list of the 60 photographers who kindly provided images is given on *page 284*. Special thanks also go to the Natural History Museum for permitting us to use their excellent photo-stacking equipment for some of the *Epipactis* images.

The following people also helped in various other ways to enable this book to be what it is: David Armstrong, Kath Castillo, Mike Chalk, Lorne Edwards, Richard Evans, David & Frances Farrell, Mike Gasson, Chris Gladman, David Gray, Michelle Green, Jonathan and Sarah Greenwood, Simon Harrap, Ian Howarth, James Hunter, Andy Jones, Mick Lacey, Paul Lambourne, David Lang, Jim and Dawn Langiewicz, Tad Lapper, Steff Leese, Louise Marsh, Mark Meijrink, Mike Parsons, Chris Raper, Juliet Regan, Tristan Reid, Tim Rich, Martin Roome, Fred Rumsey, Alan Smith, John Spencer, Mark Spencer, Jess Stone, Steve Tandy, Barry Tattershall, Rob Thatcher, Gerry Trask, John Tweddle, Rosemary Winnall, Kate Woollen and Bryan Yorke.

Finally, a number of people have requested not to be named as some very rare orchids occur on their land. We thank them sincerely for access to see these beautiful and special plants.

Sean Cole and Mike Waller, July 2020

Preface

For centuries, orchids have represented the most coveted group of all plants; their beauty, complexity and rarity has captivated the unwavering fascination of naturalists, botanists and horticulturists alike. Charles Darwin himself was intrigued by orchids and in the mid-19th century studied their highly developed pollination mechanisms to help him understand the intricacies of evolution.

This book is the result of a shared passion for orchids. Its content is the accumulation of the authors' combined 35 years of field experience and engagement with a diverse community of botanists, naturalists, conservationists and people who simply have a love of wild orchids.

Increased interest in the environment and the prevalence of social media have resulted in an explosion of interest in wild orchids. Each spring and summer, more and more people are taking to social media to share their orchid photographs and ask for help with identification, highlighting the need for a new and comprehensive overview of the subject.

We hope that this book will help those interested in orchids to find and identify these beautiful plants, and in turn also engender both a greater interest in the botanical world, and in wildlife conservation in general. Its aim is to make the identification of any wild British or Irish orchid quick and easy, taking you through logical steps to arrive at a species, or where appropriate at a subspecies, variety or hybrid. For the first time, this book will help you to identify orchids at all stages of above-ground development, with a dedicated section on identifying orchids when they are in leaf.

The pale lilac, round-topped spikes of Heath-spotted Orchid are prominent in damp heathlands, especially in the north and west.

Using this book

This book aims to provide the tools for anyone interested in orchids, whatever their level of expertise or experience, to improve their knowledge and enjoyment of these beautiful plants.

The focus is on the identification of orchids at all stages of their life-cycle, from vegetative through to seed, as well as information to assist in the identification of hybrids. In addition, tips for finding orchids are given throughout, in an attempt to encourage wider searches in locations beyond the many well-known and 'traditional' orchid sites.

The book covers 51 regular and 12 adventive species, 11 subspecies/varieties, 4 forms and 54 hybrids, most of which are illustrated with high quality photographs and botanical artwork.

As far as possible, technical terms have been avoided, although those that are used are explained in a *Glossary* (*p. 10*).

INTRODUCTORY SECTIONS

What is an orchid (*p. 12*) is a brief summary of the plants, their morphology, natural history and life-cycle, including their relationship with fungi and pollination strategies.

Orchid taxonomy (*p. 18*) is a very important section that defines the conservative position adopted in this book (see also *English and scientific names* opposite), with a detailed explanation of the reasoning behind the position taken and supporting references from the latest research.

Habitats (*p. 24*) covers the main broad habitats in which orchids are found, using photographs and a brief description of the habitat and its typical orchids.

Finding orchids (*p. 35*) offers some tips and caveats for the orchid hunter, together with a photographic collection of orchids in typical habitats, annotated with information that may help when searching for any given species.

IDENTIFYING ORCHIDS

A step-by-step guide, with caveats, to the identification of orchids when **vegetative (in leaf)**, **in bud** and **in flower**. These sections present information on differentiating orchids from similar-looking non-orchid plants, as well as introducing caveats with respect to hybrids and variation before presenting a guide to identification.

Vegetative/in bud sections (*pp. 52–79*)
A broad identification key, together with annotated photographs of the leaves of most species, and scaled illustrations of the buds arranged for ease of comparison.

In flower (*pp. 80–100*)
A detailed key that results in a direction to the relevant species account(s) for confirmation and further information. There is also a set of illustrated plates that depict typical examples, in terms of colour and average size, of similar-looking species together, to scale, which can be used as an initial comparison guide if required.

A note about size and scale (see also *p. 35*)
Size is not a primary identification feature for most species as there is considerable variation in size within species. However, in the species accounts a typical recorded height (with extreme maximum recorded given in brackets) is provided as a guide. There is also a ruler provided on both cover flaps for convenience. Where helpful, a '20p' icon is shown for scale: a 20p coin has a diameter of 21·4 mm and is therefore effectively a 2 cm scale marker for the purposes of this book.

'20p' icon at actual size

English and scientific names
Unless otherwise qualified, the English and *scientific* (in italics) names used for the orchids (and all other plants) in this book follow the standard names used in *New Flora of the British Isles*, 4th edition (2019) by Clive Stace.

SPECIES ACCOUNTS – see also *p. 101*

Species Each species is covered in full with an illustration of a flowering plant, and photographs, where appropriate, of the plants in bud and in seed as well as in flower – these typically show the whole plant in its habitat, and close-ups of the inflorescence and individual flowers. The illustrations are annotated with key identification features, as are some photographs where useful. The GB Red List and Irish Red List statuses are given (see *p. 280*).

Phenology Each species has a chart that is divided into 52 weeks, with broad month markers. The charts indicate for both Britain and Ireland when a species may be seen at each stage of development. For many there are times when both in-leaf and flowering individuals are indicated as 'can be seen'. These may or may not be within a single colony, and are more likely to indicate different areas of the country. Orchid flowering times throughout the region can vary from season to season depending on a range of consistent and variable factors and, as such, these charts should only be used as a guide – see *When flowering* (*p. 36*) for more information on these factors.

Distribution Each species has a map, showing recent, rather than historical, distribution, based on data from the Botanical Society of Britain & Ireland (BSBI) covering the period 2000–2019. The maps should be used as a guide only and, as such, not regarded as indicative of a species being present or absent in a particular area. Furthermore, and for obvious reasons, the locations given for rarer species are not precise. Where useful the maps also give an indication of any consistent regional variance in flowering, which may be down to location or ecotype – see *When flowering* (*p. 36*).

Detailed identification Where useful, introductory sections for some taxa are provided, together with a detailed guide to those species that are more difficult to identify.

Taxonomy and variation Where applicable, subspecies, varieties and forms are covered, with an explanation for the approach taken (see also *Orchid taxonomy* opposite). It is impossible and counter-productive to show the full range of variation, so photographs have been chosen that show both the extremes and selected intermediate examples of the range of variation that may be encountered.

HYBRIDS

All known, confirmed hybrids are covered, most with photographs of the plant concerned as well as the parent species, with text and annotations that may help in the often difficult, sometimes impossible, challenge of identifying hybrids in the field. A selection of older records, including some that have been re-identified as not being hybrids, is included for completeness.

SUPPLEMENTARY SECTIONS

Extinct/adventive species (*p. 274*) provides brief information, with some photographs, on those native species that are considered extinct, as well as species that have been recorded but are of dubious or unknown origin. **Threats and conservation (*p. 280*)** gives an overview, with some examples, of the latest situation relating to orchids, including current blanket and specific legislation, together with a **List of British and Irish orchids (*p. 282*)**, which includes the recognized subspecies, varieties and forms, that summarizes their Red List status and any associated specific legislation. **References (*p. 285*)**, **Sources of further information (*p. 286*)** and an **Index (*p. 287*)** complete the book.

Glossary

There are inevitably some technical terms used when referring to particular features of an orchid or its habitat, taxonomy and 'lifestyle'. These terms are defined below and highlighted in **bold text** where first used in the book.

acid	water or soils with a **pH** value less than 7
alkaline	water or soils with a **pH** value greater than 7
back-cross	where a species hybridizes with one of its own, or another's, **hybrid** offspring. Also known as an 'F2' or second-generation hybrid.
bosses	raised areas at the base of the outer lip on the flowers of some *Epipactis* helleborines
bulbil	minute bulb-like growth on the outer rim of leaves that falls off and produces a new plant
bract	a modified leaf at the base of the flower where it joins the stem, often smaller than foliage leaves
bracteoidal leaf	small leaf structures clasping the stem between the main foliage leaves and the flower stem
calcareous	soil that is partly or mostly composed of calcium carbonate, meaning it is **alkaline** (**pH** value greater than 7)
cilia	tiny tooth-like structures along the leaf margin
discrete (features)	feature with distinct boundary, rather than being part of a range or continuum
discrete (population)	a group of individuals of the same **taxon** that exist in a population of their own, rather than mixing with others of a similar/related taxon
DNA	deoxyribonucleic acid, a long molecule that contains the genetic code
downland	an area of open chalk hills. This term is especially used to describe the chalk countryside in southern England. Areas of downland are often referred to as downs
endemic	native and restricted to a defined area
epichile	outer part of lip on *Epipactis* helleborines
epiphyte	a plant that grows on another plant
family (taxonomy)	a major **taxonomic** rank of organisms, below an order and above **genus**
flush	an area where water from under ground flows out onto the surface to create an area of saturated ground, rather than a well-defined channel
form, forma, (f.)	the taxonomic rank below **variety** (**var.**), classifying a variance from the normal appearance of a species – *e.g.* in colour such as the white-flowered forms of various species
genus [pl. genera]	a major **taxonomic** category of organisms that ranks above **species** and below **family**
'glue blob'	a sticky pad located at the base of the pollinia that enables the pollinia to become attached to a pollinating insect
gryke	deep fissure between blocks of limestone pavement
'hair'	a cellular structure on the lips of some orchid species that look like hairs
hedgebank	an earth or rubble bank topped with shrubs and occasional trees, forming a hedge at the top, often alongside a road or lane
hybrid	an individual resulting from a cross between two **species**

hybrid swarm	a colony of orchids formed mainly or exclusively by hybrids of various generations
hypochile	cup-shaped inner part of lip of *e.g.* the *Epipactis* helleborines
labellum	the lip of the flower (in most orchids, the lower of the three petals)
lax	loosely spaced (flowers or leaves on a stem)
lowland	land that is < 200 m above sea level – see **upland**
morphology	the form, shape or structure of the plant or parts of it (hence the term morphological differences)
mycorrhiza [pl. mycorrhizae]	underground fungal network that provides nutrition to orchids
neutral	water or soils with a **pH** value of 7; neither **acid** nor **alkaline**
nominate	the **species** or **subspecies** that is the same name as the genus or species respectively (this is usually the first form described)
ovary	the part of the female organ of the flower where the seeds develop following fertilization; the ovary connects the flower to the stem.
pH	scale that gives a measure of the **alkalinity** (greater than 7) or **acidity** (less than 7); pH 7 is **neutral**
pollinium [pl. pollinia]	a coherent mass of pollen grains on a single flower that are usually transferred as a single unit, except on self-pollinated species
raceme	an inflorescence with flowers attached to the stem by stalks; a raceme flowers from the base upwards (the oldest flowers at the bottom) – see **spike**
rosette	group of leaves arranged around the base of a stem, often flat on the ground
speciation	the process of becoming a **species**
species (sp.) [pl. spp.]	the basic unit of **taxonomic** classification that describes a group of similar organisms which have similar genes and are capable of interbreeding and producing viable offspring
speculum	shiny bluish pattern on the lip of the *Ophrys* orchids, evolved to mimic the wings of a female wasp or bee
spike	a form of **raceme** inflorescence in which the flowers are unstalked – *i.e.* attached directly to the stem
subspecies (ssp.)	a division of a **species**, distinguished by only very slight variation that is insufficient to afford it the rank of species
taxon (pl. taxa)	a general term for a unit of biological classification (*e.g.* a **family**, **genus** or **species**)
taxonomy	the science of classifying groups of organisms (such as **species**, **subspecies**) based on their relatedness. This is most effectively done using a combination of laboratory study using **DNA** and in-field studies of the plants themselves using measurements of multiple individuals over multiple populations.
upland	land that is > 200 m above sea level – see **lowland**
variety (var.) (taxonomy)	a distinguishable form of a plant, with no or minimal genetic differences, that occurs with consistency within a **species**
vegetative	relating to the green, mainly leafy parts of a plant (*i.e.* the parts other than the flowers)
viscidium	see **'glue blob'**

What is an orchid?

Orchids are the most biologically diverse **family** of flowering plants in the world, with an estimated 27,000 species. The vast majority are **epiphytes**, growing high up in the canopy of tropical forests, but in temperate regions like Britain and Ireland, orchids grow on the ground. Many species are highly specialized and require specific conditions to thrive, although some are much less demanding and can be very common in a wide range of habitats. As with any family of plants, there are specific 'lifestyle' and structural traits that define orchids – most notably the special relationship they have with fungi, which to this day remains mysterious and hard to fathom.

Photosynthesis and the relationship with fungi

The orchid germination process is unique. Most flowering plants produce seeds pre-packed with protein to enable the embryonic plant to grow if in a suitable location. Orchids, however, produce tiny seeds that have no energy reserves and instead rely on a **mycorrhizal** relationship with particular species of fungi to provide the nutrients they need to germinate. This relationship between orchids and fungi is one of the key factors that has enabled orchids to conquer a very wide range of nutrient- and light-poor habitats, where other plants struggle to survive.

Bird's-nest Orchid

As they mature, most orchids begin to generate their own nutrients through photosynthesis, with continued support from their fungal 'partner', although the extent of this reliance varies widely between species. One species – Coralroot Orchid – has a small amount of chlorophyll that enables limited photosynthesis when in bloom, but is otherwise reliant on fungi that can be found clustered at its base. Two species – Bird's-nest Orchid and Ghost Orchid – completely lack chlorophyll and as such are unable to photosynthesize. They are therefore totally dependent upon a fungal relationship to sustain their entire life-cycle, with these fungal 'partners' in turn extracting nutrients from *e.g.* nearby tree roots. This does, however, give these orchids the advantage of being able to grow largely unchallenged in the darkest parts of woodlands. Until recently it was assumed that the relationship between orchids and mycorrhizal fungi was mutually beneficial, or symbiotic. However, in the case of the two species mentioned above, which produce no food, it is hard to see what the fungi stand to gain: it seems more likely that the orchids parasitize the fungi, hijacking their white, root-like hyphae for their own gain.

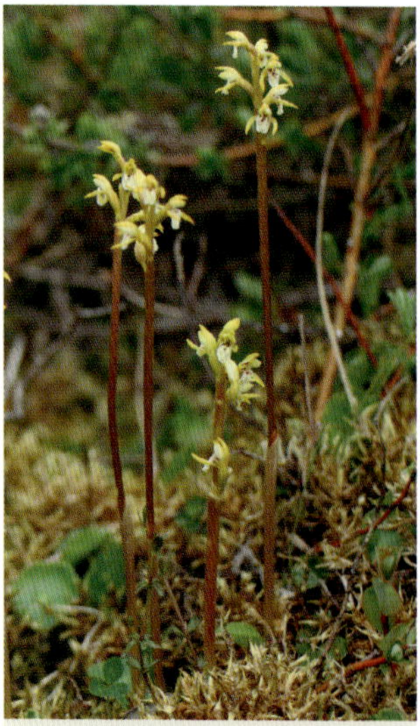

Coralroot Orchid

Orchid structure

Orchids are perennial plants, with fleshy roots, tubers or rhizomes. For identification purposes the most important features are their leaves and flowers.

Leaves

Orchids are monocotyledons, in which the young plant produces a single leaf (cotyledon) on germination, whereas the majority of other plant species are dicotyledons, and produce a pair of leaves on germination (*e.g.* salad cress). In keeping with other 'monocots' (*e.g.* grasses, lilies and onions) orchids have leaves that are unstalked and undivided, and which typically have straight, longitudinal veins, although in some species a faint network of veins running across the leaf may also be visible. A large number of orchids have a leaf **rosette**, which is a roughly circular arrangement of leaves that lies close to or flat on the ground, that may be visible, although dormant, during the colder months of the year. Stem leaves of the photosynthetic species are arranged alternately up the stem either in two opposing rows or, *e.g.* in a typical Broad-leaved Helleborine, spiralling. In some species the stem leaves are clasping; species with little or no chlorophyll have leaves reduced to scales that sheath the stem.

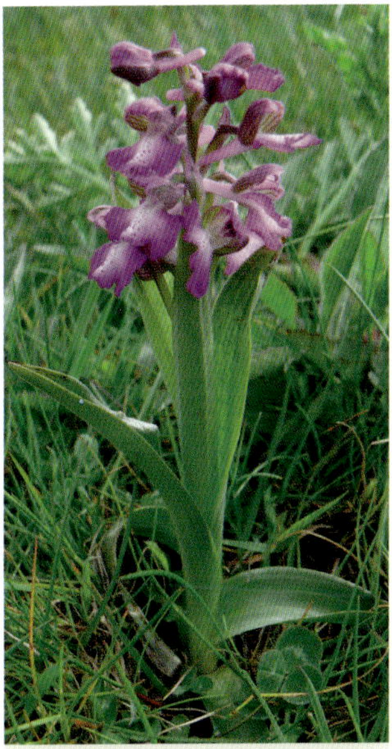

Green-winged Orchid: Most leaves basal; stem leaves clasping.

Broad-leaved Helleborine: Leaves showing the longitudinal veins.

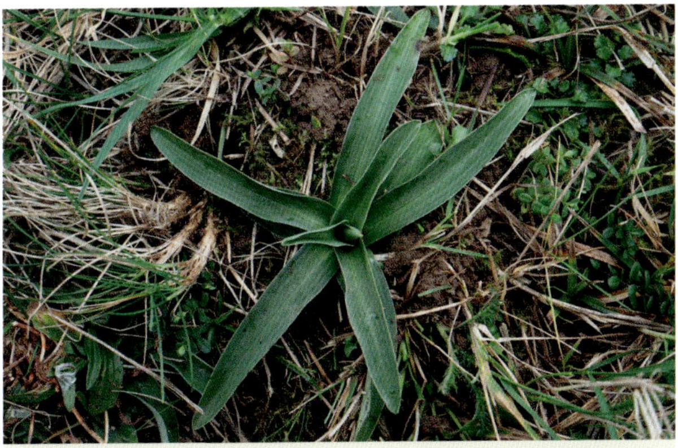

Green-winged Orchid: Rosette of a vegetative plant (February).

Sword-leaved Helleborine: Leaves without stalks arranged alternately up the stem in two rows.

Flowers

Orchids typically have multiple flowers borne on a stem, in an inflorescence that is known as a **raceme** if flowers (including the ovaries) are joined to the stem by a stalk (pedicel), or a **spike** if the flowers (including the ovaries) are attached directly to the stem without a stalk. Each flower has a **bract** (a modified leaf) immediately below the insertion point of the flower (or stalk) into the stem. The **ovary** is located beneath the flower (termed inferior) – unlike *e.g.* Bramble *Rubus* spp. in which the ovary that produces the berry is located above the flower (termed superior).

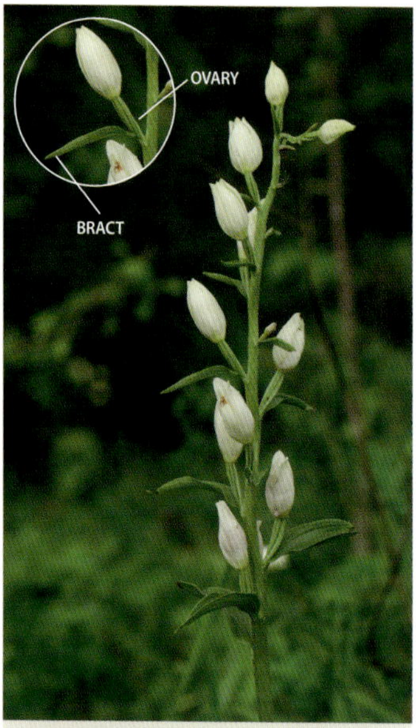
OVARY
BRACT

White Helleborine: Spike inflorescence – flowers that are attached directly to the stem by their ovary.

Although it may appear complex, an orchid's flower structure is quite simple. Each individual flower is vertically symmetrical and comprises an outer whorl of three sepals (2 lateral, 1 dorsal), that protect the flower in bud, and an inner whorl of three petals (2 lateral and 1 central 'lip'). On a facing, open flower the sepals sit behind the petals. In most British and Irish species, the flower is twisted through 180° such that the central petal (the lip or labellum) is positioned as the lowest petal. Exceptions, in which the lip is the topmost petal, include the Ghost Orchid, which is not twisted at all; the Fen Orchid, which has flowers rotated 180° but tilted back such that the labellum points upwards; and the Bog Orchid, which has the central petal (lip) positioned at the top not because the flower is untwisted, but because it is actually twisted through 360°.

Sepals can look similar to petals in some species (*e.g.* Sword-leaved Helleborine (*p. 108*)) and very different in others (*e.g.* Fly Orchid (*p. 238*)), in which the lateral petals are the 'antennae' (both species shown on *p. 16*).

BRACT
PEDICEL
OVARY

Marsh Helleborine: Raceme inflorescence – flowers (including the ovary) are attached to the stem by a stalk.

Orchid labella are usually highly modified in shape and in many are strikingly coloured/patterned to attract insects and other pollinators. In some species the dorsal sepal and lateral petals converge to form a 'hood' that protects the reproductive organs. In many species the base of the lower lip extends backwards, forming a spur that may contain nectar. The shape of spur and details of the shape and colour of the lip are intrinsic to orchid identification.
In *Epipactis* helleborines the flower shape, although in principle the same, has a morphology characteristic of that genus, with a constricted lip: the base – a bowl-like structure (**hypochile**) that contains a nectar-like substance; and the tip – a flattened near-triangle (**epichile**) with raised **bosses** (caruncles) that serves as a perch for a pollinator.

A distinguishing feature of orchids is that the male and female reproductive organs are borne on a single structure (column). All British and Irish orchids (except Lady's-slipper) have a single stamen (male) that bears 2–4 pollen masses (**pollinia**), which is stalked in some species and also may have a sticky '**glue-blob**' (viscidium) at the base. There are three stigmas (female), the two lateral stigmas being fertile and the central one sterile and forming a beak-like projection (rostellum) that, in many species, serves to separate the pollinia from the stigma to prevent self-pollination. Lady's-slipper differs in having two stamens that hold many single grains of pollen and the three stigmas all being fertile. In all other flowering plants, these parts (*e.g.* stamens and stigmas) are formed as separate structures in the flower.

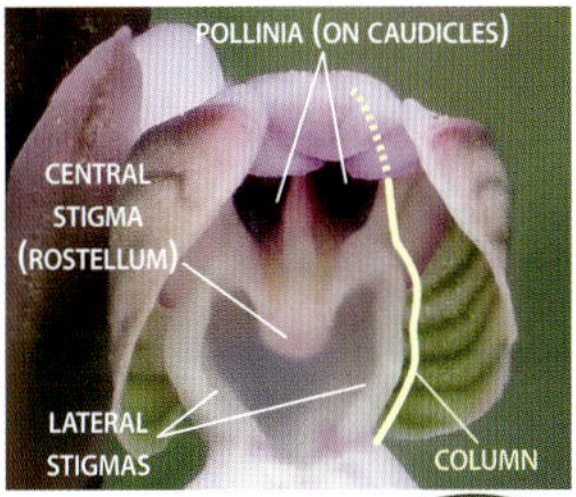
POLLINIA (ON CAUDICLES)
CENTRAL STIGMA (ROSTELLUM)
LATERAL STIGMAS
COLUMN

DS
LS
LS
LP
LP
OVARY
HOOD
SPUR
LATERAL SEPAL
BRACT
LIP
DORSAL SEPAL
LATERAL SEPAL
HOOD
LATERAL SEPAL
LIP
BRACT
CENTRAL LOBE
SIDE LOBE
SIDE LOBE

Green-winged Orchid showing the parts of a typical orchid flower and hood formed from the convergence of the dorsal sepal (DS), lateral sepals (LS) and the lateral petals (LP).

twisted
LATERAL SEPALS
LIP
LATERAL PETAL
LATERAL PETAL
DORSAL SEPAL

Bog Orchid: The lip is the uppermost petal due to the flower being twisted 360° (other orchids are only twisted 180°). The net result is that the Bog Orchid has its petals in a position found on a non-orchid flower with similar petal topology.

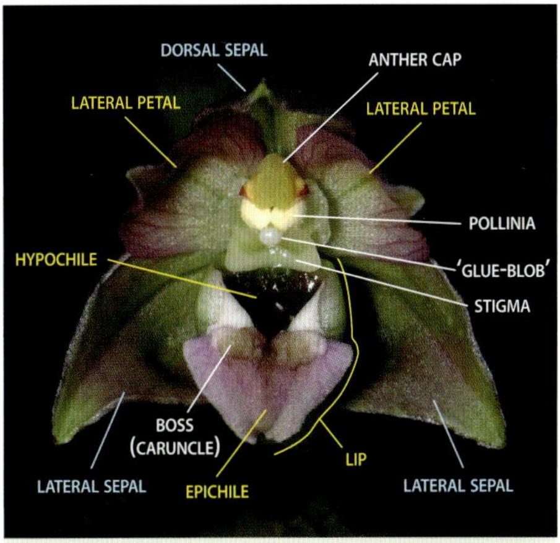
DORSAL SEPAL
ANTHER CAP
LATERAL PETAL
LATERAL PETAL
POLLINIA
HYPOCHILE
'GLUE-BLOB'
STIGMA
BOSS (CARUNCLE)
LIP
LATERAL SEPAL
EPICHILE
LATERAL SEPAL

***Epipactis* helleborine**: The lip is a single lobe, although constricted near the middle transforming the base of the lip into a cup-like structure (hypochile) and a more or less triangular tip (epichile) – see *p. 116* for more details of *Epipactis* reproductive structure.

Pollination strategies and seed dispersal

Despite having been studied for centuries, many aspects of orchid pollination mechanisms remain a mystery, as the fleeting interactions involved are so difficult to observe in detail. Some species, such as the fragrant-orchids and butterfly-orchids, produce a reward of nectar for their pollinator that is held in the long spur characteristic of the species. *Cephalanthera* helleborines are more deceitful – the yellow patch on the lip is designed to look like pollen and thus tricks solitary bees into visiting the flowers. Bee Orchids and other members of the *Ophrys* genus go a step further: they have evolved flowers that look, smell and even feel like the females of specific bee or wasp species, encouraging males to attempt to mate with the flower and inadvertently trigger pollination. Other orchids have done away with attracting pollinators altogether and instead self-pollinate, sometimes even before the flowers have opened.

The appearance, feel and smell of the Fly Orchid are highly evolved to attract specific pollinators; in this case male digger wasps (see *below*).

Once a flower has been pollinated, the ovary at its base ripens into a fruit capsule that contains thousands of dust-like seeds. These tiny seeds can be carried on the wind for great distances (see *Extinct and adventive species* (*p. 276*) for potential examples of long-distance dispersal).

SPUR

A butterfly-orchid's remarkably long spur is filled with nectar that only butterflies and moths with a long proboscis can reach.

A yellow patch on the labellum of a Sword-leaved Helleborine mimics pollen to attract soiltary bees.

Male Two-girdled Digger Wasp *Argogorytes mystaceus* – one of the two digger wasp species lured by Fly Orchid (*above*).

Broad-leaved Helleborine has a bowl-shaped lip containing nectar-like fluid; the pollinia stick to a wasp's head as it reaches in to sip.

The self-pollinating Green-flowered Helleborine has no need to attract insects, so the flowers do not always open.

A mining bee *Andrena nigroaenea* with the pollen of an Early Spider-orchid on its head after trying to mate with the flower.

Growth strategies and longevity

All British and Irish orchids are perennial, flowering each year for a period during March to October, depending on the species. One or more flowering spikes are produced from a cluster of fleshy roots or a bulb-like tuber. Orchids can live for a long time: some individual plants of Violet Helleborine are known to be forty years old and Lady's-slipper at least eighty years old. Where conditions are optimal, some species of orchids will form colonies, which can cover a large area and number into the thousands. These conditions will often be suitable for more than one orchid species, and it is particularly in these situations that hybrids occur.

EARLY APRIL
MID-APRIL
MAY 9
VEGETATIVE (' IN LEAF')
IN BUD
MAY 16
MAY 22
MAY 24
IN BUD
MID-JUNE
MID-JUNE
EARLY JULY
IN FLOWER
IN SEED/POST FLOWERING

A Common Spotted-orchid (*p. 190*) typically appears above ground in March, with buds developing from early May; the flowers open from the bottom of the inflorescence upwards over a period of around 4–6 weeks; by late June/early July many plants will have set seed, although some may still be in flower into mid-July.

Orchid taxonomy

Orchid taxonomy is constantly changing and developing, especially as a result of the increased scope and sophistication of genetic analysis that can reveal new, and sometimes surprising, relationships between taxa – often countering previous field-based conclusions and historical, more limited, genetic studies.

In the biological hierarchical system, orchids are a family of flowering plants that is subdivided into multiple genera (singular: genus), each of which is further subdivided into four lower ranks: **species**, **subspecies**, **variety** and **forma**. The term taxon (plural: taxa) is often used when referring to a recognizable group of a biological entity, which can be within any of the ranks in this hierarchy. For orchids, there are no internationally recognized definitions as to what might fall within any of these categories, although there are often commonly accepted interpretations. In order to apply consistency and clarity, while at the same time complying with international rules of nomenclature, this book focuses on three of the four lower ranks. The term forma is applied exclusively to the named Bee Orchid types (*e.g.* f. *bicolor*). Otherwise, the vernacular 'form' – as in 'colour form' or 'wide-lipped form' – is used where appropriate (see *below*) to describe the extreme colour and morphological forms that exist within the typical range of variation for a given taxon.

Ecotypes

Varieties, subspecies and species can all form their own ecotypes (growth forms that have developed to suit the prevailing conditions of their local environment). The growth form of an individual orchid can change annually depending on the seasonal conditions. For example, plants growing in shady, moist habitats tend to grow taller and have larger, more horizontal leaves to catch as much sunlight as possible. Correspondingly, those growing in exposed, dry habitats tend to be shorter and have closely bunched leaves to avoid wind damage and to collect water. Ecotypes are commonly seen in species that occur in a range of habitats, *e.g.* Early-purple Orchid and Common Twayblade. Where an ecotype has been isolated for a long period of time in a different habitat type it will gradually, through the process of natural selection, develop distinct genetic traits. This represents the early stages of speciation, such as is becoming apparent with 'Dutch Helleborine' *Epipactis helleborine* ssp. *neerlandica* (see *p. 130*). Various local ecotypes have often been confused or regarded as distinctive taxa in the past but, in the absence of genetic testing to prove otherwise, ecotypes are not given a formal name in this book.

Marsh Helleborines *Epipactis palustris* growing in fens are often tall and lanky, although in dune slacks, shown here to scale (INSET), they are typically a fraction of the size of their fenland counterparts.

Orchid classifications

The taxonomic ranks, as used in this book, are defined below. It is important to note that taxonomy is largely subjective and highly interpretive, and there is no system that will be fully acceptable to all. Where taxonomic changes have been made in this book that differ from previous guides, the rationale behind them is explained at the beginning of the relevant section. In general, a cautious approach is taken, *i.e.* not adopting any formal recognition in the absence of compelling (usually genetic) evidence.

A complete list of the British and Irish orchids that are recognized in this book appears on *p. 282*.

Species

A group of living organisms consisting of similar individuals capable of exchanging genes or interbreeding, that is genetically distinctive as a coherent group. The species is the principal natural taxonomic unit, ranking below a genus and denoted by a scientific binomial, *e.g. Cypripedium calceolus* (Lady's-slipper). A species will not usually share genes (cross-breed) with another species, but when this does happen the resultant hybrids will often be sterile (but see discussion on the *Dactylorhiza* marsh-orchids and spotted-orchids on *p. 261*). Defining a species that occurs in isolated locations – *e.g.* 'Lindisfarne Helleborine' (*p. 132*) – is tricky as hybridization cannot be easily tested; in cases like these, genetic evidence has been used to support the categorization.

Subspecies

A taxonomic category that ranks below species, defined as a taxon that consists of populations that are clearly separate, **occupy a different habitat or micro-habitat, and show at least two consistent morphological features that differ from the nominate form.** Critically, there should also be evidence to show that the taxon in question is genetically distinctive. A consistent difference in colour may be a supporting feature but is not sufficient in isolation. Applying these criteria rigorously has resulted in only a few subspecies being recognized in this book.

NOTE: SUBSPECIES NAMES Species that are subdivided into subspecies will have one form (typically the first to be discovered), which is the base taxon against which other subspecies are compared. This base taxon is known as the nominate subspecies (or form), and is denoted by a (qualified) scientific trinomial, with the same specific and subspecific names (*e.g.* Broad-leaved Helleborine *Epipactis helleborine* ssp. *helleborine* (*p. 126*)). The subspecies of Broad-leaved Helleborine known as 'Dutch Helleborine' (*p. 130*) has the name *Epipactis helleborine* ssp. *neerlandica*. Subspecies often have their own English names and, if this is the cases, they are differentiated from the species' name by the use of closed quotes.

Variety

A taxonomic rank that falls below subspecies level but still denoted in the form of a trinomial, such as *Epipactis dunensis* var. *tynensis* (*p. 133*). Varieties are less clearly defined than subspecies but must have **at least one consistent morphological feature that differs from the nominate form** and occur in discrete populations. Importantly, a variety will show no significant genetic differences from the typical form. The exclusion of colour forms from this category – often used inconsistently to create varietal names in the past – means that many fewer names have been used in this book than in other recent guides. However, as much variation as reasonably possible is shown to illustrate the diversity and beauty of each species – see also *Colour forms and other variations p. 20.*

Forma

The lowest of the four ranks in the taxonomic hierarchy used in this book, which is denoted in the form of a trinomial, such as *Ophrys apifera* f. *trollii*. This taxonomic rank is reserved exclusively here for several distinctive and consistent forms of Bee Orchid that are outside the typical range of variation of lip shape or colour pattern for the species but crop up randomly within populations of the typical form (see *Ophrys* variation, *p. 246*). They therefore do not fit the criteria required to be classed as varieties (which they have long been considered as) but are nonetheless retained in this book, under this lowermost rank, for completeness.

Ophrys apifera f. *trollii* ('Wasp Orchid'), a form of Bee Orchid with a narrower, longer lip than usual and lacking a **speculum** when fully open.

Colour forms and other variations

There are two pigment types, chlorophylls and anthocyanins, found in many orchids that affect their overall colours and patterns.

Chlorophylls (two types found in plants) give plants their green colour, and their presence is evidence that most orchids are, at least in part, able to photosynthesize (*i.e.* create their own 'food' (sugars synthesized from carbon dioxide and water) rather than rely on a host fungus to provide it).

Anthocyanins are pigments that may appear red, purple, blue or black, depending on their pH (they are found, for example, in blueberries and raspberries). Increased heat and/or drought may cause plants to produce higher levels of anthocyanin, either in the flowers and/or in the leaves in those species that have leaf patterns. Many of the orchids in Britain and Ireland that are purple or pink in colour vary in hue and pattern, even within a population, because of highly localized differences in the amounts of anthocyanins.

Over the years, orchids with extreme anthocyanin pigment levels have often been named as distinct taxa, often based on individual plants. This has resulted in an accumulation of poorly defined named types, old and new, with minimal scientific justification.

A good illustration of this is found in Common Spotted-orchid, where anthocyanin-rich individuals with purple flowers are often called '*rhodochila*', while anthocyanin-deficient individuals with white flowers are often called '*alba*'. However, it is clear that many of these varietal names, based on colour extremes, have no defined limits within which to categorize individual plants – partly as a result of the

A particularly anthocyanin-rich Common Spotted-orchid, with both leaves and flowers heavily pigmented. The rich colour can occur anywhere in the plant, meaning dark-flowered individuals do not necessarily show darker leaf patterning.

The 'rhodochila' conundrum – how much dark solid colour does a Common Spotted-orchid require on its lip to be named as a '*rhodochila*'? 51%? 80%?

'TYPICAL' RANGE

original published descriptions often being vague and lacking clearly defined, measurable criteria. As a result, many names are effectively of no use. These forms are simply part of the typical colour variation of Common Spotted-orchid, with every colour shade in between. It therefore seems logical to treat these as part of the normal range of colour variation within the species and avoid attempting to apply names to them.

The problem with names

In order to illustrate the problem with the liberal naming of colour forms, below is a list of varietal names given to different orchid species, each with the same anthocyanin-deficiency that sometimes manifests as white or green flowers, depending on the species:

Marsh Helleborine var. *albiflora*
Dark-red Helleborine var. *albiflora*
Chalk Fragrant-orchid var. *albiflora*
Heath Fragrant-orchid var. *albiflora*
Southern Marsh-orchid var. *albiflora*
Pugsley's Marsh-orchid var. *albiflora*
Northern Marsh-orchid var. *albiflora*
Burnt Orchid var. *albiflora*
Pyramidal Orchid var. *albiflora*
Common Spotted-orchid var. *alba*
Dense-flowered Orchid var. *alba*
Early-purple Orchid var. *alba*
Green-winged Orchid var. *alba*
Bee Orchid var. *chlorantha*
Heath Spotted-orchid var. *leucantha*
Early Marsh-orchid var. *ochranthra*
Fly Orchid var. *ochroleuca*
Broad-leaved Helleborine var. *chlorantha*

The lack of naming consistency means an observer needs to already know, or look up, the name of the anthocyanin-deficient form of a species. In addition, for some species, varietal names are even given to examples that almost entirely lack anthocyanin – but not quite. For example, Bee Orchid 'var. *flavescens*' is like the anthocyanin-deficient 'var. *chlorantha*' but has *some* anthocyanins – although the level is undefined. This hair-splitting not only causes definition confusion but also places an over-importance on colour variants that are simply a response to local conditions, while potentially deflecting from actual conservation and protection issues.

A similar situation applies to chlorophyll levels. For example, some Violet Helleborine plants develop without chlorophyll, which results in the entire plant being a striking pink colour – often named 'var. *rosea*'. These plants are able to develop and grow entirely without sunlight, instead gaining all their nutrients from their host fungus that is attached to the roots of nearby trees. However, some plants classed as this type have hints of green here and there, indicating the presence of some chlorophyll, which, for the purist, excludes them from being attributed as 'var. *rosea*'. Equally, at the other end of the scale, some Violet Helleborines are entirely green, with just a few streaks of pink on the leaves where chlorophyll is absent. The reality is that '*rosea*' types are just plants at the extreme end of a continuum of variation within Violet Helleborine and, even though they are worthy of note, do not justify being regarded as a variety.

As well as colour, the same logic applies to morphological features, such as lip width or bract length, that show a range of variation and have been attributed a range of arbitrarily chosen varietal names in the past.
For example, Fly Orchids with a flaring, wide lip have previously been given

Two anthocyanin-deficient examples of Bee Orchid. The plant on the *left* would typically be called 'var. *chlorantha*', the one on the *right* 'var. *flavescens*'. However, experience shows that these colour forms are part of a continuum with numerous intermediates. The all-too-easily published descriptions of named Bee Orchid varieties can be frustratingly vague with poorly defined limits, often resulting in identification turmoil for the observer.

the name '*subbombifera*', but experience shows this is just one extreme of a range of side-lobe shapes. Similarly, large examples of Frog Orchid have previously been given the name '*longibracteatum*' on the basis that the bracts are longer than smaller individuals – but this is simply a feature of more robust plants and are part of the standard variation within the species.

A more logical approach would perhaps be to refer to all of these types as *e.g.* an 'anthocyanin-lacking form', 'chlorophyll-lacking form', 'white-flowered form' or 'wide-lipped form' and this is the approach taken in this book.

Violet Helleborines lacking chlorophyll are sometimes termed 'var. *rosea*', but upon closer inspection many individuals show a hint of green in various places, disqualifying them from the epithet on a technicality, even though they are equally as striking in appearance. The same lack of chlorophyll in Broad-leaved Helleborine results in creamy or ice-white, rather than pink, individuals.

Most species of orchid can vary greatly in size. These two Common Spotted-orchids were found within two metres of each other, and yet one (LEFT) has flowers almost three times the size of those of the other (RIGHT).

Colour and shape can be highly variable within certain species, with appearance changing as the plant develops. The inflorescence of a Pyramidal Orchid is initially pyramid-shaped (LEFT) but as more flowers open it becomes increasingly torpedo-shaped (RIGHT).

Fly orchid lips can be very variable in size, shape and colour. Over the years, many of the more extreme forms, some examples of which are shown on *page 247*, have been described as distinct varieties, resulting in a long list of weird and wonderful names (although these are not followed in this book).

Individuals in the *Epipactis* and *Cephalanthera* genera, such as this White Helleborine, can sometimes appear without any chlorophyll, with the entire plant a ghostly yellow or pink colour. These plants can continue to grow, and even flower, via nutrients supplied by the fungal partner connected to their root system.

Habitats

Orchids occupy a wide variety of habitats across Great Britain and Ireland, from gardens and road verges to upland moorland and ancient woodland. All orchids require nutrient-poor soils and most prefer soils that are **neutral** or **alkaline** (often referred to as 'calcareous' or 'base-rich'), but a small minority are specialists of **acid** soils.

Associated orchid species

Different species of orchid often associate with each other, so when you find an orchid its presence may itself be a clue as to what else you might find. This section provides a summary of the orchid species associated with the main habitat types.

Familiarizing yourself with different habitat types is a key aspect of looking for orchids. With field experience you can develop useful skills for finding new species at existing sites, and indeed may even discover completely new sites. Over time, you will come to recognize 'good' orchid habitats, often by subconsciously noticing associated plant species, particular vegetation structure and favoured topography. For example, a short grassland sward with patches of bare ground and plenty of bright yellow Common Bird's-foot-trefoil *Lotus corniculatus* indicates there is a good chance that Bee Orchids might be present. Similarly, a boggy mountain flush with distinctive plants such as Cross-leaved Heath *Erica tetralix* and Bog Asphodel *Narthecium ossifragum* is a good place to look for Bog Orchids.

Aside from soil nutrient levels and pH (the level of acidity or alkalinity), many other elements also determine the suitability of a habitat for orchids, including vegetation height and density, light levels, the presence of fungal hosts for germination, and soil moisture. Orchids compete poorly with other plants and have evolved to occupy niches where the vegetation is less vigorous. For example, some species grow only in shady areas, whereas others disappear if their favoured open, grazed grassland becomes overgrown with coarse grasses and other dense vegetation. In many cases this means that careful, active management of special sites is required to optimize orchid populations.

By and large, orchids grow where the underlying soil is left undisturbed. While light soil disturbance by winter-grazing livestock may be helpful to some species, for most ploughing is often the death knell. Well-managed habitats that have remained in the same condition for decades are generally better for orchids than those that have changed significantly over recent years.

The rest of this section describes typical orchid habitats in Britain and Ireland and the species that can be found within them. Be aware that not all orchid species will be found in every location that might appear suitable, and that habitats often grade into one another! For more information on specific habitat requirements of individual species, see the relevant species accounts.

Grassland and heathland

Chalk and limestone grassland

This is undoubtedly one of the most productive orchid habitats, particularly in southern England and western Ireland, where some sites can host up to 15 species, typically in large numbers. The soil is usually very shallow, with short, flower-rich turf and patches of whitish bedrock often visible at the surface. The bedrock is especially prominent in the 'limestone pavement' regions of the Yorkshire Dales, Lancashire and the Burren in Co. Clare, Ireland.

Characteristic species include **Autumn Lady's-tresses**, **Common Twayblade**, **Common Spotted-orchid**, **Greater Butterfly-orchid** and **Bee**, **Chalk Fragrant-**, **Early-purple** and **Pyramidal Orchids**. Older, high-quality areas may contain **Burnt**, **Fly**, **Man**, **Frog** and **Musk Orchids**, **Dense-flowered Orchid** in Ireland, and occasionally **Dark-red Helleborine** in northern Britain and western Ireland. Chalk grasslands also host some of Britain and Ireland's rarest species, including **Late** and **Early Spider-orchids**, and **Monkey** and **Military Orchids**.

Heathland and acid grassland

Heathlands, and the adjacent stretches of acid grassland, are often relatively poor in orchids, particularly in the drier lowland areas of southern England. However, the damp peaty areas of upland Britain, often referred to as moorland, can be more productive.

The most prominent and widespread species is **Heath Spotted-orchid**, but **Heath Fragrant-orchid**, **Lesser Butterfly-orchid** and **Small-white Orchid** are occasionally present, particularly in Scotland. Areas of mature, often boggy, upland heathland are the principal habitat of **Lesser Twayblade**, which favours the sheets of *Sphagnum* mosses that form beneath the heather.

Heathland often occurs in association with bogs (see *Bogs, p. 31*).

Meadows and pastures

Meadows and pastures that are lightly grazed, or traditionally managed for hay production, can be particularly species-rich and appear in a variety of forms: they may be alkaline, neutral or acidic depending on the soil type and vary from dry to damp.

Species characteristic of lowland areas include **Common Spotted-orchid**, **Green-winged Orchid**, **marsh-orchids** and, occasionally, **Burnt Orchid**. Northern and western species largely replace their southern lowland counterparts in upland meadows and pastures, where **Heath Spotted-orchid**, **Northern Marsh-orchid** and **Heath Fragrant-orchid** can be abundant, with occasional **Frog Orchid**, **Lesser Butterfly-orchid** and **Small-white Orchid** in especially high-quality areas. **Greater Butterfly-orchid** is often a consistent presence in both upland and lowland areas.

Dunes and machair

Dunes and machair are two of the most orchid-rich habitat types in Britain and Ireland, both in terms of the number of species and in the sheer quantity of plants. This is due to the strongly alkaline substrate derived from wind-blown shell fragments, and also the variety of micro-habitats that develop between the higher, drier ground and the low-lying damp areas. Consequently, dunes and machair often support species typical of both limestone grasslands and fens.

Sand dune systems

Sand dune systems are widely scattered around the coasts of Britain and Ireland, often forming vast landscapes. The largest number of orchids occur in low-lying damp areas, or 'slacks', where the characteristic species are **Marsh Helleborine** and the brick-red var. *coccinea* of **Early Marsh-orchid**, both of which can number tens of thousands. Other orchids that are often well represented include **Southern**, **Northern** and **Irish Marsh-orchids**, **Common Spotted-orchid** and, less frequently, **Marsh Fragrant-orchid**. In South Wales, this is the primary habitat of **Fen Orchid**, which favours newly developed slacks, while in the dunes of northern Britain, **Coralroot Orchid** also occurs sporadically.

Higher, drier grassland areas less prone to water inundation are often home to **Common Twayblade** and **Early-purple**, **Pyramidal**, **Bee**, **Green-winged** and **Frog Orchids**, and, in northern Ireland, **Dense-flowered Orchid**. Scrubby zones may also support *Epipactis* helleborines, such as **Green-flowered** and **Dune Helleborines** and, in South Wales, the *neerlandica* subspecies of **Broad-leaved Helleborine**.

Dry dune grasslands in southern Britain are an important habitat for **Autumn Lady's-tresses** and, very rarely, **Lizard Orchid** (in Kent and Somerset).

Machair

Unique to the northwest coastlands of Scotland and northern Ireland, machair is a type of damp dune grassland habitat that is traditionally grazed with livestock, creating a rolling turf rich in orchids and other wildflowers. **Frog Orchid** and **Common Spotted-orchid var. *hebridensis*** are often abundant, and the Scottish machair can hold impressive numbers of **marsh-orchids**, including rarities such as **Pugsley's Marsh-orchid**, including the variant '**Hebridean Marsh-orchid**' of North Uist.

Woodland

Coppice

Coppicing is a woodland management technique that involves the rotational cutting-back, close to the ground, of certain shrub species, particularly Hazel *Corylus avellana*; the subsequent straight stems that develop from the 'stools' being harvested for the production of fencing, tool handles and furniture. As a result, the canopy is opened-up every few years, allowing more light to reach the woodland floor – which coincidentally creates favourable conditions for a variety of orchids. Shortly after an area has been coppiced, orchids previously lying dormant can flower in profusion, particularly on alkaline soils. Coppice can be a feature of any of the ancient broadleaved woodland types described in this section.

Ancient broadleaved woodland

Ancient woodland is defined as an area that has been continuously wooded since at least 1600. It is characterized by the presence of mature or 'veteran' trees, with undisturbed soil layers and high levels of associated fungal diversity – both important elements for several orchid species. Correspondingly, woodland orchids are often referred to as good indicators of ancient woodland.

When looking for orchids in woodlands, focus your searches in areas that are open and rich in other woodland wildflowers.

Limestone Ash woods

Ash-dominated woods, which develop on exposed limestone bedrock, can support several orchid species. **Common Twayblade**, **Broad-leaved Helleborine**, **Early-purple Orchid** and **Greater Butterfly-orchid** are found most commonly, with the occasional appearance of **Fly Orchid** and **Dark-red Helleborine** in northern England. This is one of the lost habitats of **Lady's-slipper**, that once thrived in the open Ash woods of Yorkshire, Lancashire and County Durham.

Beech woods

The chalk and limestone Beech woods of southern England are a classic orchid habitat, with several specialist species.

At the lighter woodland edges, and within rides and glades, **Common Twayblade**, **Early-purple Orchid**, **Greater Butterfly-orchid**, **Common Spotted-orchid** and **Fly Orchid** can be common, with **Sword-leaved Helleborine**, **Lady Orchid**, **Lesser Butterfly-orchid** and **Military Orchid** in a few sites in Hampshire, Kent and the Chilterns.

In the leaf-litter of darker, shady areas, **White Helleborine** and **Bird's-nest Orchid** can be abundant, and there are occasional **Violet**, **Broad-leaved** and **Green-flowered Helleborines**. This is the principal habitat of **Narrow-lipped Helleborine**, and also the rarest species in Britain and Ireland – **Ghost Orchid** – which favours the deep leaf-litter in damp hollows and ditches.

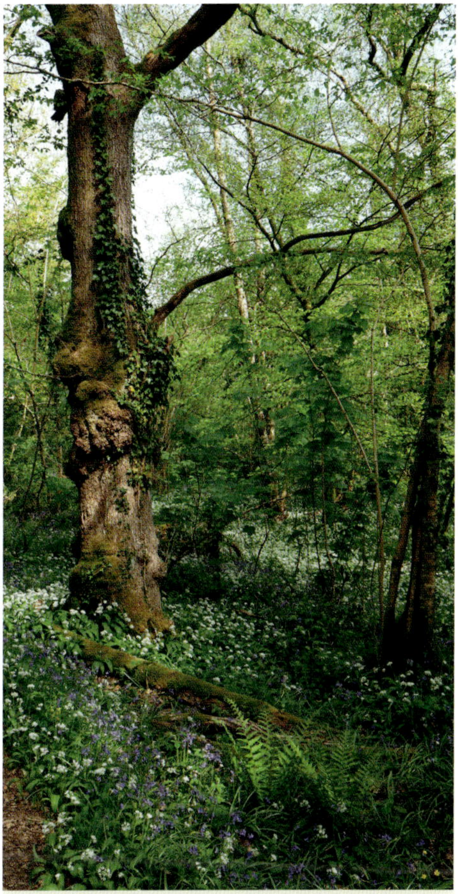

Lowland mixed oak woods

Away from the chalk and limestone regions, most lowland woods are dominated by oaks, along with a mixture of other broadleaved tree species.

These woodlands are generally orchid-poor. However, those on slightly more alkaline soils, such as the clay woodlands of the English Midlands, can support several orchid species, including **Broad-leaved Helleborine**, **Common Twayblade**, **Early-purple Orchid**, **Bird's-nest Orchid** and **Greater Butterfly-orchid**, and also sometimes **Violet** and **Green-flowered Helleborines**. Although rare, **Sword-leaved Helleborine** can also be found in this habitat, notably in the Wyre Forest, Worcestershire, but it also favours the Atlantic oak and Hazel woodlands characteristic of Snowdonia, Cumbria and Argyll.

Wet woodlands (willow, Alder and birch carr)
Permanently wet (carr) woodlands develop on waterlogged soils at the base of river valleys and around the edges of lakes, marshes and bogs. Typically dominated by willows, Alder and birches, they can occur on alkaline, neutral or acidic soils, depending on the bedrock, and therefore vary greatly in their orchid richness.

In lowland Britain and Ireland, wet woodlands can be important for several species, such as **Common Twayblade**, **Southern Marsh-orchid**, **Common Spotted-orchid** and, less frequently, **Green-flowered** and **Dune Helleborines**. In northern and upland Britain, swampy acidic woodland with a thick layer of *Sphagnum* mosses is the principal habitat for **Coralroot Orchid**, often alongside **Lesser Twayblade** and, more rarely, **Creeping Lady's-tresses**.

Coniferous woodlands
Although widespread across Britain and Ireland, most coniferous woodland habitats outside Scotland are commercial plantations. For the most part, these plantations are ecologically poor, usually being very dark with even-aged trees. Nevertheless, in parts of Lancashire and North Wales, where conifers have been planted widely spaced on dune systems, such plantations can be important habitats for **Green-flowered** and **Dune Helleborines**. However, the native 'Caledonian' pinewoods of Scotland hold the most orchids, **Creeping Lady's-tresses** often being extremely common, alongside occasional **Lesser Twayblade** and **Coralroot Orchid**.

Wet habitats

Bogs

There are several types of bog, all of which develop in heavily waterlogged areas fed by rainwater. The waterlogging allows peat to accumulate over many years, usually covered by a thick layer of *Sphagnum* mosses. Blanket bogs are common in the uplands and can cover enormous areas. Although most lowland bogs have now been drained, some raised bogs and valley mires remain in parts of lowland Britain and Ireland.

Being acidic and low in nutrients, bogs are a hostile environment to most orchids. However, a few species, such as **Heath Spotted-orchid** and **Early Marsh-orchid var. *pulchella***, are able to thrive. **Lesser Butterfly-orchid** and **Heath Fragrant-orchid** may be found growing on tussocks within bogs, while **Pugsley's Marsh-orchid** favours flushes flowing from surrounding slopes. **Bog Orchid** is, of course, the main specialist of this habitat, although it is usually found in bogs on sloping ground where the surface water is flowing.

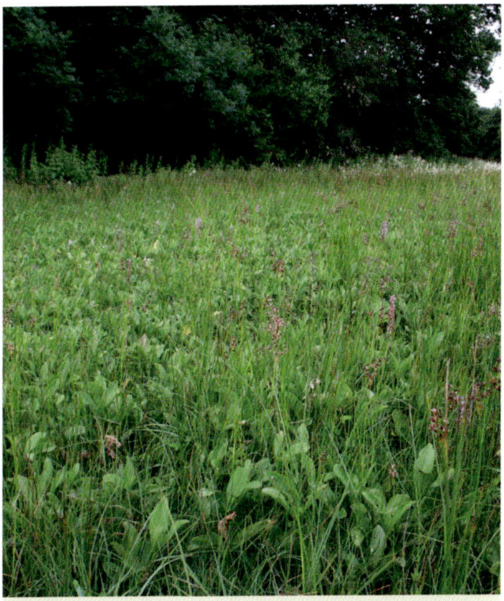

Fens

Fens also develop in waterlogged areas that allow peat to accumulate, but differ from bogs in that they are fed by groundwater, and where this is alkaline they are often particularly rich habitats for orchids.

Fen is a rather rare habitat in Britain and Ireland, with some of the best sites being found in East Anglia, North Wales and Ireland. These often support the commoner marsh-orchid species but also several specialists, such as **Fen Orchid**, **Marsh Helleborine**, **Marsh Fragrant-orchid** and **Pugsley's Marsh-orchid**, as well as the very rare **Early Marsh-orchid var. *ochroleuca***. **Fly Orchid** occasionally grows on the tussocks within fens in Ireland and on Anglesey.

Marshes

For simplicity, this book uses a fairly loose definition of a marsh, which covers a wide range of permanently wet or seasonally inundated open habitats, such as coastal grazing marshes and swampy lake margins. As such, marshes vary in orchid richness, but can be important for the commoner **marsh-orchids**. These may occur in large numbers, and can be with **Marsh Helleborine** where the soil is slightly more alkaline. **Bee Orchid** regularly occurs at the edges of lakeside reedbeds and, in Ireland and western Scotland, marshy lakeshores are a key habitat for **Irish Lady's-tresses**.

Human-made habitats

A range of habitats have been created as a result of human activities and although not natural these can support diverse ecosystems. In today's increasingly fragmented landscape, such areas have become valuable habitats for orchids. As conservation practices become more embedded in the day-to-day management of human-made habitats, we can expect to see more orchids turning up in unexpected places in the future.

Churchyards
The undisturbed nature and often consistent management of churchyards can result in conditions that are very favourable to several species of grassland orchid. Sensitively managed areas sometimes support significant populations of **Autumn Lady's-tresses** and **Green-winged Orchid**, both of which seem particularly fond of these locations. **Common Twayblade**, **Southern** and **Northern Marsh-orchids**, **Common** and **Heath Spotted-orchids**, **Early-purple**, **Pyramidal** and **Bee Orchids** can also be common, depending on the geographical location.

Road verges and hedgebanks
Newly landscaped banks and cuttings can create excellent habitats, especially if south-facing. Here, large numbers of **Common Twayblade**, **Bee** and **Pyramidal Orchids**, **Southern** and **Northern Marsh-orchids**, and **Common** and **Heath Spotted-orchids** can occur. On chalk and limestone, **Fly** and **Man Orchids** may also be present. Where roads pass through high-quality woodland habitats, the break in shade from trees can provide just the right light levels for a wide variety of woodland orchids such as **Greater Butterfly-orchid** and **Broad-leaved Helleborine**.

The tall, earth hedgebanks of western Britain can provide an excellent habitat for **Early-purple Orchid**, which can be more abundant here than in nearby woodlands. In recent years, several new **Lizard Orchid** colonies have appeared along strips of roadside grassland in heavily agricultural landscapes devoid of other orchid species.

Urban environment

A few orchid species have taken advantage of urban green spaces, including those in city centres. Parks, gardens, green roofs and brownfield sites can all support orchids. **Northern Marsh-orchid** and **Broad-leaved Helleborine** are now very common in some Scottish cities, even growing up through drain covers and cracks in the pavement (above). Similarly, **Bee** and **Green-winged Orchids** have become established on several green roofs in London, with the latter even colonizing a few of the skyscrapers.

Excavations and spoil tips

Quarries and pits can become highly productive orchid habitats. By exposing the bedrock, excavation removes the nutrient-rich upper soil layers, reducing competition and providing orchids with opportunities to become established. Significant variations in moisture, light and aspect mean that a wide range of orchids can sometimes be found in a relatively small area. Chalk and limestone quarries, such as those in Flintshire in north-east Wales, the Chiltern Hills, and also Hampshire, Derbyshire, Yorkshire and County Durham, all tend to be rich in orchids. Indeed, such sites may support virtually all the species found in natural grasslands and, over time, as they are gradually colonized by trees, woodland orchids as well. Water often collects at the base of derelict gravel pits, where a rich marshland habitat can sometimes develop, supporting large numbers of marsh-orchids.

Similarly, spoil from excavations and industrial practices can become valuable habitats for orchids and, depending on the alkalinity, can be colonized by numerous species. The industrial spoils of the English Midlands regularly support large numbers of **Bee Orchid**, while the birch woodlands that develop on spoil heaps in Northern England and Scotland have become vital habitats for **Broad-leaved** and **Dune Helleborines.**

Such is the quality of some of these habitats for wildlife that many have become nature reserves and are considered to be of equal value to the 'natural' habitats around them.

Finding orchids

Code of Conduct

Remember that uprooting any plant is illegal unless you have the landowner's permission, and that some orchids (as well as other plants) are specifically protected by law (*p. 281*) and cannot be picked or disturbed unless you have the appropriate licence. In addition, it goes without saying that care and consideration for the plant and its surroundings, especially when taking photographs (see *p. 37*) are of prime importance.
A full code for anyone interested in wild plants can be found at:
bsbi.org/wp-content/uploads/dlm_uploads/Code-of-Conduct-v5-final.pdf

Although many people will travel to 'traditional' orchid sites to enjoy these spectacular flowers, some may explore (*e.g.* their local area) in detail in an attempt to discover orchids, and others may not even be looking for orchids when they come across them.

Even though some orchids may seem to be restricted to a handful of known and protected sites there is always the chance, when exploring the British and Irish countryside, that a new colony in a well-known area or a previously undiscovered site can be stumbled upon – perhaps even a Ghost Orchid.

The aim of this book is to both provide the means of identifying any orchid you may find, whether the diminutive Bog or the impressive Lizard Orchid, but also to offer a few pointers to make the most of any search for orchids.

When and where flowering *p. 36*

For those who wish to find a particular species, as well as providing a guide to supplement identification, the 'in leaf', 'in flower' and 'in seed' periods for all British and Irish orchids are shown together on *pp. 38–39*. Naturally, these can vary year-on-year due to a range of factors so it is worth checking online social media where the latest information about orchids in flower can be found, often on a day-to-day, basis during the flowering season.

Orchids in their habitats *pp. 40–50*

The ability to spot plants within surrounding vegetation is key, and the more hours spent 'getting one's eye in', the more improved that ability becomes. Everyone sees things differently, and it is hoped that looking at these images in conjunction with the information pointers will help enhance any search for orchids.

A Lizard Orchid rosette and flowering Bog Orchid highlight the size range of Britain and Ireland's orchids.

LIZARD ORCHID
⅕ life size

BOG ORCHID
⅕ life size

BOG ORCHID
life size

When flowering

When planning trips to see particular species, it is important to bear in mind that there is a huge annual variation in flowering times, depending on many factors, both consistent (*e.g.* longitude/latitude, altitude and habitat) and variable (*e.g.* spring temperature, current rainfall, the prevailing conditions of the previous growth and dormant seasons). Ongoing research shows that many orchids are highly sensitive to seasonal weather change. Anecdotal evidence also suggests that British and Irish orchids are already flowering earlier as a result of climate change, as well as expanding and contracting their distributions as prevailing weather patterns alter. This can make flowering times for a particular species at a particular site even more difficult to predict.

mid-JUN
mid-MAY
MAY
APR
early APR

Average annual first-flowering dates by region of Early-purple Orchid. These can differ from year to year depending on local factors.

In general, flowering times will vary according to latitude and altitude, with populations in the warmer south flowering first and those in the north flowering last. Similarly, populations of orchids at higher elevations will generally flower later than those at lower elevations. For example, Early-purple Orchid begins flowering in early April in coastal southern England but will not begin flowering until mid-June in the northern Scottish mountains. Habitat, as well as the weather, can influence timing of flowering during critical growth periods during an individual season. Late frosts, a cold spring or a warm, wet spell might, for example, delay flowering or bring it forward, with the season reverting to 'normal' the following year.

With as much accuracy as possible, the annual growth charts on *pp. 38–39* show the timing of each species' development stage – when in leaf, in flower and in seed.

Where flowering

As well as flowering times, the distribution of many orchid species has changed dramatically over recent decades. For this reason, the maps on the species accounts show the known current distribution of each species based on records from 2000–2019 (rather than reflecting their historical distribution). Nonetheless, it is always possible to find new, or re-find old populations outside the distribution ranges presented here and therefore these should be used only as an indication of distribution. The number of records submitted online is increasing and providing a more accurate picture of any changes in distribution, so it is worth accessing 'real-time' data for the latest information.

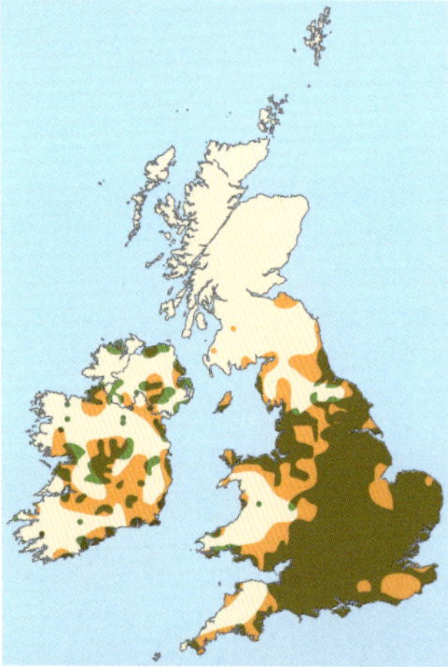

Historical (1930–1999 ■■) and current (2000–2019 ■■) distribution of Bee Orchid showing its recent expansion northwards.

Photography and recording

Photographic advice

This book is designed to help with the identification of an orchid when it is in front of you. However, if for any reason you have to leave the plant unidentified, hoping to name it later, it is important to take a photographic record showing as many of the following aspects in as much detail as possible:

- Several flowers, from the front and side if possible
- Several individual leaves, including from above to show shape and any pattern
- The whole plant from the side
- The plant in the context of its habitat
- The very base of the plant to show the lowermost leaf, which can often be very small
- The stem and ovary of more than one flower, to show colour, shape and any hairs
- Any particular striking feature you notice at the time

Photographing a Dense-flowered Orchid.

When taking pictures please be mindful of the surrounding vegetation, which may include rare species. Avoid trampling and 'gardening' as this could affect the plant by *e.g.* exposing it to grazing, or changing the immediate micro-habitat/climate.

Try and include something for scale in each image.
Also make sure you note the date, exact location and the presence of other known species of orchid close by.

Submitting records

New orchid discoveries are being made every year, and the hope is that this book will encourage further such discoveries in future. Distribution data are vital to the conservation of orchids, so you are strongly encouraged to submit information of new sightings to the relevant Botanical Society of Britain & Ireland (BSBI) recorder. This will add to the valuable species database, from which distribution maps, such as those included in this book, can be prepared. Local BSBI recorders are listed at **bsbi.org/local-botany**.

Examining a challenging *Epipactis* hybrid.

Annual growth cycle

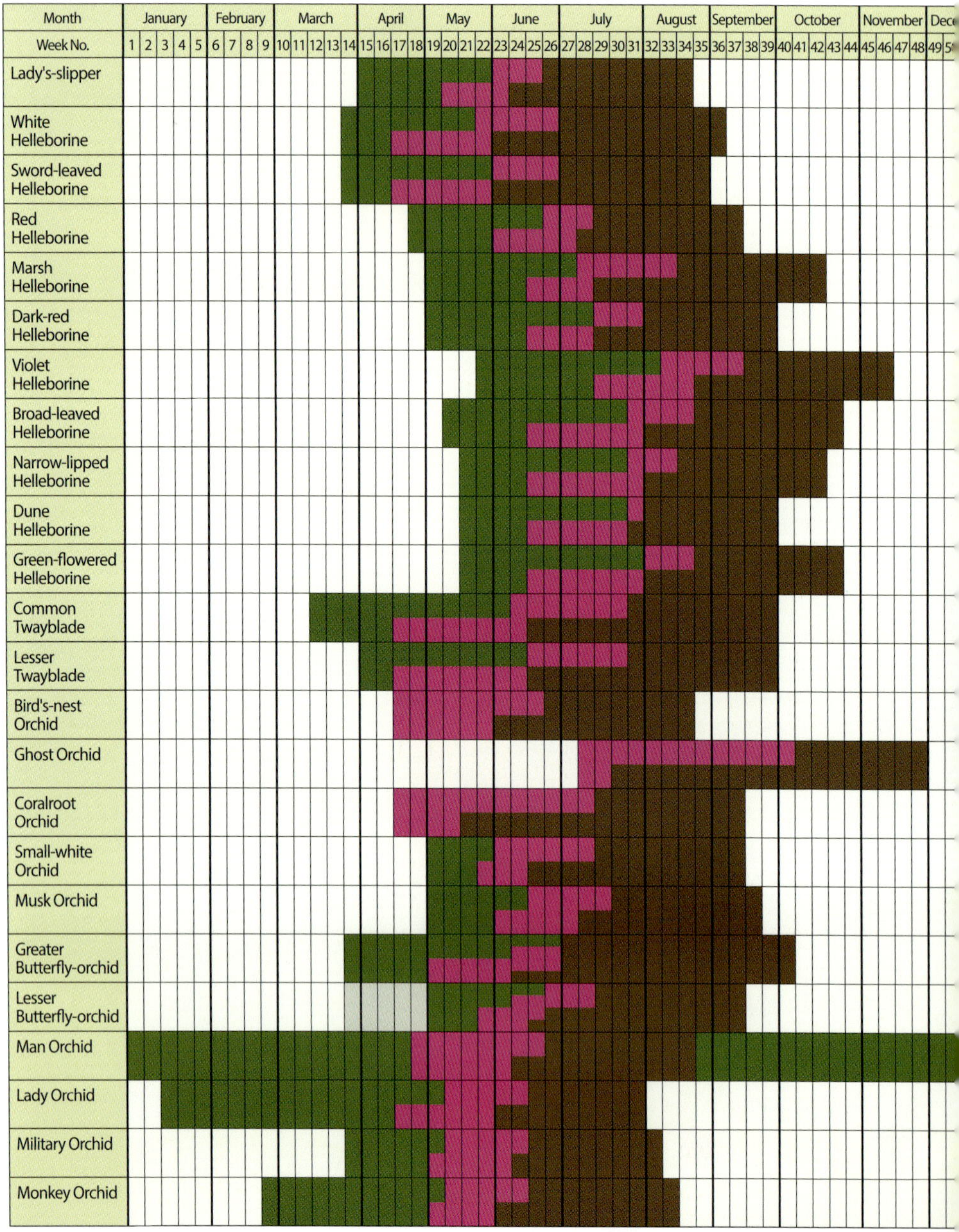
Month
January
February
March
April
May
June
July
August
September
October
November
Week No.
1 2 3 4 5 6 7 8 9 10 11 12 13 14 15 16 17 18 19 20 21 22 23 24 25 26 27 28 29 30 31 32 33 34 35 36 37 38 39 40 41 42 43 44 45 46 47 48 49
Lady's-slipper
White Helleborine
Sword-leaved Helleborine
Red Helleborine
Marsh Helleborine
Dark-red Helleborine
Violet Helleborine
Broad-leaved Helleborine
Narrow-lipped Helleborine
Dune Helleborine
Green-flowered Helleborine
Common Twayblade
Lesser Twayblade
Bird's-nest Orchid
Ghost Orchid
Coralroot Orchid
Small-white Orchid
Musk Orchid
Greater Butterfly-orchid
Lesser Butterfly-orchid
Man Orchid
Lady Orchid
Military Orchid
Monkey Orchid

NOTE: The time periods given are necessarily general and show when a plant **may** be seen in a particular stage throughout the region covered by the book and not necessarily that plants can be seen *e.g.* in flower and in seed at the same time in the same location. **Additionally, dead flower heads, particularly of some species, may persist well into the winter and beyond**, depending on prevailing weather and other facto

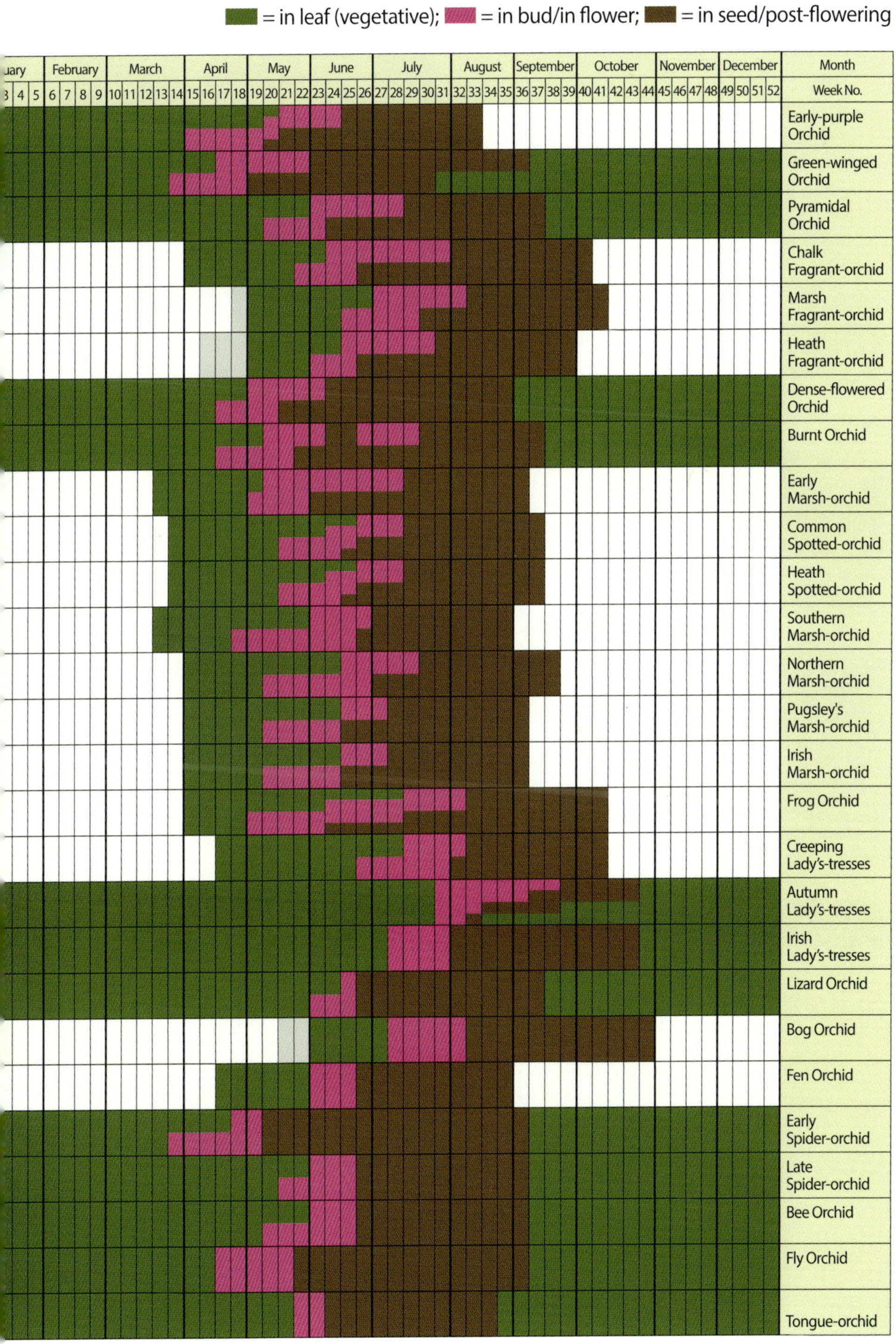
= in leaf (vegetative); = in bud/in flower; = in seed/post-flowering
uary
February
March
April
May
June
July
August
September
October
November
December
Month
3 4 5 6 7 8 9 10 11 12 13 14 15 16 17 18 19 20 21 22 23 24 25 26 27 28 29 30 31 32 33 34 35 36 37 38 39 40 41 42 43 44 45 46 47 48 49 50 51 52
Week No.
Early-purple Orchid
Green-winged Orchid
Pyramidal Orchid
Chalk Fragrant-orchid
Marsh Fragrant-orchid
Heath Fragrant-orchid
Dense-flowered Orchid
Burnt Orchid
Early Marsh-orchid
Common Spotted-orchid
Heath Spotted-orchid
Southern Marsh-orchid
Northern Marsh-orchid
Pugsley's Marsh-orchid
Irish Marsh-orchid
Frog Orchid
Creeping Lady's-tresses
Autumn Lady's-tresses
Irish Lady's-tresses
Lizard Orchid
Bog Orchid
Fen Orchid
Early Spider-orchid
Late Spider-orchid
Bee Orchid
Fly Orchid
Tongue-orchid

Orchids in their habitats

The following is a collection of photographs showing orchids in their habitats. This is not an exhaustive library of the all the habitats in which each species occurs but is instead intended to help by showing the species in context, as you may encounter them, with notes, where useful, on any micro-habitat details that will help narrow down a search.

Lady's-slipper (*p. 102*) | Limestone pavement, Lancashire; one of the reintroduced colonies.

Sword-leaved Helleborine (*p. 108*) | Beech woodland, Hampshire. Favours lighter areas such as glades and woodland edges.

Sword-leaved Helleborine (*p. 108*) | Oak woodland, Gwynedd. Favours lighter areas such as glades and woodland edges.

White Helleborine (*p. 106*) | Beech woodland, Oxfordshire. Can occur at woodland edges or in darker areas.

Red Helleborine (*p. 110*) | Beech woodland, Buckinghamshire. Favours glades or openings on sloping ground.

Marsh Helleborine (*p. 120*) | Dune slacks, Ceredigion. Often occurs in very large numbers in this habitat.

Marsh Helleborine (*p. 120*) | Fen, Shropshire (with Marsh Fragrant-orchids).

Dark-red Helleborine (*p. 122*) | Limestone grassland, County Durham. Also favours the 'grykes' (cracks) in limestone pavement.

Violet Helleborine (*p. 124*) | Beech woodland, Oxfordshire. Usually occurs in the darkest areas where little else can grow.

Broad-leaved Helleborine (*p. 126*) | Mixed plantation woodland, Ceredigion.

Narrow-lipped Helleborine (*p. 134*) | Beech woodland, Oxfordshire. Always occurs in the darkest areas where few other plants are able to grow.

Dune Helleborine (*p. 130*) | Wet birch woodland, Yorkshire.

Dune Helleborine – var. *tynensis* 'Tyne Helleborine' (*p. 133*) | Riverside scrub, Northumberland.

Green-flowered Helleborine (*p. 136*) | Wet willow woodland, Lincolnshire.

Bird's-nest Orchid (*p. 144*) | Beech woodland, Oxfordshire. Usually occurs in the darkest areas where few other plants are able to grow.

Common Twayblade (*p. 140*) | Wet birch woodland, Denbighshire.

Lesser Twayblade (*p. 142*) | Wet upland heathland, Gwynedd. Favours boggy areas of mature heathland, growing on beds of *Sphagnum* moss beneath the heath

Ghost Orchid (*p. 146*) | Dark Beech woodland, Oxfordshire. Favours damper areas in or on the edges of ditches, tracks or shallow depressions.

Fen Orchid (*p. 150*) | Dune slacks, Glamorgan. Occurs most abundantly in 'new' wet dune slacks that have very short, sparse vegetation.

Bog Orchid (*p. 152*) | Acidic bog, Ceredigion. Usually within small 'streams' or flushes on gently sloping ground where there is some movement of surface water.

Musk Orchid (*p. 154*) | Limestone grassland, Gloucestershire. Favours areas where the turf is short and sparse.

Coralroot Orchid (*p. 148*) | Dune slacks, Cumbria. Often hidden among a dense carpet of Creeping Willow *Salix repens*.

Coralroot Orchid (*p. 148*) | Wet birch and Alder woodland, Inverness-shire. Usually occurs in boggy areas on beds of moss, rather than among leaf-litter.

Autumn Lady's-tresses (*p. 166*) | Dune grassland, Devon. Favours areas where the turf is very short.

Lesser Butterfly-orchid (*p. 173*) | Acidic bog, Ceredigion. Occurs in a huge variety of other habitats but in bog habitats is associated with slightly more alkaline tussock in this case 'floating' on the bog itself.

Irish Lady's-tresses (*p. 168*) | Damp rush pasture, Co. Antrim.

Greater Butterfly-orchid (*p. 172*) | Lowland meadow, Ceredigion.

Creeping Lady's-tresses (*p. 164*) | Pine woodland, Inverness-shire.

Greater Butterfly-orchid (*p. 172*) | Limestone Ash woodland, Shropshire. Favours lighter areas such as coppiced glades and woodland edges but can survive i darker woodland.

Chalk Fragrant-orchid (*p. 176*) | Chalk grassland, Hampshire.

Small-white Orchid (*p. 156*) | Upland pasture, Yorkshire. Occurs in areas that are particularly rich in other upland flowers.

Heath Fragrant-orchid (*p. 176*) | Upland meadow, Powys.

Dense-flowered Orchid (*p. 158*) | Limestone pavement, Co. Clare.

Marsh Fragrant-orchid (*p. 177*) | Fen, Shropshire.

Burnt Orchid (*p. 160*) | Limestone grassland, Gloucestershire. Favours areas where the turf is short.

Lady Orchid (*p. 234*) | Mixed chalk woodland, Kent. Favours lighter areas such as coppiced glades and woodland edges but can survive in darker woodland.

Military Orchid (*p. 232*) | Chalk grassland, Oxfordshire. Favours sheltered grassy glades but can survive in darke woodland.

Monkey Orchid (*p. 230*) | Chalk grassland, Kent.

Man Orchid (*p. 228*) | Chalk grassland, Kent. Sometimes also occurs in scrub and light woodland.

Pyramidal Orchid (*p. 218*) | Hay meadow, Wiltshire. Always occurs on drier grasslands.

Green-winged Orchid (*p. 220*) | Hay meadow, Worcestershire. Favours slightly damper areas of grasslan

ommon Spotted-orchid (*p. 190*) | Hay meadow, /iltshire.

Heath Spotted-orchid (*p. 192*) | Upland meadow, Powys.

ommon Spotted-orchid (*p. 190*) | Limestone grassland, nropshire.

Heath Spotted-orchid (*p. 192*) | Heathland, Ceredigion.

ommon Spotted-orchid var. *hebridensis* (*p. 190*) | une grassland, Cornwall.

Heath Spotted-orchid (*p. 192*) | Wet rush pasture, Powys.

Northern Marsh-orchid (*p. 196*) | Upland pasture, Cumbria.

LOCHS
GLENS

Northern Marsh-orchid (*p. 196*) | Roadside verge, Cumbria. Often abundant in a variety of grassland habitats.

Southern Marsh-orchid (*p. 198*) | Marsh in re-landscaped industrial spoil, Staffordshire. Often abundant in a variety of grassland habitats.

Southern Marsh-orchid (*p. 198*) | Upland hay meadow, Powys.

Early Marsh-orchid (*p. 202*) | Fen, Hampshire.

Early Marsh-orchid var. *coccinea* (*p. 213*) | Dune slacks with Northern Marsh-orchid, Ceredigion. Usually occurs in large numbers in this habitat.

Pugsley's Marsh-orchid (*p. 206*) | Coastal flush, Co. Donegal. Typically associated with Black Bog-rush *Schoenus nigricans*.

Early-purple Orchid (*p. 226*) | Hedgebank, Ceredigion.

Irish Marsh-orchid (*p. 204*) | Limestone grassland, Co. Clare. Can be common in a variety of other grassland types, including roadside verges.

Early-purple Orchid (*p. 226*) | Limestone grassland, Yorkshire.

Frog Orchid (*p. 188*) | Disused limestone quarry, Flintshire.

Early-purple Orchid (*p. 226*) | Limestone ash woodland, Shropshire.

Lizard Orchid (*p. 214*) | Golf course on dune grassland, Somerset. Favours grasslands that are very dry and prone to drought.

Bee Orchid (*p. 242*) | Roadside grassland, Northamptonshire. Often associated with Common Bird's-foot-trefoil *Lotus corniculatus* and Oxeye Daisy *Leucanthemum vulgare* in this habitat.

Fly Orchid (*p. 238*) | Limestone grassland, Gloucestershire.

Fly Orchid (*p. 238*) | Fen, Anglesey. Grows on tussocks c Black Bog-rush *Schoenus nigricans* in this habitat.

Early Spider-orchid (*p. 240*) | Coastal limestone grassland, Dorset. Favours areas with very short turf.

Late Spider-orchid (*p. 244*) | Chalk grassland, Kent.

Identifying orchids

The majority of Britain and Ireland's orchids, once found (see *p. 35*), are relatively straightforward to identify – the remainder range from 'needing care' to 'difficult', especially in the case of species that are variable and/or prone to hybridizing.

The following sections cover orchids 'in leaf', 'in bud' and 'in flower', all of which are cross-referenced to the main species accounts and, where relevant, more detailed identification information.

When identifying an orchid, especially the more variable groups and those prone to hybridization, it is not always just a case of looking at its physical characteristics; it very often involves considering other supporting information, such as:

- Geographical location
- General habitat type
- Aspect and location of a plant within a habitat
- Associated species, both orchids and others
- Time of year/date of observation and stage of development at that point in time
- Overall shape and development of the plant, taking into account variation between several individuals
- Appearance of similar plants in the immediate vicinity
- Pollination method

Relevant supporting information is described in the main species accounts, as appropriate. The accounts group similar species together rather than being in strict taxonomic order, with expanded sections covering subspecies, varieties and variations that may be encountered, together with a cross-referenced list of hybrids.

It is intended that, having found an unfamiliar orchid, you should be able to narrow down the options using the information in this section, *e.g.* for a plant in flower by using the chart and/or key before checking the main species account and, if necessary, the variations and hybrids.

However, due to the nature of some species, particularly the *Dactylorhiza* spotted-orchids and marsh-orchids it may only be possible to arrive at a 'most likely' identification in the field.

In relation to a scaled 20p coin (*top right*) the relative size of a Pyramidal Orchid *Anacamptis pyramidalis* compared to a typical, tiny Burnt Orchid *Neotinea ustulata* can really be appreciated.

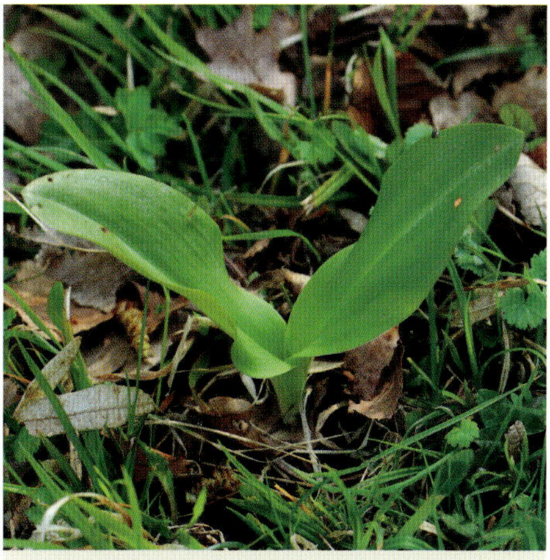

Although there are no features that unequivocally distinguish Greater (*shown*) and Lesser Butterfly-orchids when in leaf, habitat and associated species may provide good clues.

Identifying orchids in leaf

This section is designed to help you identify orchids when they are in a vegetative state – or in leaf. Some species are visible above ground virtually all year round (see *pp. 38–39*), whereas others lie dormant below ground until a month or two before flowering. When not flowering, orchids can be observed in a range of different states, described below. **Ghost**, **Coralroot** and **Bird's-nest Orchids** do not photosynthesize (or not significantly), so lack green leaves and are therefore not covered here.

Rosette

Prior to flowering, all photosynthetic orchid species produce a rosette – a roughly circular arrangement of leaves more or less flat to the ground – or leafy spike (helleborines). Warmth-loving species tend to produce a rosette a month or two after flowering and can therefore be found from autumn through winter into the following spring or summer, when the leaves may then begin to die back and wither as the plant comes into flower.

Non-flowering or 'blind'

In some years an orchid may, for whatever reason, not flower and instead rest as a rosette or short stem with several leaves. This is a particularly common trait among the helleborines, where a significant proportion of a colony may be found in this condition.

Immature

Young plants can be found occasionally within a population of mature orchids. Young plants are always much smaller with fewer, often narrower leaves. Accurate identification of these based on physical features alone can be difficult – so, where possible, always examine mature plants in the immediate vicinity, as the probability is that the nearest mature orchids will be the same species.

Preparing to flower (in bud)

Orchids that are preparing to flower will have buds that are not fully visible and often sheathed by bracts or leaves. The size and shape of the bracts and sheathing leaves, and texture of the stem, can be used in conjunction with features of the leaf and the habitat in which the plant is growing to attempt an identification. Buds are illustrated by photographs in the species accounts.

Will it flower?

Judging whether an orchid is going to flower can be tricky – those that will do so during the forthcoming season typically have a small leaf, or several small leaves, unfurling from the centre of the rosette or from the top of the stem. These will continue to unfurl and extend until the flowering spike begins to ascend from this central point. However, non-flowering plants lack these small unfurling leaves and do not develop further, retaining a reduced number of leaves (see *below*).

A mature Sword-leaved Helleborine that is not flowering this season (*i.e.* 'blind').

An immature Lady Orchid looks very different to a mature plant (see *p. 73*).

Orchid 'lookalikes' in leaf

Only a few plants have leaves that could be confused with an orchid. Many of these can immediately be ruled out by the presence of a stalk (lacking in orchids), leaf veins in a network (longitudinal in all but Creeping Lady's-tresses (*p. 68*)), or by some other obvious feature. **The most commonly encountered 'lookalike' species that could be confused with in-leaf orchids are shown opposite; others are shown on the following pages for comparison.**

single leaf; no veins

Adder's-tongue (fern)
Ophioglossum vulgatum
[immature orchids]

leaves atop stem with purplish base

Lily-of-the-Valley
Convallaria majalis
[Butterfly-orchids *p. 62*,
Common Twayblade *p. 63*]

leaves ±equal; held in flat plane

Solomon's-seal
Polygonatum multiflorum
[Helleborines *pp. 58–61*]

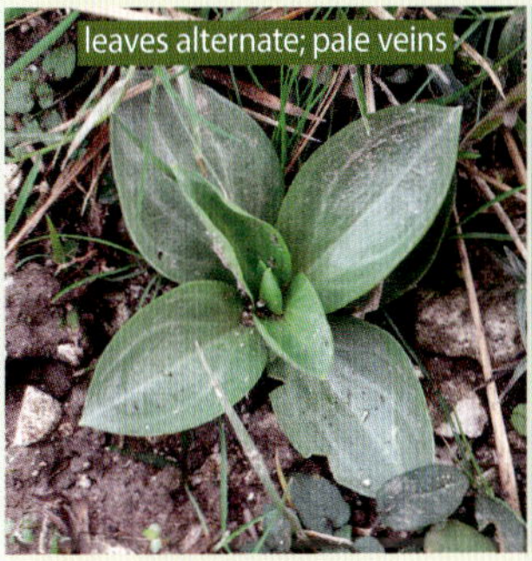
leaves alternate; pale veins

Centauries
Centaurium spp.
[*Ophrys pp. 74–75*]

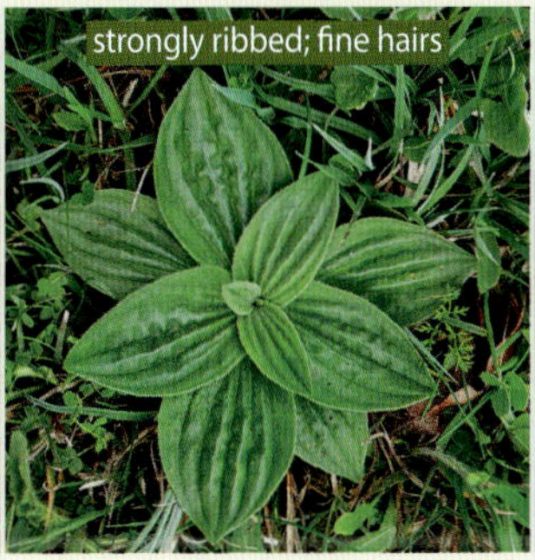
strongly ribbed; fine hairs

Plantains
Plantago spp.
[*Ophrys*, in particular, *pp. 74–75*]

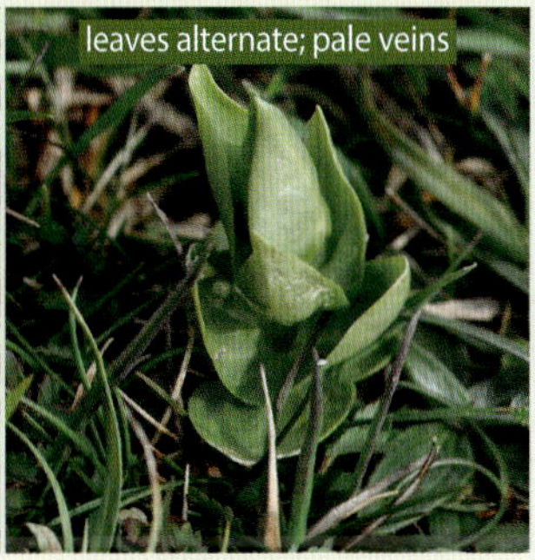
leaves alternate; pale veins

Yellow-wort
Blackstonia perfoliata
[*Ophrys pp. 74–75*]

Bluebell *Hyacinthoides non-scripta* (LEFT) with Early-purple Orchid (RIGHT); Bluebells have a pointed, keel-shaped leaf tip that is usually pale at the very tip.

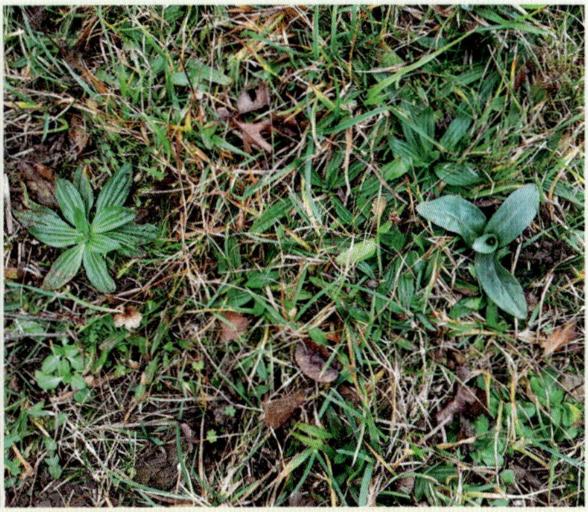

Ribwort Plantain *Plantago lanceolata* (LEFT) with Bee Orchid (RIGHT) showing the strong longitudinal veins of the plantain compared with the 'smooth' orchid.

Guide to British and Irish orchids in leaf when mature

Immature and non-flowering plants can look very different with fewer and/or narrower leaves than mature pre-flowering individuals. The page numbers refer to the relevant species 'in-leaf' account.

LEAVES along stem, not forming a rosette

Lady's-slipper
p. 56

***Cephalanthera* helleborines**
3 species *p. 57*

***Epipactis* helleborines**
7 species *pp. 58–61*

LEAVES erect

Basal leaves same size as stem leaves

Fragrant-orchids
3 species *p. 67*

Small-white Orchid
p. 64

Irish Lady's-tresses
p. 68

Basal leaves broader than stem leaves

Frog Orchid
p. 70

NB marsh-orchid leaves can be plain or spotted

Marsh-orchids, spotted-orchids
8 species *pp. 69–70*

LEAVES usually paired

Twayblades
2 species *p. 63*

Butterfly-orchids
2 species *p. 62*

Musk Orchid
p. 65

Fen Orchid
p. 64

NB A few specimens of Musk Orchid have three leaves and some Dense-flowered Orchids two. Bog Orchid (*p. 64*) is minute and unlikely to be seen unless specifically looked for in its habitat.

LEAVES 'star' arrangement

Pyramidal Orchid, Green-winged Orchid
p. 66

Tongue-orchid
p. 65

LEAVES 'rosette' of three or more leaves

Lady's-tresses
2 species *p. 68*

Burnt/Dense-flowered Orchids
p. 64

***Ophrys* orchids**
4 species *pp. 74–75*

Early-purple Orchid
p. 71

'Manikin' orchids
3 species *pp. 72–73*

Lizard Orchid
p. 67

Lady's-slipper *p. 76*, p. 102
Cypripedium calceolus APRIL–MAY

COMPARE WITH: Broad-leaved and other helleborines.

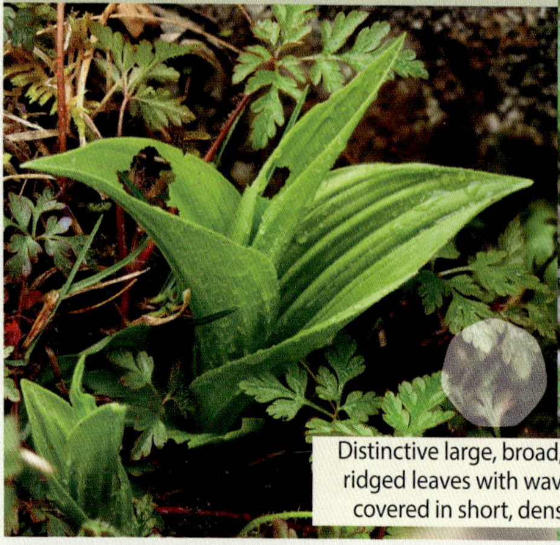
Distinctive large, broad, strongly ridged leaves with wavy edges, covered in short, dense hairs.

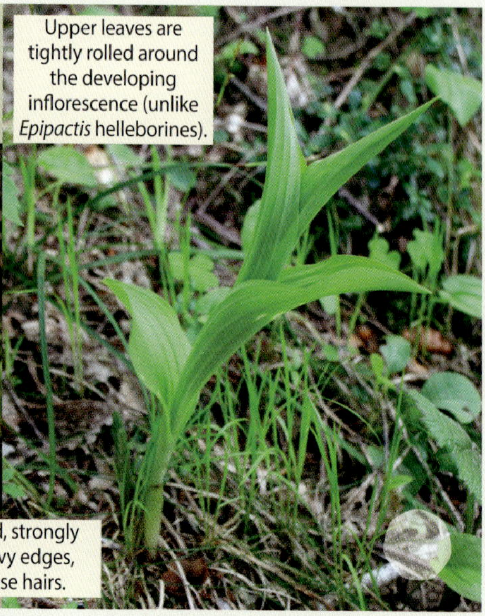
Upper leaves are tightly rolled around the developing inflorescence (unlike *Epipactis* helleborines).

Cephalanthera and *Epipactis* helleborines

Cephalanthera and *Epipactis* helleborines emerge in spring and summer respectively, as a spike of rolled or tightly clasping leaves. As the plant matures, the leaves are spaced along the stem, usually in an alternate or spiral arrangement. However, the developing flower spikes of *Cephalanthera* are always held straight until flowering, whereas in *Epipactis* the developing flower spike is held in an arching position. Both genera can look superficially like other woodland plants such as Lily-of-the-valley *Convallaria majalis*, which has paired leaves that protrude from the ground separately with no stem, and Solomon's-seals *Polygonatum* spp., which are always entirely arching with leaves arranged alternately along the top of the stem (see *p. 53*).

BUDS: upright

***Cephalanthera* helleborine**

BUDS: arch downwards

BASAL LEAF: second lowermost leaf smaller and more rounded than leaves above.

***Epipactis* helleborine**

Cephalanthera helleborines

COMPARE WITH: Each other, and *Epipactis* helleborines (*pp.* 58–59) not in bud,

BASAL LEAF:
purplish

STEM: base whitish

BASAL LEAF: green

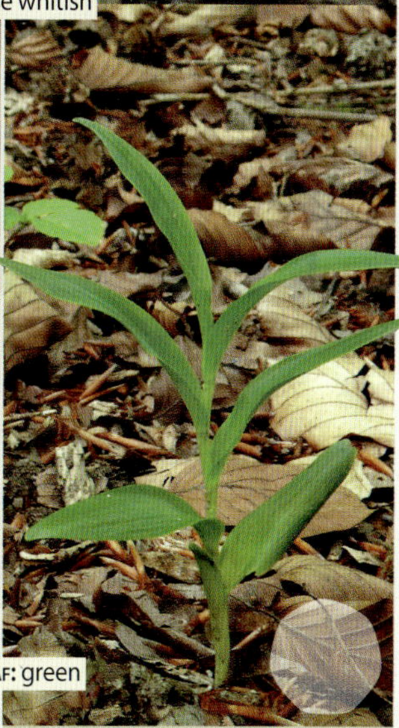

Red Helleborine *p. 76*, *p. 110*
Cephalanthera rubra APRIL–JUNE

Darker green leaves than others in the genus; arranged alternately up the stem.

Small clasping basal leaf is purplish with dark veins (unlike other members of the genus).

Sword-leaved Helleborine *p. 76*, *p. 108*
Cephalanthera longifolia LATE MARCH–MAY

Long, narrow leaves arranged alternately or spirally up the stem. Mature plants have leaves with strong veins that form ridges on the underside.

White Helleborine *p. 76*, *p. 106*
Cephalanthera damasonium LATE MARCH–MAY

Fewer, broader leaves than Sword-leaved Helleborine; arranged alternately; second lowermost leaf relatively long and thin, almost the same size as leaves above *cf. Epipactis* helleborines.

Epipactis helleborines

Marsh, Dark-red and Violet Helleborines are somewhat distinctive; the remaining four are similar to one another. All four can occur with each other, but occurrence with the widespread Broad-leaved Helleborine is more likely. For this reason, it is useful to become familiar with Broad-leaved Helleborine and it is used here as the basis for comparison with the other similar *Epipactis*.

Broad-leaved Helleborine

p. 77, p. 126

Epipactis helleborine

MAY–JULY

Variable but typically with **rather broad leaves arranged in a spiral around the stem**, the base of which always has a purplish wash. **COMPARE WITH:** Narrow-lipped, Dune and Green-flowered Helleborines.

Shoot (INSET) and emerging plant

Leaves arranged in a **spiral** around the stem and sometimes floppy.

Rosette from side

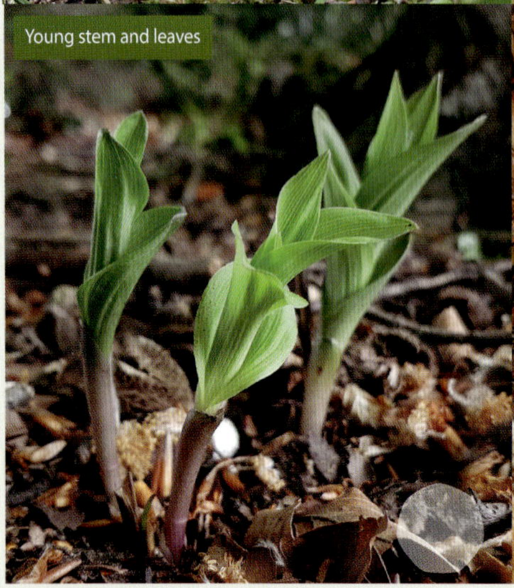

Young stem and leaves

Leaves usually rather broad and dark green.

Rosette from above

Leaves usually arranged alternately up the stem.

Narrow-lipped Helleborine *p.77*, *p.134*
Epipactis leptochila MAY–JULY

Paler green in every part of the plant than Broad-leaved Helleborine (with which it often co-occurs). **COMPARE WITH:** Broad-leaved, Dune and Green-flowered Helleborines (*p.60*).

Leaves usually arranged alternately up the stem and often held rather erect.

Dune Helleborine *p.77*, *p.130*
Epipactis dunensis MAY–JULY

Usually paler, olive to yellowish-green in every part of the plant than Broad-leaved Helleborine (with which it often co-occurs). **COMPARE WITH:** Broad-leaved and Green-flowered Helleborines (*p.60*).

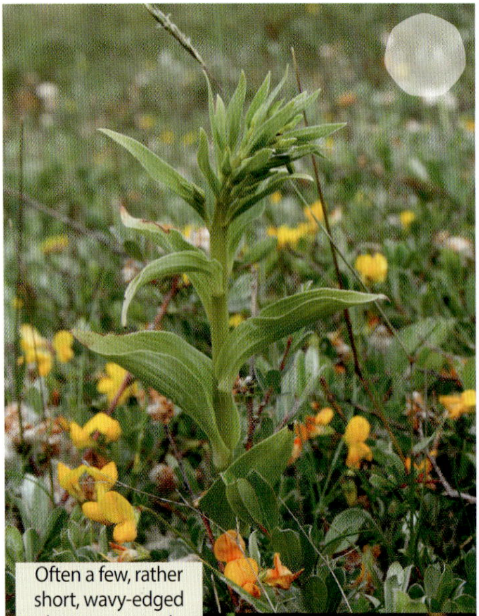
Often a few, rather short, wavy-edged leaves arranged alternately up stem.

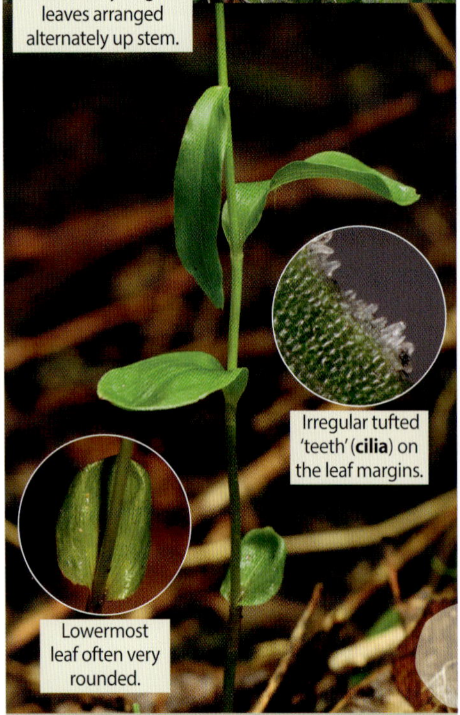
Irregular tufted 'teeth' (**cilia**) on the leaf margins.
Lowermost leaf often very rounded.

Green-flowered Helleborine *p. 77*, *p. 136*

Epipactis phyllanthes MAY–JULY

COMPARE WITH: Broad-leaved, Dune and Narrow-lipped Helleborines (may co-occur with all) (*pp. 58–59*).

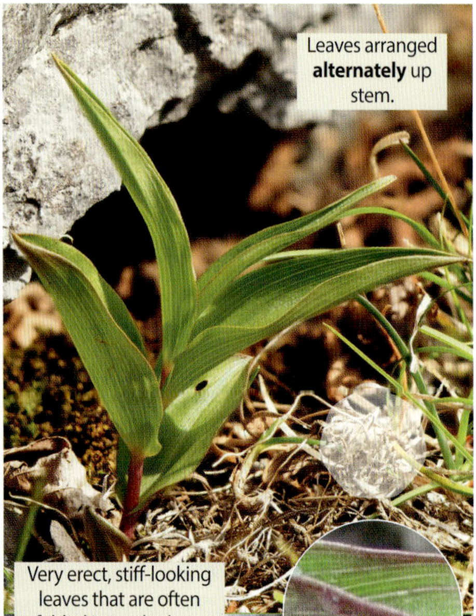
Leaves arranged **alternately** up stem.
Very erect, stiff-looking leaves that are often folded inwards along their length.

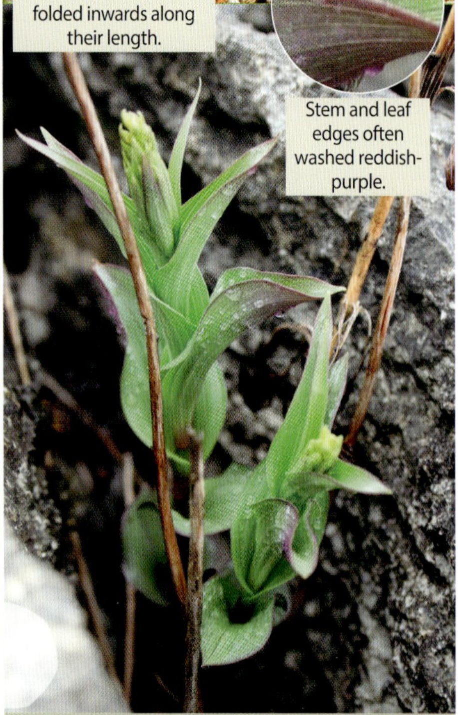
Stem and leaf edges often washed reddish-purple.

Dark-red Helleborine *p. 77*, *p. 122*

Epipactis atrorubens MAY–JULY

COMPARE WITH: Broad-leaved Helleborine (*p. 58*), although Dark-red Helleborine's habitat makes it a relatively distinctive species.

Whole plant generally washed dark pink or purple on first emergence; turning a dull purple colour as the plant matures through the season.

Violet Helleborine *p.77*, *p.124*

Epipactis purpurata LATE MAY–EARLY AUGUST

Purplish wash distinctive when not in flower. Curiously, Violet Helleborine does not appear to produce non-flowering plants, neither as resting mature individuals nor young plants that are yet to flower. **COMPARE WITH:** None.

The leaves are held rather erect but closer to horizontal in taller fen vegetation.

Star-shaped rosette.
Long, pointed leaves.

Marsh Helleborine *p.77*, *p.120*

Epipactis palustris MAY–EARLY JULY

In open habitats, leaves clustered in rosette unlike other *Epipactis*; similar to *Dactylorhiza* orchids with which it often co-occurs. **COMPARE WITH:** Marsh-orchids (*p.69*).

Butterfly-orchids

Distinctive long, usually paired leaves, although non-flowering plants may only produce a single leaf. In woodland habitats, the base of the leaves often taper to become very narrow where they meet the ground. The upper surface may show pale spots. It is not possible to identify in-leaf butterfly-orchids to species with any confidence. Although they have slightly different habitat preferences, there is significant overlap in their ranges. On average, Lesser Butterfly-orchid has smaller leaves than Greater Butterfly-orchid, but this feature is not diagnostic. **COMPARE WITH:** Common Twayblade, the leaves of which have a pointed tip and the buds are not covered by large bracts.

Some plants produce a single leaf.
Developing buds covered by large bracts.
Tip blunt-ended.
Typical paired leaf.
Leaf edges usually wavy.
life size

BUTTERFLY-ORCHIDS *p. 170*

Greater Butterfly-orchid *p. 78*, *p. 172*
Platanthera chlorantha
LATE MARCH–JUNE

Lesser Butterfly-orchid *p. 78*, *p. 173*
P. bifolia
MAY–JUNE

Twayblades

The common name refers to the number of leaves, as 'tway-blade' means 'two-leaves' in old English although, rarely, some plants have three leaves. Common Twayblade can be confused with young Beech *Fagus sylvatica* seedlings. Non-flowering Lesser Twayblades can look like young Bilberry *Vaccinium myrtillus* plants, which differ in having oval leaves with a serrated edge.

Beech *Fagus sylvatica*

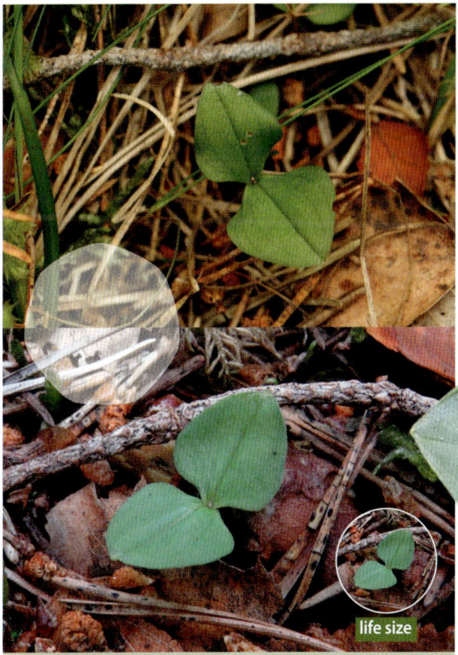
life size

Lesser Twayblade

p. 77, *p. 142*

Neottia cordata

APRIL–MID-JUNE

Tiny paired heart-shaped leaves that are faintly net-veined (an unusual feature in British and Irish orchids). Typically hidden among mosses and heather. **COMPARE WITH:** Very similar to young Bilberry plants, with which it co-occurs.

Developing buds not covered by large bracts.

The leaf tip has **a tiny pointed projection**, which is lost as it matures.

life size

Common Twayblade

p. 77, *p. 140*

Neottia ovata

MID-MARCH–EARLY JUNE

Large paired oval-shaped leaves with two prominent veins either side of the midrib. Developing buds clearly visible once leaves unfurl. **COMPARE WITH:** Butterfly-orchids; similar to emergent cotyledons of Beech (*top left*).

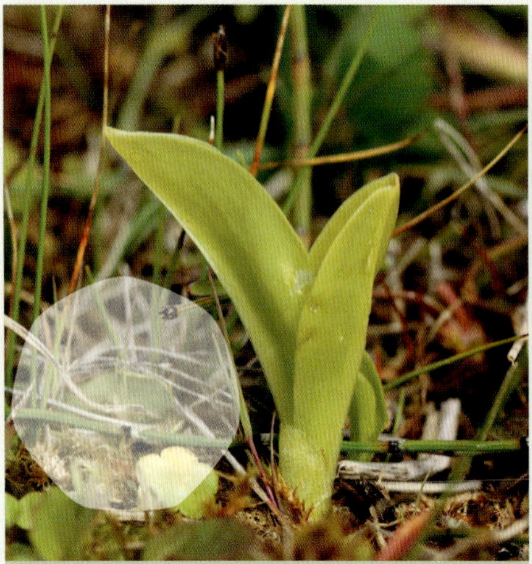

Fen Orchid *p.76, p.150*

Liparis loeselii MID-APRIL–MAY

Paired leaves with a distinctive and unique waxy texture. Leaves usually folded, forming a shallow trough and usually very erect – only rarely flattened-out in fen habitats. Dune plants tend to have shorter, rounder leaves with a blunt tip; those in fens have narrower leaves with a more pointed tip. **COMPARE WITH:** Twayblades (*p.63*).

Edges of the leaves often lined with tiny ball-like structures called '**bulbils**' that can break off and develop into new plants.

Bog Orchid *p.76, p.152*

Hammarbya paludosa JUNE–EARLY JULY

Smallest leaves of all British and Irish orchids, forming minuscule rosettes that rest precariously on bare peat or *Sphagnum* moss carpets. Because of their size, non-flowering plants are near impossible to spot but can be found by closely looking in the vicinity of a flowering plant. **COMPARE WITH:** Only likely to be mistaken for other bog plants (not other orchids).

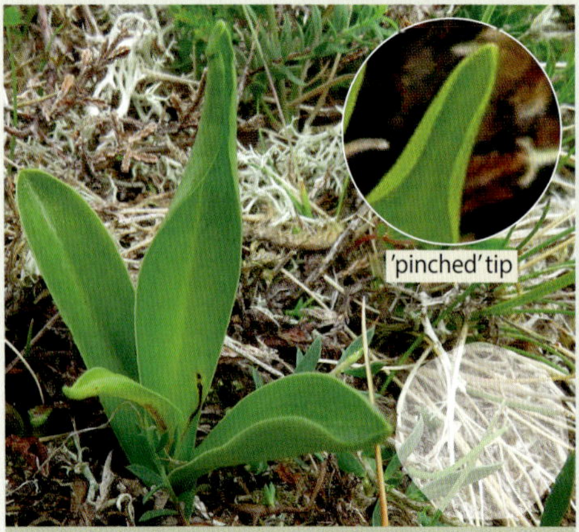
'pinched' tip

Small-white Orchid *p.76, p.156*

Pseudorchis albida MAY

Small, pale green rosette comprising thin, erect upper leaves and broader basal leaves. **Leaves have a unique 'pinched' tip** – rolled inwards with the whole leaf tip bent back away from the stem. **COMPARE WITH:** Fragrant-orchids (*p.67*) and marsh-orchids (*p.69*).

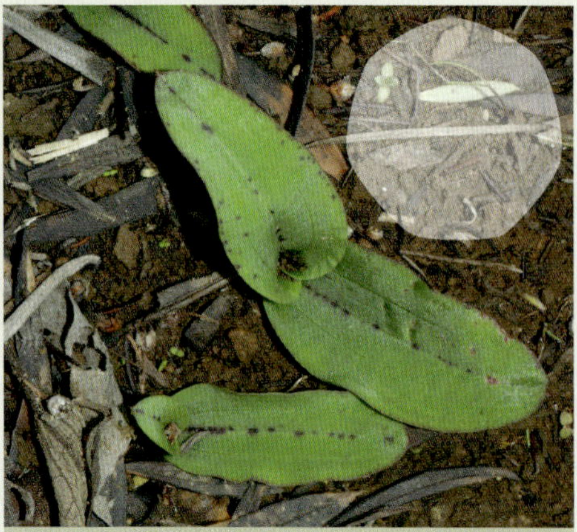

Dense-flowered Orchid *p.76, p.158*

Neotinea maculata SEPTEMBER–APRIL

Small, nondescript rosette, most easily identified by the two or three wavy-edged leaves lying rather flat to the ground. The leaves may be unmarked or covered in small spots with dark edges. **COMPARE WITH:** Bee Orchid (*p.75*).

Some have reddish leaf edges and tips.

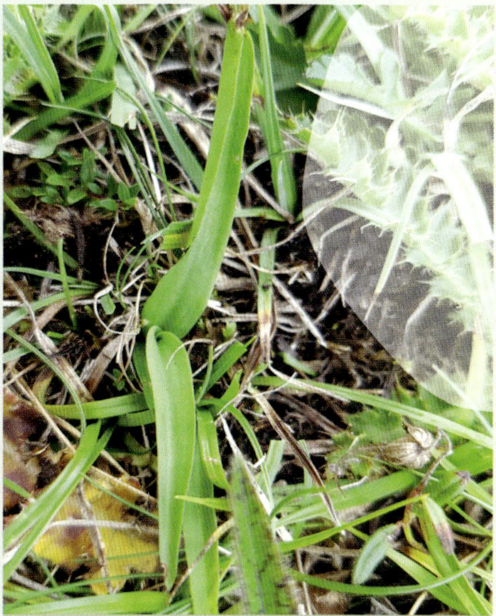

Musk Orchid *p. 78*, p. 154

Herminium monorchis MAY–MID-JUNE

Rosettes are very small and difficult to spot, so are unlikely to be found by accident. They usually have two (sometimes three) leaves held more or less flat to the ground. **COMPARE WITH:** Fragrant-orchids (*p. 67*).

Burnt Orchid *p. 78*, p. 160

Neotinea ustulata SEPTEMBER–APRIL

A hard-to-spot rosette that looks very similar to that of a small Bee Orchid in colour, shape and leaf number but is a third to a fifth of the size. The rosette overwinters and is held flat to the ground. **COMPARE WITH:** Bee Orchid (*p. 75*).

Tongue-orchid *p. 78*, p. 216

Serapias lingua LATE AUGUST–MAY

Simple rosette of three or four very long, narrow leaves arranged oppositely. **COMPARE WITH:** Fragrant-orchids (*p. 67*), Musk Orchid.

During autumn and winter, both species show small, black leaf-tip projections to their **keeled leaves**. However, beware, as this feature may disappear as the leaves begin to die back during spring and early summer. Other species may develop damaged leaf tips as they age and can look similar, but leaf-tip blackening will not have the consistent form as shown. Several leaves and (if possible) rosettes should be examined to differentiate between genuine morphology and random leaf damage.

Small, straight, black projection on leaf tip.

Small, hooked, black projection on leaf tip.

Very narrow; pale green to greyish-green.

Dark green.

Pyramidal Orchid *p. 78*, *p. 218*

Anacamptis pyramidalis MID-SEPTEMBER–MAY

Distinctive rosette with very narrow, pointed and sometimes curled leaves held flat to the ground – giving it the appearance of a 'green starfish'. Sometimes several rosettes may be clustered together to create a mass of tufted leaves. **COMPARE WITH:** Green-winged Orchid, Man Orchid (*p. 73*) and fragrant-orchids.

Green-winged Orchid *p. 79*, *p. 220*

Anacamptis morio LATE JULY–MID-APRIL

Rosette similar to Pyramidal Orchid, being rather flat with many long leaves. Sometimes several rosettes may be clustered together to create a mass of tufted leaves. **COMPARE WITH:** Pyramidal Orchid, Man Orchid (*p. 73*) and fragrant-orchids.

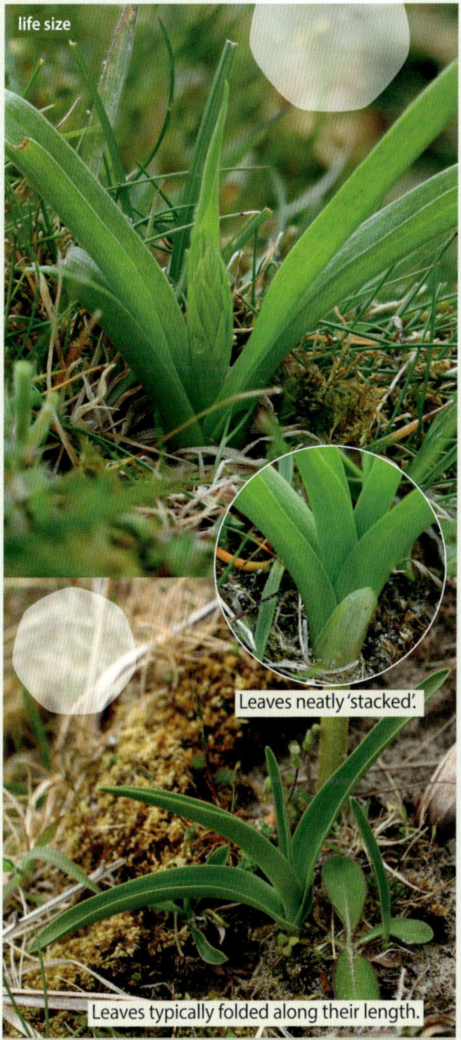
life size
Leaves neatly 'stacked'.
Leaves typically folded along their length.

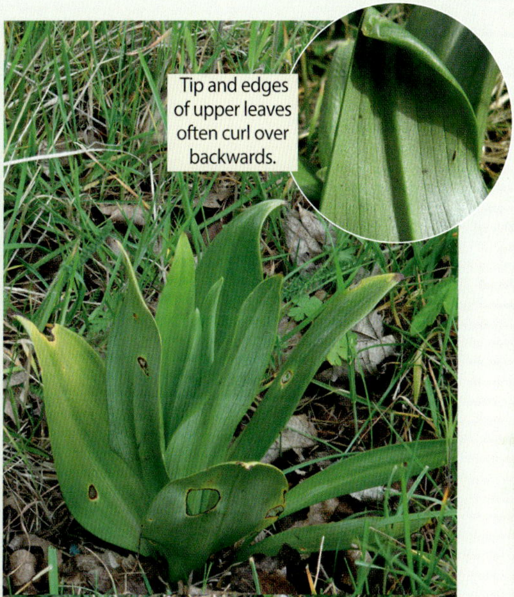
Tip and edges of upper leaves often curl over backwards.

Leaves usually damaged and blackened at their edges and tip.

Fragrant-orchids *p. 78*, *pp. 174–179*

Gymnadenia spp. APRIL–JUNE

Despite their quite different habitat preferences, the fragrant-orchids – Chalk, Heath and Marsh – are virtually impossible to separate on vegetative features alone, and so are treated here together.

Rosette formed of thin, arching leaves that look as if they have been neatly stacked on top of each other. The leaves are typically folded along their length, making them appear even narrower and more pointed. **COMPARE WITH:** Green-winged Orchid, Pyramidal Orchid.

Lizard Orchid *p. 78*, *p. 214*

Himantoglossum hircinum SEPTEMBER–MID-JUNE

Often produces a very large rosette (matched in size only by large Lady Orchid plants) comprising very glossy leaves reminiscent of those of Cherry Laurel *Prunus laurocerasus* in colour, shape and glossiness. **COMPARE WITH:** Bee Orchid (*p. 75*), Lady Orchid (*p. 73*).

Lady's-tresses

Each of the Lady's-tresses has a very different rosette and occurs in a different habitat. Irish Lady's-tresses is extremely hard to find as a rosette as it can easily be confused for a grass or sedge. Creeping Lady's-tresses cannot easily be confused with other orchids but could be mistaken for other plants, particularly wintergreen species. Autumn Lady's-tresses is superficially like a Bee Orchid, but is very small and lies very flat – so is unlikely to be confused.

Round-leaved Wintergreen *Pyrola rotundifolia*

Irish Lady's-tresses

p. 76, *p. 168*

Spiranthes romanzoffiana OCTOBER–EARLY JULY

An extremely difficult species to spot when not in flower on account of its long, hairless grass-like leaves that blend into the tall marshland vegetation in which it occurs. Overwinters as a tiny, shoot-like rosette, just 2 cm tall. **COMPARE WITH:** Grasses and sedges, which differ in having a serrated leaf edge or ligule, or both.

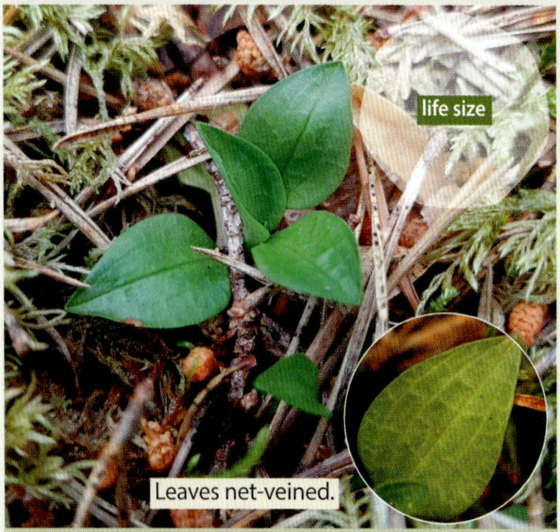
life size
Leaves net-veined.

Creeping Lady's-tresses

p. 76, *p. 164*

Goodyera repens MAY–MID-JULY

The clustered groups of rosettes, with faintly net-veined leaves, on a pine forest floor make this species distinctive. **COMPARE WITH:** Species in the wintergreen genera *Pyrola* and *Orthilia* can initially look similar in size, arrangement and colour but on close inspection their leaves clearly have a stalk and serrated edges.

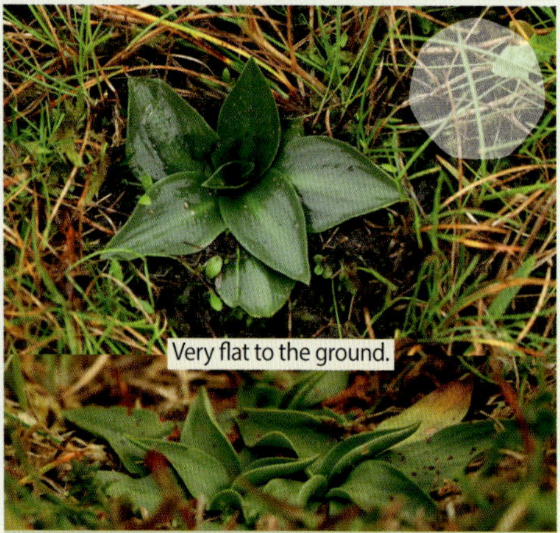
Very flat to the ground.

Autumn Lady's-tresses

p. 76, *p. 166*

Spiranthes spiralis MID-AUGUST–JULY

Small, neat rosettes so flat to the ground that they are safe from mower blades and so the species flourishes on lawns and even such unlikely places as old grass tennis courts. The rosette overwinters but withers away entirely before the flowering spike appears. The following year's rosette always develops next to a flowering spike. **COMPARE WITH:** Burnt Orchid (*p. 65*), Bee Orchid (*p. 75*).

Marsh-orchids and spotted-orchids

Marsh-orchid rosettes are distinctive, with pointed, erect upper leaves and broader, blunter basal leaves. The first leaves to emerge are opposite to one another but as the rosette matures and more leaves are produced, the rosette may develop a more spiral arrangement. However, there is a wide variation both within and between species of both leaf shape and markings, *e.g.* Early Marsh-orchid retains its hook-tipped, keeled leaves and only Southern Marsh-orchid has unmarked leaves; all other species routinely or occasionally have leaves marked with spots, blotches, rings or bar markings. **Typically, marsh-orchids have broader leaves than either of the spotted-orchid species.**

MARSH-ORCHIDS

Early Marsh-orchid — *p. 79, p. 202*
Dactylorhiza incarnata — MID-MARCH–EARLY MAY

Northern Marsh-orchid — *p. 79, p. 196*
D. purpurella — APRIL–MID-JUNE

Southern Marsh-orchid — *p. 79, p. 198*
D. praetermissa — MARCH–MAY

Pugsley's Marsh-orchid — *p. 79, p. 206*
D. traunsteinerioides — APRIL–MID-JUNE

Irish Marsh-orchid — *p. 79, p. 204*
D. kerryensis — APRIL–MID-JUNE

Due to the wide overlap in measurements of these species in a vegetative state, and the similarly wide overlap in ranges, these species are treated here together. Some orchidologists argue that it is possible to separate the species based on vegetative characteristics alone, but experience suggests otherwise: it is safest instead to rely on habitat and location to make a 'most likely' decision when observing a plant.

life size

A marsh-orchid with spotted leaves can be easily confused with those of a spotted-orchid. However, marsh-orchid leaves (ABOVE) are typically broader than those of a spotted-orchid (RIGHT) and a gentle squeeze will show the stems are hollow (solid in spotted-orchids).

life size

Frog Orchid *p. 79*, *p. 188*
Dactylorhiza viridis APRIL–MID-JULY

Small, neat rosette with **three or four short, blunt-ended leaves** held oppositely and flat to the ground. **COMPARE WITH:** Marsh-orchids (*p. 69*).

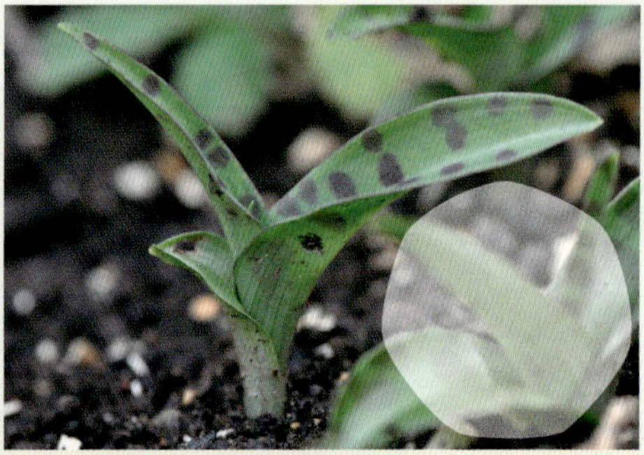

Leaves **opposite** and held **rather erect**.

Upper leaves narrower and more pointed than basal.

Leaves often
with dark edges.

SPOTTED-ORCHIDS

Common Spotted-orchid *p. 79*, *p. 190*
Dactylorhiza fuchsii LATE MARCH–JUNE

Heath Spotted-orchid *p. 79*, *p. 192*
D. maculata LATE MARCH–JUNE

Despite their usually quite different habitat preferences, these two species are virtually impossible to separate when in leaf.

Commonly encountered rosette, with characteristic spots on the leaves. **COMPARE WITH:** Early-purple Orchid; distinguished by leaf shape and arrangement (see annotations).

Early-purple Orchid

p. 79, p. 226

Orchis mascula

JANUARY–MID-MAY

A distinctive roughly star-shaped rosette that is common in late winter and spring in woodlands and calcareous grasslands. **COMPARE WITH:** Spotted-orchids; distinguished by leaf shape and arrangement (see annotations).

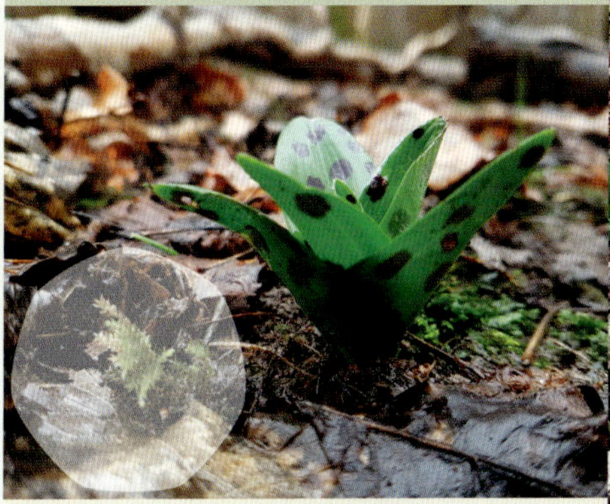

Leaves **in a spiral**; often **rather flat** to the ground.

life size

All leaves strap-like with blunt tip and glossy texture.

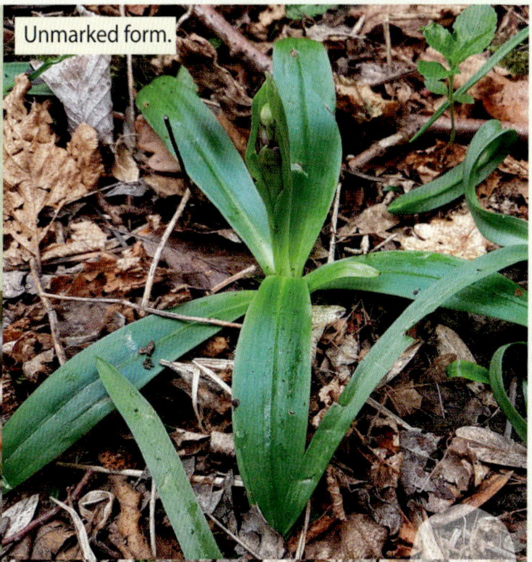

Unmarked form.

Typical spotted leaf.

Heavily spotted leaf.

Orchis orchids

Orchis species form a roughly star-shaped rosette of blunt-tipped and, sometimes, glossy leaves. All species appear in late winter and early spring, except for Man Orchid which emerges above ground in autumn.

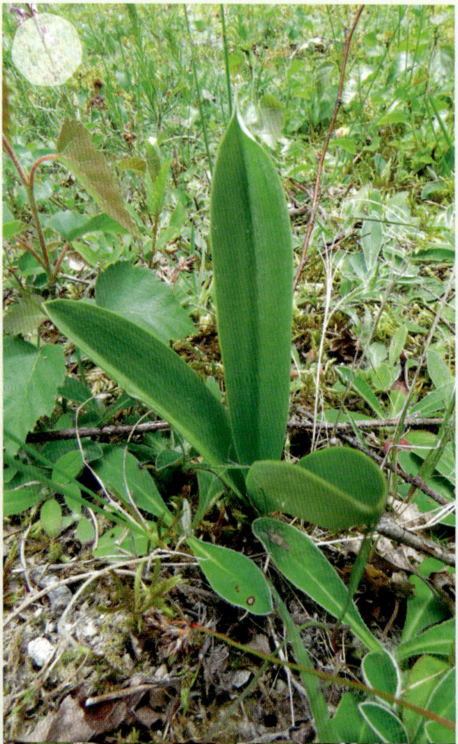

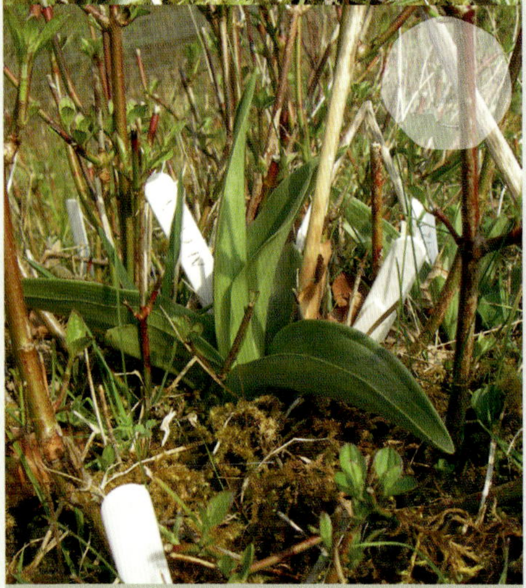

Monkey Orchid *p.79, p.230*

Orchis simia LATE FEBRUARY–EARLY MAY

Rosette very similar to Military Orchid but roughly half the size (approx. 10 cm across). **COMPARE WITH:** Military Orchid.

Military Orchid *p.79, p.232*

Orchis militaris LATE MARCH–EARLY MAY

Large, thick leaves that fold along their length to form a trough shape. **COMPARE WITH:** Monkey Orchid.

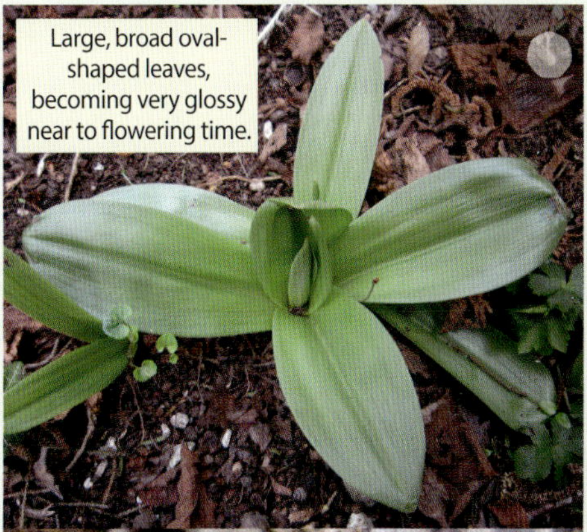
Large, broad oval-shaped leaves, becoming very glossy near to flowering time.

Upper leaf surface has many fine, pale veins.

Lady Orchid *p. 79, p. 234*

Orchis purpurea JANUARY–EARLY MAY

Large rosette of broad, blunt-ended, fresh-looking leaves. The upper surface of the leaf has many fine, pale veins and becomes very glossy nearer to flowering time. **COMPARE WITH:** Lizard Orchid (*p. 67*), other *Orchis* orchids.

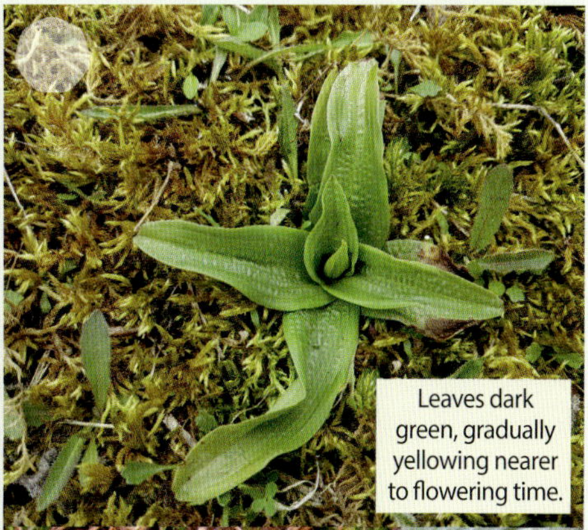
Leaves dark green, gradually yellowing nearer to flowering time.

Leaves have 'blister'-like structures on upper surface in most plants, but are not 'frosted' *cf. Ophrys*.

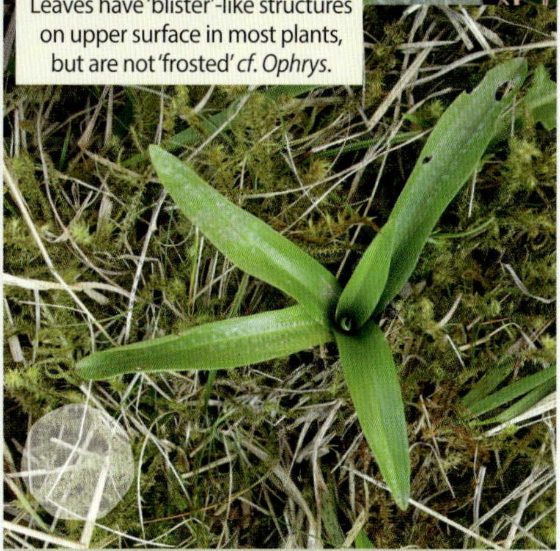

Man Orchid *p. 79, p. 228*

Orchis anthropophora LATE AUGUST–APRIL

Fairly distinctive flat rosette, with leaves that tend to be widest near the middle. The leaves often have 'blister'-like structures on their upper surface. In some locations the rosette may appear in November and overwinters, but in other areas it appears above ground a couple of months later. **COMPARE WITH:** Lady Orchid, Bee Orchid (*p. 75*), Green-winged and Pyramidal Orchids (both *p. 66*).

Ophrys orchids

Ophrys leaves are typically rather greyish-green with numerous fine, dark veins. **The upper surface often shows a silvery 'frosting' that is created by the surface layer lifting up and small air pockets forming underneath.** The tips of the leaves often blacken and break off shortly before and during flowering. Man Orchid (*p. 73*) also often has 'blisters' but the leaves are shiny with less obvious veins.

The 'frosting' caused by air pockets and the blackened tips typical of *Ophrys* leaves.

Spider-orchid rosettes are more compact and stubby than those of Bee Orchid.

Early Spider-orchid *p. 78*, *p. 240*
Ophrys sphegodes SEPTEMBER–APRIL

Leaves prominently veined and oval-shaped, reminiscent of Hoary Plantain *Plantago media*. They also look similar to Bee Orchid but the rosette is more compact and stubby, and usually consists of more leaves. Although some rosettes overwinter, most plants appear above ground in spring (unlike other *Ophrys* species, which usually overwinter as rosettes). **COMPARE WITH:** Late Spider-orchid, Bee Orchid.

Late Spider-orchid *p. 78*, *p. 244*
Ophrys fuciflora SEPTEMBER–MAY

Rosette very similar to those of both Bee Orchid and Early Spider-orchid, with several greyish-green leaves and the characteristic silvery 'frosting' on the upper surface. On average, the rosette has more leaves than that of a Bee Orchid, but is a similar size. **COMPARE WITH:** Early Spider-orchid, Bee Orchid.

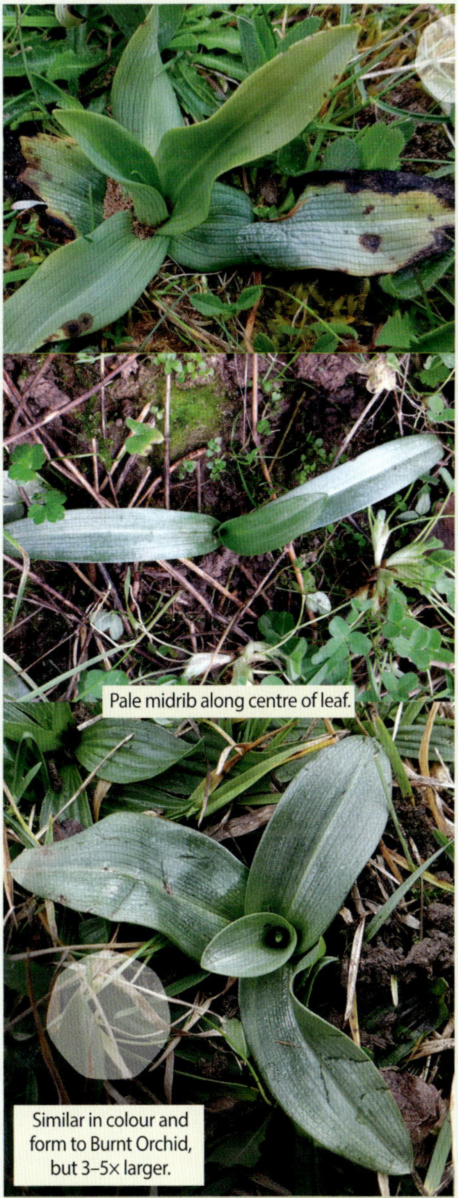
Pale midrib along centre of leaf.
Similar in colour and form to Burnt Orchid, but 3–5× larger.

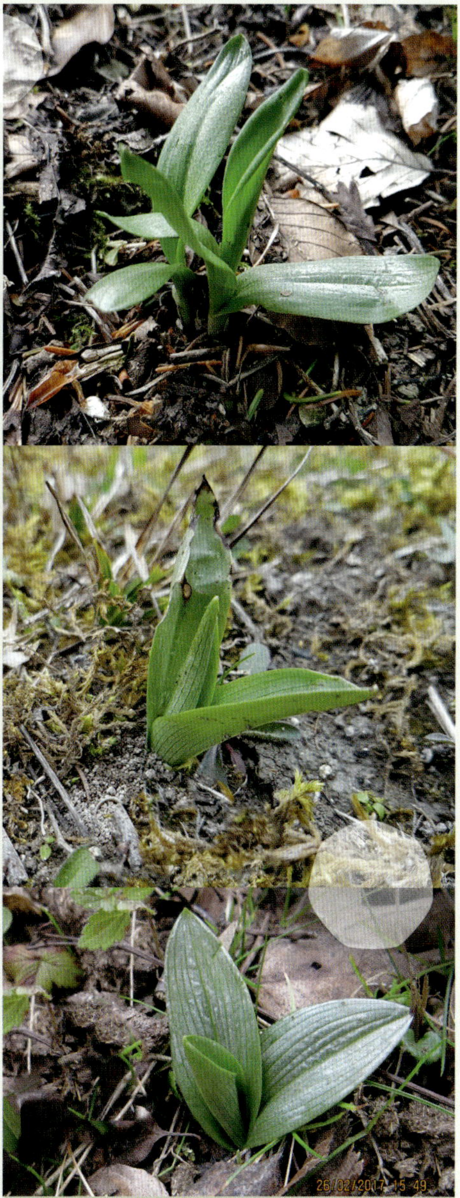

Bee Orchid
p. 78, *p. 242*

Ophrys apifera

SEPTEMBER–MAY

Probably the most frequently encountered overwintering rosette of any orchid species in Britain and Ireland. Often rather battered-looking and usually with some degree of blackening or damage to the **three or four curled, greyish-green leaves**. **COMPARE WITH:** Spider-orchids, Burnt Orchid (*p. 65*).

Fly Orchid
p. 78, *p. 238*

Ophrys insectifera

SEPTEMBER–APRIL

Overwintering rosette very small, with a distinctive, **erect, hood-shaped leaf**. As the rosette matures and gets closer to flowering, leaves that are more strap-shaped are produced. **COMPARE WITH:** Bee Orchid, Early Spider-orchid.

Identifying orchids in bud

Buds are to scale within, but not between, groups.

Fen Orchid
Liparis loeselii
p. 64, *p. 150*

Bog Orchid
Hammarbya paludosa
p. 64, *p. 152*

Creeping Lady's-tresses
Goodyera repens
p. 68, *p. 164*

Autumn Lady's-tresses
Spiranthes spiralis
p. 68, *p. 166*

Irish Lady's-tresses
Spiranthes romanzoffiana
p. 68, *p. 168*

Dense-flowered Orchid
Neotinea maculata
p. 64, *p. 158*

Small-white Orchid
Pseudorchis albida
p. 64, *p. 156*

Lady's-slipper
Cypripedium calceolus
p. 56, *p. 102*

Cephalanthera helleborines

White Helleborine
C. damasonium
p. 57, *p. 106*

Sword-leaved Helleborine
C. longifolia
p. 57, *p. 108*

Red Helleborine
C. rubra
p. 57, *p. 110*

PHOTOGRAPHS OF EACH ORCHID SPECIES IN BUD CAN BE FOUND ON THE RELEVANT SPECIES PAGE.

Neottia

Lesser Twayblade
N. cordata
p. 63, *p. 142*

Common Twayblade
N. ovata
p. 63, *p. 140*

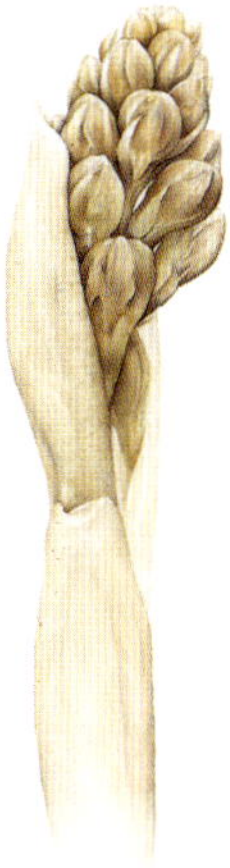

Bird's-nest Orchid
N. nidus-avis
p. 144

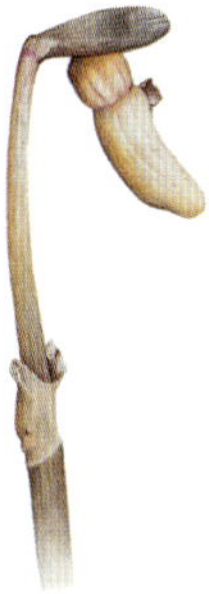

Ghost Orchid
Epipogium aphyllum
p. 146

Coralroot Orchid
Corallorhiza trifida
p. 148

Epipactis helleborines

NB In-bud **Narrow-lipped** (*p. 134*), **Dune** (*p. 130*) and **Green-flowered** (*p. 136*) **Helleborines** are all very similar to **Broad-leaved Helleborine** and identification is best attempted using vegetative features – see ***pp. 58–p. 60***.

Marsh Helleborine
E. palustris
p. 61, *p. 120*

Dark-red Helleborine
E. atrorubens
p. 60, *p. 122*

Violet Helleborine
E. purpurata
p. 61, *p. 124*

Broad-leaved Helleborine
E. palustris
p. 58, *p. 126*

Butterfly-orchids

Greater and **Lesser Butterfly-orchids** are identical when not in flower – see ***p. 62***

Musk Orchid
Herminium monorchis
p. 65, *p. 154*

Greater Butterfly-orchid
Platanthera chlorantha
p. 62, *p. 172*

Lesser Butterfly-orchid
Platanthera bifolia
p. 62, *p. 173*

Lizard Orchid
Himantoglossum hircinum
p. 67, *p. 214*

Pyramidal Orchid
Anacamptis pyramidalis
p. 66, *p. 218*

Fragrant-orchids

Chalk *Gymnadenia conopsea*, **Heath** *G. borealis* and **Marsh** *G. densiflora* **Fragrant-orchids** are identical when not in flower – see ***p. 67***, *p. 174*

Spider-orchids

Early and **Late Spider-orchids** are near identical when not in flower – see ***p. 74***

Bee Orchid
Ophrys apifera
p. 75, *p. 242*

Fly Orchid
Ophrys insectifera
p. 75, *p. 238*

Early Spider-orchid
Ophrys sphegodes *p. 240*

Late Spider-orchid
Ophrys fuciflora *p. 244*

Tongue-orchid
Serapias lingua
p. 65, *p. 216*

Burnt Orchid
Neotinea ustulata
p. 65, *p. 160*

PHOTOGRAPHS OF EACH ORCHID SPECIES IN BUD CAN BE FOUND ON THE RELEVANT SPECIES PAGE.

Frog Orchid
Dactylorhiza viridis
p. 70, *p. 188*

Spotted-orchids

Common *Dactylorhiza fuchsii* and **Heath** *D. maculata* **Spotted-orchids** are very similar when not in flower – see ***p. 70**, pp. 190–192*

Marsh-orchids

All *Dactylorhiza* **marsh-orchids** are very similar when not in flower – see ***p. 69**, pp. 196–206*

Green-winged Orchid
Anacamptis morio
p. 66, *p. 220*

Early-purple Orchid
Orchis mascula
p. 71, *p. 226*

Military Orchid
Orchis militaris
p. 72, *p. 232*

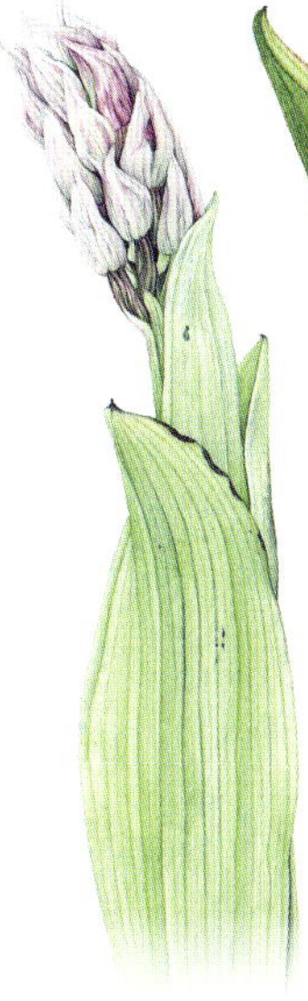

Monkey Orchid
Orchis simia
p. 72, *p. 230*

Lady Orchid
Orchis purpurea
p. 73, *p. 234*

Man Orchid
Orchis anthropophora
p. 73, *p. 228*

Identifying orchids in flower

Is it an orchid?

With their inflorescences of multiple flowers clustered near the top of a usually long stem, orchids, as a group, are reasonably distinctive. However, there are a few wildflower species that could present the opportunity for confusion.

Apart from Lady's-slipper and the lady's-tresses, orchids are hairless, with the sepals and petals in close arrangement (not separated), an ovary between the flower and stem, and obvious anthers attached to a column. If there is still doubt then a look at the leaves will confirm. The leaves of all non-orchid lookalikes, whether stalked or unstalked, are clearly net-veined and very different from those of orchids, almost all of which have longitudinal veins (see *p. 13*).

Southern Marsh-orchid

LONGITUDINAL VEINS

Orchid 'lookalikes' in flower

The most orchid-like flowers are those of the Lamiaceae family, including Bugle, Betony, Ground-ivy, woundworts, louseworts, dead-nettles and mints. Their 'lip' and 'wing' shapes are somewhat similar to the spotted-orchids, marsh-orchids, Early-purple and Green-winged Orchids but they differ from orchids in the obvious anthers, and the sepals fused into a tube. Among those species lacking chlorophyll, non-orchid lookalikes either have a very different flower structure and/or are hairy.

Ground-ivy *Glechoma hederacea*

ANTHERS
FUSED SEPALS

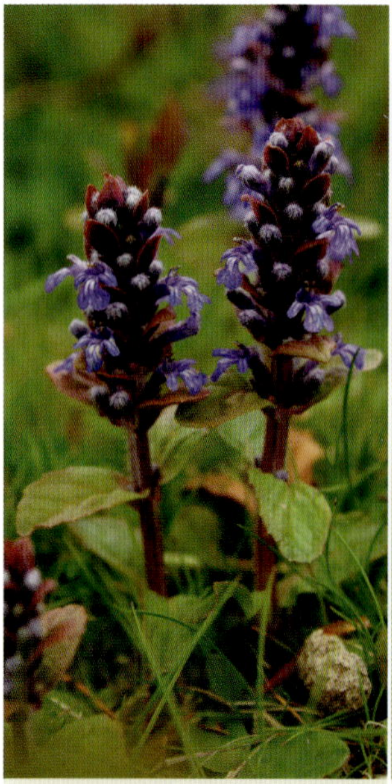

Bugle
Ajuga repens
[Early-purple Orchid *p. 226*]

LEAVES CLEARLY NET-VEINED

Betony *Betonica officinalis*
Woundworts *Stachys* spp.
[marsh-orchids *p. 180*]

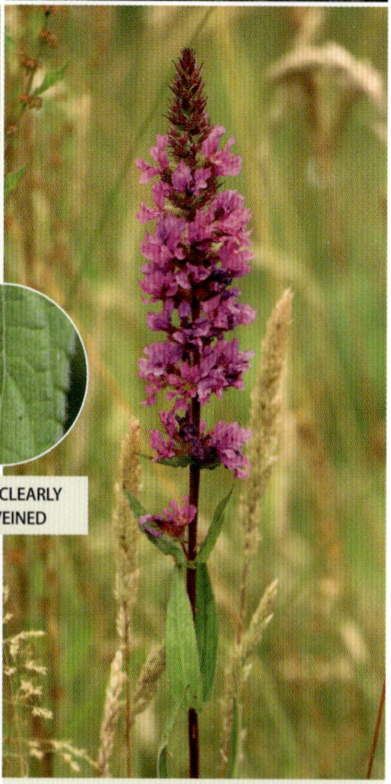

Purple-loosestrife
Lythrum salicaria
[marsh-orchids *p. 180*]

Other orchid-like species

Bluebell (in seed)
Hyacinthoides non-scripta
[Ghost Orchid *p. 146*]

Yellow Bird's-nest
Hypopitys monotropa
[Bird's-nest Orchid *p. 144*;
Ghost Orchid *p. 146*]

Toothwort
Lathraea squamaria
[Violet Helleborine *p. 124*]

BROOMRAPE
LIP: 3-lobed
BIRD'S-NEST ORCHID
LIP: 2-lobed

Broomrapes
Orobanche spp.
[Bird's-nest Orchid *p. 144*]

Common Wintergreen
Pyrola minor
[Coralroot Orchid *p. 148*]

Round-leaved Wintergreen
Pyrola rotundifolia
[butterfly-orchids *p. 170*]

Which orchid is it?

It's an orchid – but which one? Orchids may, at first glance, look very different from other plants, but their basic flower structure is the same (see *p. 16*) and this characteristic offers a straightforward pathway for identification of the vast majority of British and Irish orchids to species. However, *Epipactis* helleborines, fragrant-orchids and *Dactylorhiza* spotted-orchids and marsh-orchids can present particular challenges, as can the ever-present potential of hybrids and variation. These difficult areas are addressed within this book. The approach taken is not to use size as a primary identification feature, but to recognize that this may provide some help in supporting an identification – see *p. 8* for more information.

Identification step-by-step

Two complementary approaches are detailed: the first uses the **form and colour** of the whole plant in a 'look-and-find' section, which may be all that is needed for a confident identification. If more help is needed this section points to the second detailed section that uses **lip characters** as a starting point for identification. These two sections cross-refer, and also have references to either the relevant detailed species account or a more in-depth identification key which, in turn, will point to a species account. While there is the possibility that you may find an individual orchid that does not fit any species description, it is unlikely that there will not be a close approximation to *e.g.* a species group. In this event, a variation, aberrant form or hybrid may well be a consideration and, as far as possible, these situations are addressed in sections covering **variation** (*see box below*) at the end of relevant species groups, and a detailed photographic guide to **hybrids** (*pp. 248–273*).

Identification using form and colour

The illustrations on *pages 84–94* show all the British and Irish orchids as flowering plants **broadly to scale and grouped by both type and the typical range of lip base-colours** their flowers exhibit. For those species that have a variety of lip base-colours an indication of the range is provided in a colour bar; species without a colour bar are depicted as they are likely to be found in the field.

For the purposes of **colour** the lip base-colour of this Green-winged Orchid would be regarded as 'magenta'; the **lip characters** of this example would be described as **3-lobed with central markings.**

Identification using lip characters

Pages 95–100 use a step-by-step illustrated approach to identification by looking initially at the **shape of the lip in terms of the number and shape of the lobes**. There are a few species that may be hard to qualify using this feature and these are highlighted. Once lip shape has been broadly established, identification is then based on individual or a combination of details of *e.g.* spur, lip markings, inflorescence, fragrance and habitat.

A note about variation

Although some species are rather consistent in their appearance, others are highly variable in terms of size, and also lip shape, colour and markings. The vast majority of these variations are covered in this book. However, when faced with a non-conforming individual in a colony, it is prudent to check others around, as there will normally be a number of 'typical' individuals that will help the identification process. This strategy is also useful when assessing *e.g.* marsh-orchids where the possibility of hybrids is very real.

Identifying orchids by form and colour

Orchids come in a range of forms and colour, the details of which are, for many, enough to provide an identification. Others are more variable in form and colour, and for these the range of lip base colour that could be encountered is shown in a bar . The following 11 pages show Britain and Ireland's orchids grouped by form/colour as follows:

Distinctive and non-chlorophyllous orchids *p. 84*
Species that have unmistakable flower shapes and and/or lack any green.

***Cephalanthera* helleborines** *p. 85*
Three species with a characteristic 'half-open' flower: two white-flowered, one pink/red-flowered.

'Green-/yellow-/white-flowered' orchids *pp. 86–87*
Species that are often small, lack colourful flowers and are not shaped like an *Epipactis* helleborine or 'purple' orchid.

***Epipactis* helleborines** *pp. 88–89*
Orchids with a characteristic constricted single lip

'Pink/purple' orchids *pp. 90–93*
Flowers with 'typical' lip shape; some plants may have white or reddish flowers.

'Insect' orchids *p. 94*
Flowers of the genus *Ophrys* that broadly mimic insects.

Ghost Orchid
Epipogium aphyllum
p. 77, *p. 146*

Lizard Orchid
Himantoglossum hircinum
p. 67, ***p. 78***, *p. 214*

Lady's-slipper
Cypripedium calceolus
p. 56, ***p. 76***, *p. 102*

Bird's-nest Orchid
Neottia nidus-avis
p. 76, *p. 144*

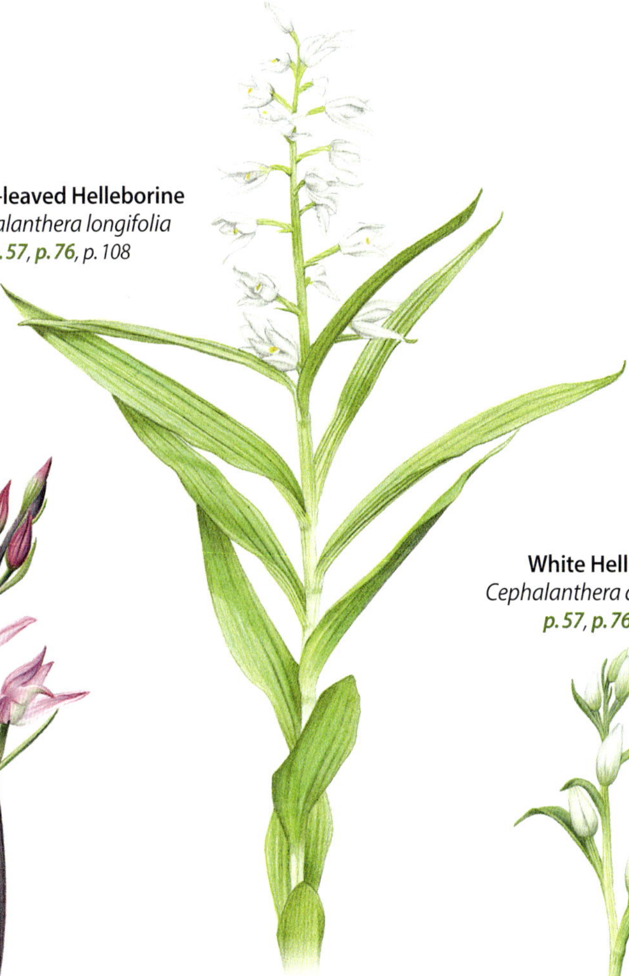

Sword-leaved Helleborine
Cephalanthera longifolia
p. 57, ***p. 76***, *p. 108*

White Helleborine
Cephalanthera damasonium
p. 57, ***p. 76***, *p. 106*

Red Helleborine
Cephalanthera rubra
p. 57, ***p. 76***, *p. 110*

Dense-flowered Orchid
Neotinea maculata
p. 64, **p. 76**, p. 158

Frog Orchid
Dactylorhiza viridis
p. 70, **p. 79**, p. 188

Small-white Orchid
Pseudorchis albida
p. 64, **p. 76**, p. 156

Creeping Lady's-tresses
Goodyera repens
p. 68, **p. 76**, p. 164

Autumn Lady's-tresses
Spiranthes spiralis
p. 68, **p. 76**, p. 166

Irish Lady's-tresses
Spiranthes romanzoffiana
p. 68, **p. 76**, p. 168

Man Orchid
Orchis anthropophora
p. 73, **p. 79**, p. 228

Fen Orchid
Liparis loeselii
p. 64, **p. 76**, *p. 150*

FEN FORM

DUNE FORM

Musk Orchid
Herminium monorchis
p. 65, **p. 78**, *p. 154*

Bog Orchid
Hammarbya paludosa
p. 64, **p. 76**, *p. 152*

Coralroot Orchid
Corallorhiza trifida
p. 77, *p. 148*

Common Twayblade
Neottia ovata
.63, **p. 77**, *p. 140*

Lesser Twayblade
Neottia cordata
p. 63, **p. 77**, *p. 142*

Lesser Butterfly-orchid
Platanthera bifolia
p. 62, **p. 78**, *p. 173*

Greater Butterfly-orchid
Platanthera chlorantha
p. 62, **p. 78**, *p. 172*

Epipactis helleborines

Violet Helleborine
E. purpurata
p. 61, ***p. 77***, *p. 124*

Dark-red Helleborine
E. atrorubens
p. 60, ***p. 77***, *p. 122*

Narrow-lipped Helleborine
E. leptochila
p. 59, ***p. 77***, *p. 134*

Green-flowered Helleborine
E. phyllanthes
p. 60, ***p. 77***, *p. 136*

Broad-leaved Helleborine
E. palustris
p. 58, ***p. 77***, *p. 126*

Dune Helleborine
E. dunensis
p. 59, ***p. 77***, *p. 130*

'Lindisfarne Helleborine'
E. dunensis
ssp. *sancta*
p. 132

Marsh Helleborine
E. palustris
p. 61, ***p. 77***, *p. 120*

Marsh Fragrant-orchid
Gymnadenia densiflora
p. 67, ***p. 78***, *p. 177*

Pyramidal Orchid
Anacamptis pyramidalis
p. 66, ***p. 78***, *p. 218*

Heath Fragrant-orchid
Gymnadenia borealis
p. 67, ***p. 78***, *p. 176*

Chalk Fragrant-orchid
Gymnadenia conopsea
p. 67, ***p. 78***, *p. 176*

Monkey Orchid
Orchis simia
p. 72, **p. 79**, p. 230

Military Orchid
Orchis militaris
p. 72, **p. 79**, p. 232

Burnt Orchid
Neotinea ustulata
p. 65, **p. 78**, p. 160

Lady Orchid
Orchis purpurea
p. 73, **p. 79**, p. 234

Green-winged Orchid
Anacamptis morio
p. 66, ***p. 79***, *p. 220*

Early-purple Orchid
Orchis mascula
p. 71, ***p. 79***, *p. 226*

Heath Spotted-orchid
Dactylorhiza maculata
p. 70, ***p. 79***, *p. 192*

Common Spotted-orchid
Dactylorhiza fuchsii
p. 70, ***p. 79***, *p. 190*

Irish Marsh-orchid
Dactylorhiza kerryensis
p. 69, **p. 79**, p. 204

Northern Marsh-orchid
Dactylorhiza purpurella
p. 69, **p. 79**, p. 196

Southern Marsh-orchid
Dactylorhiza praetermissa
p. 69, **p. 79**, p. 198

Pugsley's Marsh-orchid
Dactylorhiza traunsteinerioides
p. 69, **p. 79**, p. 206

Early Marsh-orchid
Dactylorhiza incarnata
p. 69, **p. 79**, p. 202

Early Spider-orchid
Ophrys sphegodes
p. 74, **p. 78**, p. 240

Late Spider-orchid
Ophrys fuciflora
p. 74, **p. 78**, p. 244

Tongue-orchid
Serapias lingua
p. 65, **p. 78**, p. 216

Bee Orchid
Ophrys apifera
p. 75, **p. 78**, p. 242

Fly Orchid
Ophrys insectifera
p. 75, **p. 78**, p. 238

Identifying orchids by lip characters

Although lip shape and colour can be variable, particularly within some groups, these characters are consistent enough between groups to be used as a primary identification feature. Orchids can be broadly grouped by the number of lobes the lip possesses, as detailed below.

Those shown are 'normal' examples; in some cases, lips may be less, or indeed more, well defined than a typical flower of that species. **Lady's-slipper**, **Lizard Orchid** and the non-chlorophyllous **Ghost** and **Bird's-nest Orchids** can also be defined by lip characters but they are all distinctive or unmistakable and treated separately in the following guide. The colour bar, as used in the 'by form and colour' section, is repeated here to flag up those species with a range of lip base-colours.

ORCHID LIP TYPES

The lip is one of three petals that sit inside three sepals. The lobe count of some highly modified lips can be confusing at first – for clarity, both sepals and petals are indicated for each flower type below.

■ DS = dorsal sepal; LS = lateral sepal | ■ LP = lateral petal; LIP – sL = side lobe; cL = central lobe

DS
LP
LP
LS
LS
LIP

1-lobed (not constricted)

DS
LP
LP
LS
LS
LIP (hypochile)
LIP (epichile)

1-lobed (constricted)

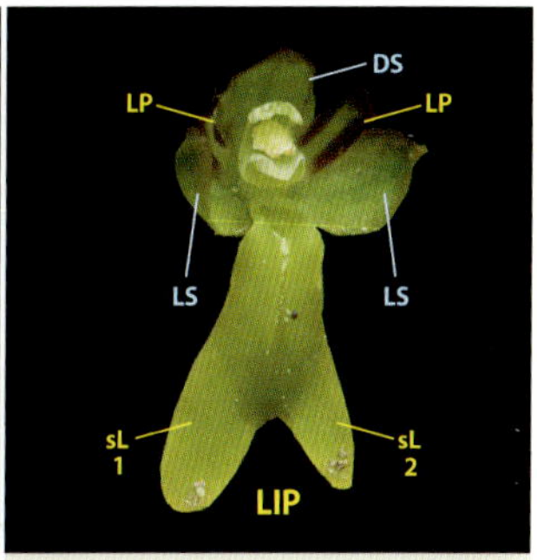
DS
LP
LP
LS
LS
sL 1
sL 2
LIP

2-lobed

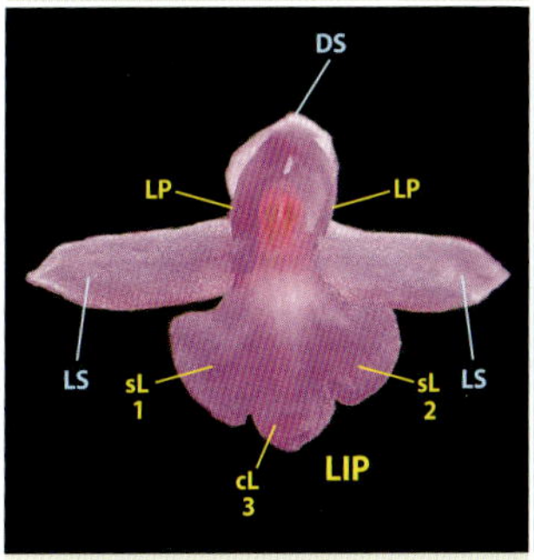
DS
LP
LP
LS
LS
sL 1
sL 2
cL 3
LIP

3-lobed

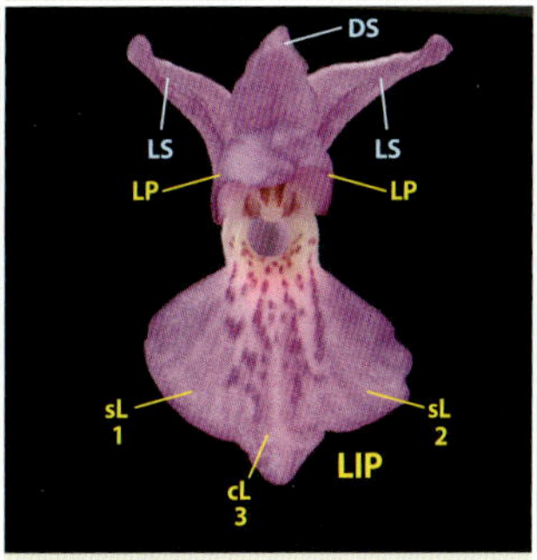
DS
LS
LS
LP
LP
sL 1
sL 2
cL 3
LIP

3-lobed (side lobes broad)

DS
LS
LS
LP
LP
sL 1
sL 2
LIP
cL
3, 4 + (tooth [5?])

'3-plus-lobed'

A NOTE ABOUT LOBES

'3-plus-lobed' | Technically, these are 3-lobed lips that have the central lip **obviously divided**. In the field they appear to have four or even five lobes, hence the qualified '3-plus' term used here. To add confusion, some individual plants of normally 'straightforward' 3-lobed species may show uneven edges or a **slight indent or division in the central lobe (but never a 'tooth')** that could lead to a four count, as in the Green-winged Orchid shown (RIGHT). **If not deeply indented, assume the lobe count is 3.**

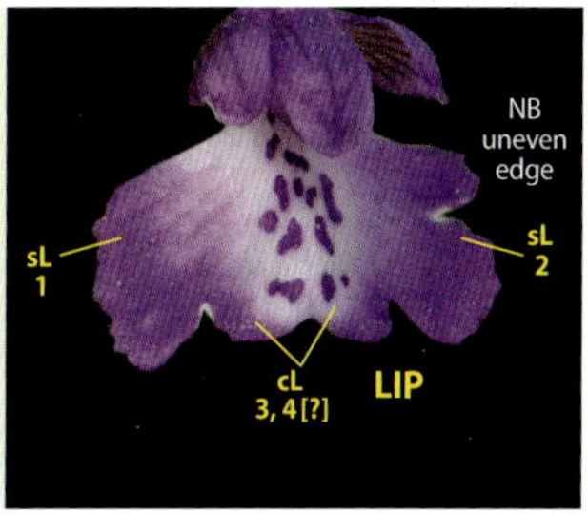
NB
uneven
edge
sL 1
sL 2
cL
3, 4 [?]
LIP

PLANTS WITHOUT CHLOROPHYLL

Two very distinctive orchids

Ghost Orchid is unmistakable: frilly, purple-ridged lip at top of flower, bent back and almost touching the spur; long, thin, yellowish lateral petals and sepals hang below. **Bird's-nest Orchid** looks 2-lobed, but lack of any green separates it from other orchids (see *Orchid lookalikes in flower, p. 80*).

NB Coralroot Orchid has a small amount of chlorophyll and is covered opposite.

Ghost Orchid *p. 146*

Bird's-nest Orchid *p. 144*

PLANTS WITH CHLOROPHYLL

LIP SHAPE HIGHLY MODIFIED – UNMISTAKABLE

Two 'green' orchids which have lip shapes that are unmistakable. Both orchids are named after their shapes.

Lady's-slipper has a 'slipper'-like 1-lobed lip.
Lizard Orchid has a 3-lobed lip with the side lobes reminiscent of a lizard's legs and the extremely elongated central lobe the body/tail.

Lady's-slipper *p. 102*

Lizard Orchid *p. 214*

LIP 1-LOBED (OBVIOUSLY CONSTRICTED) | *EPIPACTIS* HELLEBORINES

FLOWERS drooping well below horizontal

OUTER LIP green, some with pink-tinged edge; **FLOWER** barely open; **OVARY** broad, hairless

Green-flowered Helleborine *p. 136*

OUTER LIP narrow, off-white with green/pink tone; **FLOWER** opening; **OVARY** narrow, hairy

Narrow-lipped Helleborine *p. 134*

OUTER LIP (EPICHILE) frilled

OUTER LIP typically creamy white

Marsh Helleborine *p. 120*

OUTER LIP dark red with purplish edge

Dark-red Helleborine *p. 122*

FLOWERS ± horizontal; colour variable

LEAVES dark green, rounded – often as wide as long, arranged spirally up stem

Broad-leaved Helleborine *p. 126*

LEAVES dull sickly-green, ovate – longer than wide, arranged alternately up stem

Dune Helleborine *p. 130*

LEAVES greyish-green, lower leaves with purple tinge, small and narrow

Violet Helleborine *p. 124*

***Epipactis* helleborines** are very variable in form and colour. In addition, most species hybridize with Broad-leaved Helleborine (see *pp. 250–253*). Consequently many plants that are not typical can be encountered and a more detailed approach to identification may be required for these.

Identifying *Epipactis* p. 115

DS = dorsal sepal; LS = lateral sepal | LP = lateral petal; LIP – sL = side lobe; cL = central lobe

LIP 1-LOBED (NOT OBVIOUSLY CONSTRICTED) 1/2

FLOWERS small; **SEPALS** white; **PETALS** white or mainly white

LEAVES oval to triangular, net-veined; **FLOWER** very hairy; **LIP** white

Creeping Lady's-tresses *p. 164*

LEAVES absent when flowering; **FLOWER** short hairs; **LIP** green with white frilly edge

Autumn Lady's-tresses *p. 166*

LEAVES long, grass-like; **FLOWER** slightly hairy; **LIP** white with green veins

Irish Lady's-tresses *p. 168*

FLOWERS small; **SEPALS** yellow-green

LEAVES scale-like, on stem; **LIP** white with crimson spots

Coralroot Orchid *p. 148*

NOTE: Musk Orchid flowers (3-lobed, small, greenish/yellow (*p. 98*)) can look 1-lobed.

NOTE: Coralroot Orchid lip is actually 3-lobed, but side lobes are so small, as is the flower, that it appears 1-lobed.

FLOWERS small, yellow–green

LIP tongue-like, edge frilled; **FLOWERS** face upwards

DS
LP
LS
LP
LS
LIP

Fen Orchid *p. 188*

LIP at top of flower, edge frilled; **FLOWERS** face upwards

LS
LIP
LS
LP
LP
DS

Bog Orchid *p. 152*

NOTE: Fen Orchid occurs in two forms; the dune form has much broader leaves than the fen form.

Greater × Lesser Butterfly-orchid hybrids have the pollinia intermediate in position (*p. 253*).

LIP long and narrow | **BUTTERFLY-ORCHIDS**

POLLINIA diverge

Greater Butterfly-orchid *p. 172*

POLLINIA parallel

Lesser Butterfly-orchid *p. 173*

FLOWERS 'half-open' | ***CEPHALANTHERA* HELLEBORINES**

FLOWERS pinkish-red

Red Helleborine *p. 110*

LEAVES long, narrow << **FLOWERS** white >> **LEAVES** oval

FLOWERS more open; **BRACTS** tiny

Sword-leaved Helleborine *p. 108*

FLOWERS less open; **BRACTS** large, obvious

White Helleborine *p. 106*

Sword-leaved × White Helleborine hybrids have open flowers with bracts and intermediate leaves (*p. 250*).

LIP APPEARING 1-LOBED – 'INSECT'-LIKE | *OPHRYS* ORCHIDS 2/2

SEPALS pink

UPPER PETALS pink or greenish; **LIP** tip rounded with yellow, backward-pointing appendage

Bee Orchid
p. 242

UPPER PETALS pink; **LIP** tip broad with yellow, flat or forward-pointing appendage

Late Spider-orchid
p. 244

SEPALS green

UPPER PETALS green or reddish; **LIP** usually with variable but distinctive 'H' shape, tip rounded

Early Spider-orchid
p. 240

***Ophrys* orchids** show considerable variation in lip shape and markings (*p. 246*). In addition, various hybrids have been recorded, all of which show mixed/intermediate characters of the parents (*p. 272*).

LIP 1-LOBED, LARGE tongue-like, pointed tip

Tongue-orchid
p. 216

NOTE: *Ophrys* orchid lips are actually 3-lobed, but the side lobes are so reduced that they appear 1-lobed in the field. One, **Fly Orchid**, has green sepals and a clearly multiple lobed lip (see red box below and *p. 100*).

LIP 2-LOBED

PLANT very small, usually <10 cm tall; **FLOWERS** reddish-brown

Lesser Twayblade
p. 142

PLANT typically 20–75 cm tall; **FLOWERS** green

Common Twayblade
p. 140

3-lobed and '3-plus-lobed' confusion species

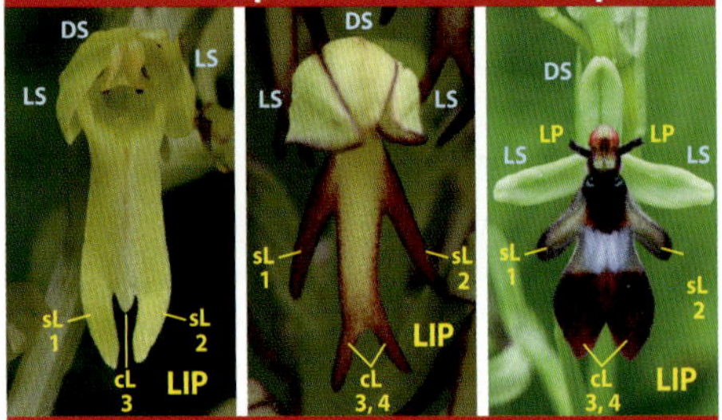
DS
LS
LS
sL 1
sL 2
cL 3
LIP
DS
LS
LS
sL 1
sL 2
LIP
cL 3, 4
DS
LS
LP
LP
LS
sL 1
sL 2
cL 3, 4
LIP

Frog Orchid (LEFT – see *below*), **Man Orchid** (CENTRE) and other 'manikin' orchids (see *p. 100*) and **Fly Orchid** (RIGHT – see *p. 100*) may be considered 2-lobed, but the lip is 3-lobed in **Frog** and 3-plus-lobed in **Man** and **Fly Orchids**, with the lateral petals hidden under the hood (Frog and Man) and forming the 'antennae' (Fly Orchid).

LIP 3-LOBED – FLOWERS WHITE

SIDE LOBES thin; **CENTRAL LOBE** longer, square-ended/slight indent or tiny tooth

Dense-flowered Orchid
p. 158

SIDE LOBES small; **CENTRAL LOBE** larger, tongue-like

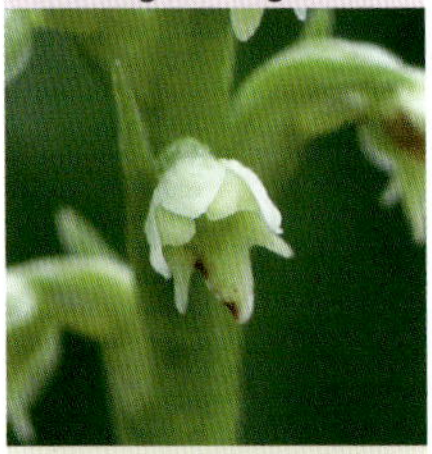

Small-white Orchid
p. 156

Hybrids (*p. 260*).

LIP 3-LOBED – GREENISH-YELLOW

SIDE LOBES short; **CENTRAL LOBE** longer, pointed

can appear 1-lobed

Musk Orchid
p. 154

SIDE LOBES long; **CENTRAL LOBE** smaller, tooth-like

Frog Orchid
p. 188

Hybrids (*p. 262*).

LIP 3-LOBED (side lobes broad) – WHITE–PINK–PURPLE–DEEP RED | NB typical plants shown

SPUR medium length, broad, **downcurved**

DACTYLORHIZA ORCHIDS
downcurved
bracts large, rigid

LEAVES typically narrow and spotted, unmarked on a few plants

SPOTTED-ORCHIDS

LOBES distinct; **MARKINGS** strong dark 'loops' and dashes

Common Spotted-orchid *p. 190*

LOBES not well defined, central much smaller; **MARKINGS** speckles and spots, no strong 'loops'

Heath Spotted-orchid *p. 192*

Both **Common Spotted-orchid** and **Heath Spotted-orchid** are very variable in lip shape, colour and markings and can be difficult to identify (see *p. 194*). In addition, both species hybridize with a range of species, producing an array of intermediate plants (see *pp. 261–272*).

LEAVES unmarked or spotted; broader leaves than in spotted-orchids

MARSH-ORCHIDS

MARKINGS across all lobes

LOBES shallow, side lobes strongly bent back; **MARKINGS** double 'loops' and spots

Early Marsh-orchid *p. 202*

LOBES distinct; central long, pointed; **MARKINGS** bold 'loops', spots

Pugsley's Marsh-orchid *p. 206*

LOBES all rounded, edges often ragged; **MARKINGS** bold 'loops' and spots

Irish Marsh-orchid *p. 204*

SPUR medium length, **upcurved**

upcurved
LS green lines

LATERAL SEPALS marked with green parallel lines in all flower colours

Green-winged Orchid *p. 220*

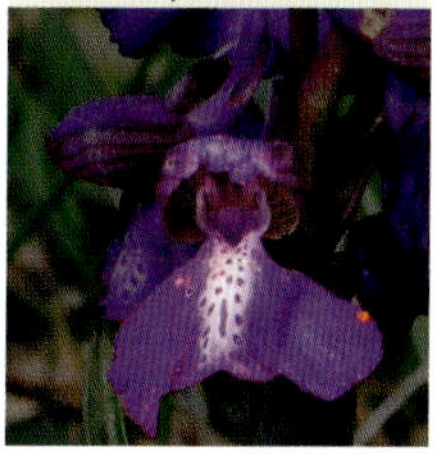

upcurved
LS unmarked

LATERAL SEPALS unmarked

Early-purple Orchid *p. 226*

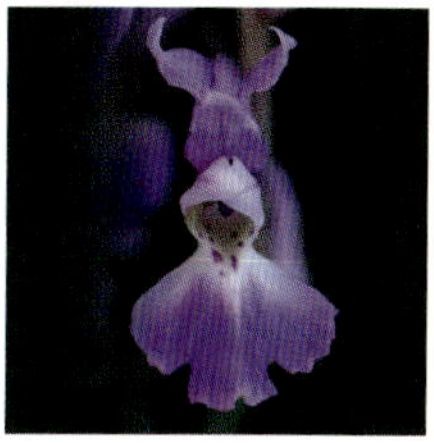

NOTE: Both Green-winged and Early-purple Orchids are highly variable in colour and lip shape (*p. 222*). The central lobe can be frilly, or slightly indented, and could appear to be 4-lobed.

MARKINGS central ± inner area of side lobes

LIP barely lobed 'diamond'; **MARKINGS** spots, blotches, 'loops'

see also *p. 200*

Northern Marsh-orchid *p. 196*

LIP weakly lobed; central pointed; **MARKINGS** spots, speckles ('loops' rare)

Southern Marsh-orchid *p. 198*

All the **marsh-orchids** are very variable in lip shape, colour and markings (see *Identifying Dactylorhiza* and species accounts for details). In addition, all species readily hybridize with one or more other species. Consequently, many plants that are not typical can be encountered, which may require a more detailed approach to their identification.

Dactylorhiza* hybrids *p. 261

Identifying *Dactylorhiza* *p. 185*

LIP 3-LOBED – PINK–MAUVE–MAGENTA (WHITE) FLOWERS WITH LONG, NARROW SPUR

INFLORESCENCE pyramidal

LIP 2 erect 'guide' plates at base; **LOBES** variable, but typically ± equal

'guide' plate

Pyramidal Orchid
p. 218

FLOWERS noticeably fragrant | **FRAGRANT-ORCHIDS**

LIP about as long as wide; **LOBES** clearly defined; **SCENT** sweet, not clove-like

Chalk Fragrant-orchid
p. 176

LIP longer than wide; **LOBES** weakly defined; **SCENT** clove-like, sweet

Heath Fragrant-orchid
p. 176

LIP wider than long; **LOBES** clearly defined; **SCENT** clove-like, spicy

Marsh Fragrant-orchid
p. 177

Fragrant-orchids show habitat preferences and some differences in inflorescence shape. Despite this, all three species show considerable variation in form, lip shape and colour. Consequently, some plants may be difficult to identify with certainty. In addition intergeneric hybrids occur, typically having the long spur of a fragrant-orchid, with the flower characteristic of the other parent (*p. 254*).

Identifying fragrant-orchids *p. 174*

LIP '3-PLUS-LOBED'

PLANT large <20 cm; **LIP** 4-lobed (additional central 'tooth' may be present); 'humanoid' **'MANIKIN' ORCHIDS**

LIP 'soldier'-like, side lobe 'arms' thinner than central 'legs'; **MARKINGS** two rows of purple 'spots' of tiny hairs

Military Orchid
p. 232

LIP 'lady in a dress', side lobe 'arms' thin, central very broad 'dress'; **MARKINGS** purple 'spots' of tiny hairs

Lady Orchid
p. 234

LIP 'monkey'-like with 'tail'; **MARKINGS** dark purple 'hands and feet'

Monkey Orchid
p. 230

LIP 'humanoid' form, side lobe 'arms' and central 'legs' thin; **MARKINGS** 'limbs' may be tinged reddish-brown

Man Orchid
p. 228

'Manikin' orchids, particularly Lady Orchid, show considerable variation in lip shape and markings (*p. 236*). In addition, various hybrids have been recorded, all of which show mixed/intermediate characters of the parents (*p. 270*).

PLANT small, typically ≤15 cm;

LIP 4-lobed, white with crimson–purple markings

Burnt Orchid
p. 160

FLOWER 'insect'-like

UPPER PETALS 'antennae'; **LIP** 'wing' side lobes and central divided 'body' (division may be weak)

Fly Orchid
p. 238

***Ophrys* orchids** show considerable variation in lip shape and markings (*p. 246*). In addition, various hybrids have been recorded, all of which show mixed/intermediate characters of the parents (*p. 272*).

The species accounts

Most species have a double-page spread, formatted as shown below. The exceptions are the butterfly-orchids and fragrant-orchids which, to aid comparison, are formatted slightly differently.

Phenology codes

- in leaf/ in bud
- in flower
- in seed

English name | *Scientific name*
Alternative and former names given where relevant

Cross-references to further information

Full plant illustration

Legal protection – see *p.* 282

Phenology chart

Conservation status:
IUCN Red List (see *below*)

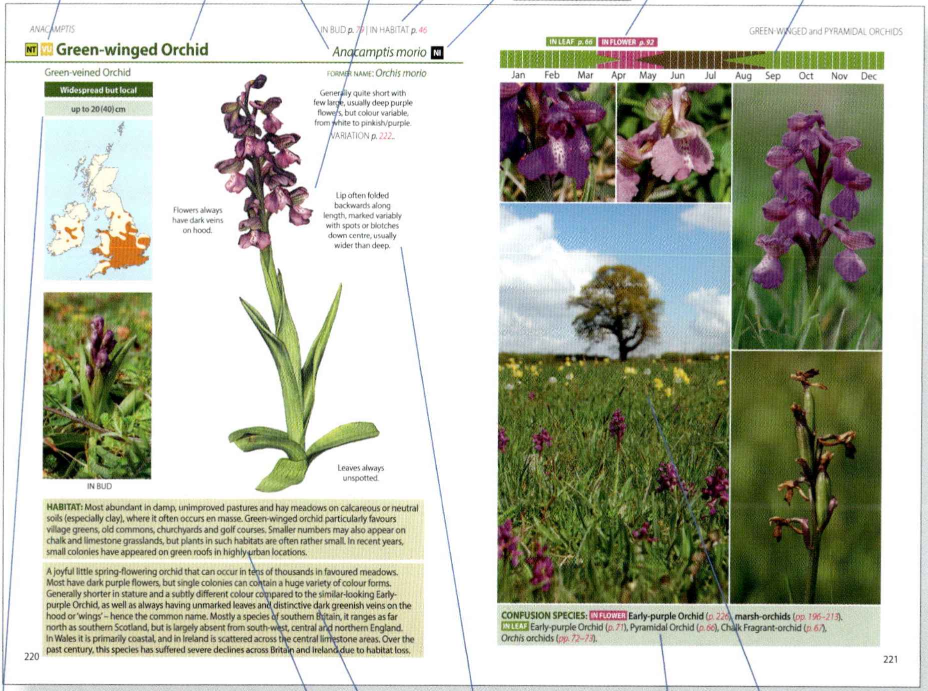

ANACAMPTIS
NT VU Green-winged Orchid
IN BUD p. 79 | IN HABITAT p. 46
Anacamptis morio NI
Green-veined Orchid
FORMER NAME: Orchis morio
Widespread but local
up to 20 (40) cm
Generally quite short with few large, usually deep purple flowers, but colour variable, from white to pinkish/purple.
VARIATION p. 222..
Flowers always have dark veins on hood.
Lip often folded backwards along length, marked variably with spots or blotches down centre, usually wider than deep.
Leaves always unspotted.
IN BUD
HABITAT: Most abundant in damp, unimproved pastures and hay meadows on calcareous or neutral soils (especially clay), where it often occurs en masse. Green-winged orchid particularly favours village greens, old commons, churchyards and golf courses. Smaller numbers may also appear on chalk and limestone grasslands, but plants in such habitats are often rather small. In recent years, small colonies have appeared on green roofs in highly urban locations.
A joyful little spring-flowering orchid that can occur in tens of thousands in favoured meadows. Most have dark purple flowers, but single colonies can contain a huge variety of colour forms. Generally shorter in stature and a subtly different colour compared to the similar-looking Early-purple Orchid, as well as always having unmarked leaves and distinctive dark greenish veins on the hood or 'wings' – hence the common name. Mostly a species of southern Britain, it ranges as far north as southern Scotland, but is largely absent from south-west, central and northern England. In Wales it is primarily coastal, and in Ireland is scattered across the central limestone areas. Over the past century, this species has suffered severe declines across Britain and Ireland due to habitat loss.
220
GREEN-WINGED and PYRAMIDAL ORCHIDS
IN LEAF p. 66
IN FLOWER p. 92
Jan Feb Mar Apr May Jun Jul Aug Sep Oct Nov Dec
CONFUSION SPECIES: IN FLOWER Early-purple Orchid (p. 226), marsh-orchids (pp. 196–213).
IN LEAF Early-purple Orchid (p. 71), Pyramidal Orchid (p. 66), Chalk Fragrant-orchid (p. 67), Orchis orchids (pp. 72–73).
221

Status, plant height and distribution
Maps based on BSBI Distribution Database using 2000–2019 data plus key additional 2020 data. Some sensitive distribution data are modified. Where relevant, extreme heights are given in parentheses.

Key identification features

Species information

Habitat description

Confusion species in flower and in leaf, and a list of hybrids

Photographs
showing the species in situ; the inflorescence in bud, in flower and in seed, and close-ups of the flower.

Conservation status codes
From: *GB Red List for Vascular Plants*, BSBI (2019) [black outline]; *Ireland Red List No. 10: Vascular Plants*, NPWS (2016) [pale green outline].

CR	Critically Endangered	LC	Least Concern
EN	Endangered	DD	Data Deficient
VU	Vulnerable	NE	Not Evaluated
NT	Near Threatened	WL	Wait Listed (Ireland only)

Cross-referencing
to the in-leaf section, in-flower comparison pages and any confusion species, and any relevant subspecies, variation, comparison and hybrid pages.

IN BUD *p. 76* | IN HABITAT *p. 40*

CR Lady's-slipper *Cypripedium calceolus*

Extremely rare; 1 native site

30–50 cm

Large, showy, yellow-and-maroon flowers.
Large, broad, heavily ridged leaves sheathing stem.

IN BUD

HABITAT: Rocky limestone hillsides: on sheltered grasslands in open Ash *Fraxinus excelsior* woodland on north- or north-west-facing slopes. Its precise habitat preferences in Britain are still poorly understood.

Large and showy, producing multiple stems as it matures, each with one or two flowers. Never common, this beautiful species was, up until recently, one of Britain's rarest orchids following a rapid decline as a direct result of over-collecting during the 19th and early 20th centuries. Lady's-slipper formerly occurred in the limestone regions of Derbyshire, Lancashire, Yorkshire, Cumbria and County Durham but by the 1930s it was reduced to a single native site in the Yorkshire Dales, where it is heavily protected. Fortunately, Lady's-slipper has been successfully re-established at 11 sites across its former range, at two of which public access to see the plants has been arranged.

IN LEAF p. 56
IN FLOWER p. 84
Jan
Feb
Mar
Apr
May
Jun
Jul
Aug
Sep
Oct
Nov
Dec

CONFUSION SPECIES: **IN FLOWER** None. **IN LEAF** Broad-leaved Helleborine (*p.* 58).

Cephalanthera and *Epipactis* helleborines compared

The helleborine genera *Cephalanthera* and *Epipactis* (*pp. 112–139*) are closely related and consequently share several structural characteristics. Despite having very different flower forms and colours they can be a challenge to separate when not in flower. The two genera also often share the same woodland habitat and are frequently found together.

FLOWERS: unstalked; dull; various colours

Epipactis

FLOWERS: stalked; white, cream or rose-pink

Cephalanthera

IN BUD

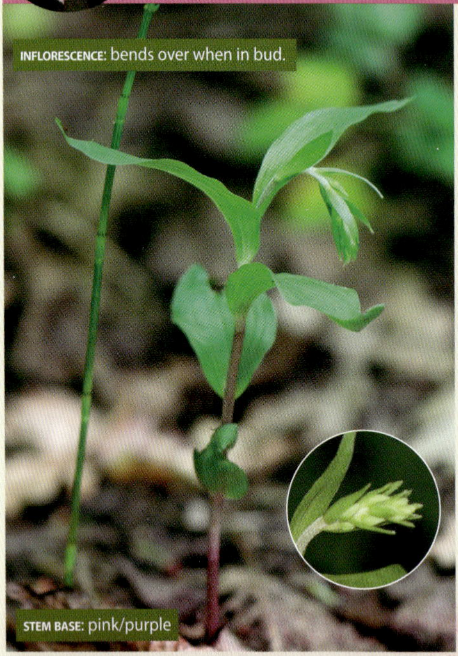
INFLORESCENCE: bends over when in bud.
STEM BASE: pink/purple

INFLORESCENCE: vertical when in bud.
STEM BASE: whitish

POST-FLOWERING

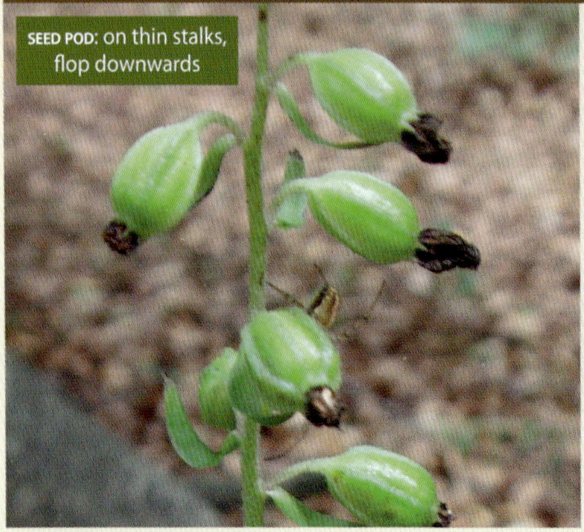
SEED POD: on thin stalks, flop downwards

SEED POD: unstalked, point upwards

Cephalanthera helleborines

The genus *Cephalanthera* contains three species that are straightforward to recognize when in flower. The flowers are large and either white (White and Sword-leaved Helleborines) or pink (Red Helleborine). The leaves are typically arranged alternately up the length of the stem. All three species are associated with woodlands, especially their edges and glades, but can often be found in adjacent grasslands if conditions are favourable.

Hybrids White × Sword-leaved Helleborine (*p. 250*)

White Helleborine *p. 106* **Sword-leaved Helleborine** *p. 108* **Red Helleborine** *p. 110*

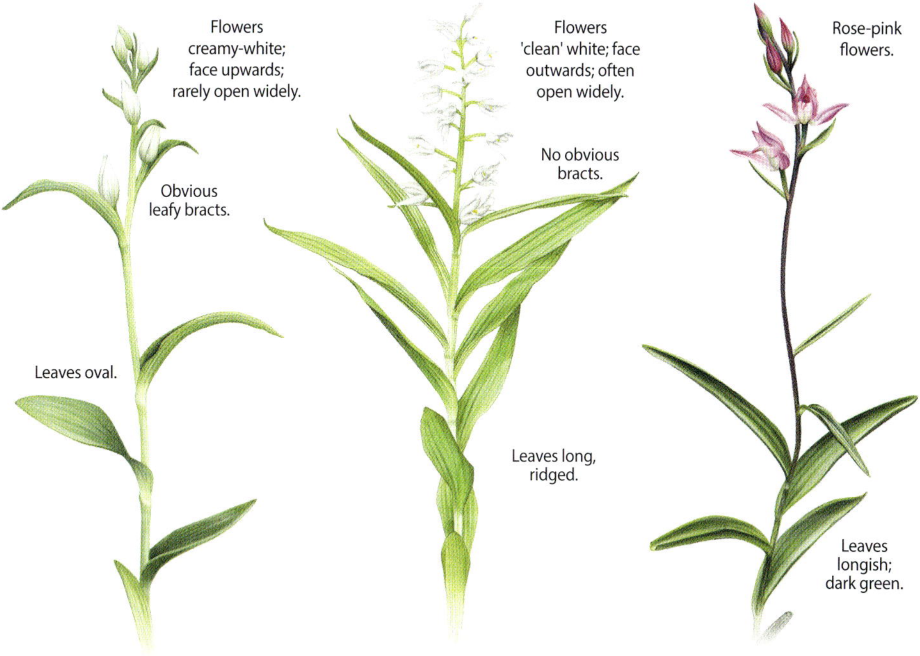
Flowers creamy-white; face upwards; rarely open widely.
Obvious leafy bracts.
Leaves oval.
Flowers 'clean' white; face outwards; often open widely.
No obvious bracts.
Leaves long, ridged.
Rose-pink flowers.
Leaves longish; dark green.

IN BUD

VEGETATIVE

Cephalanthera species are straightforward to identify in their vegetative state during late March–April. See *opposite* and also *p. 57* for comparative descriptions.

IN BUD *p. 76* | IN HABITAT *p. 40*

VU White Helleborine *Cephalanthera damasonium*

Large White Helleborine

Locally common

up to 60 cm

Creamy-white flowers face upwards and rarely open widely; arranged alternately along stem.
Each flower has an obvious leafy bract.
Oval-shaped leaves arranged alternately up the stem.
Base of stem whitish.

IN BUD

HABITAT: Chalk and limestone woodlands, mainly in southern Beech woods. Usually among leaf-litter in deep shade, but can stray onto woodland edges, roadside verges, scrub and grassland, and even gardens.

A characteristic, often common, species in the Beech woods of southern England, with spikes of skyward-facing, usually closed, creamy-white flowers that self-pollinate. It can form colonies into the hundreds, where it is often the only plant species present on the woodland floor. Recorded from Lincolnshire (2014), well north of its core range.

IN LEAF *p. 57* IN FLOWER *p. 85*

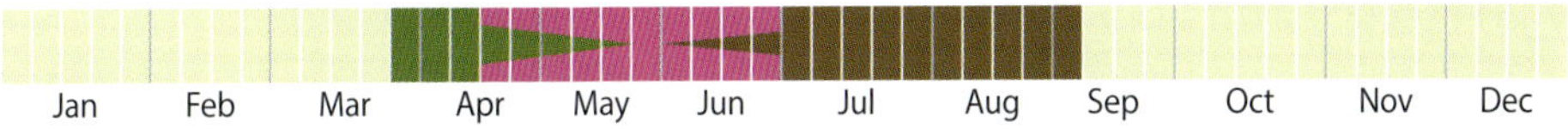
Jan
Feb
Mar
Apr
May
Jun
Jul
Aug
Sep
Oct
Nov
Dec

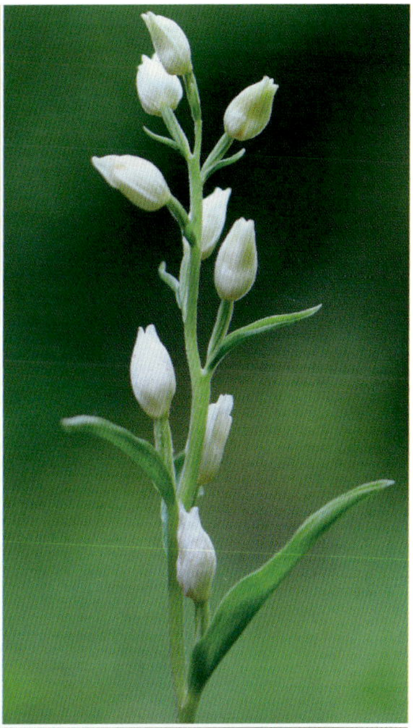

CONFUSION SPECIES: IN FLOWER **Sword-leaved Helleborine** (*p. 108*). IN LEAF Sword-leaved and Red (*p. 110*) Helleborines; *Epipactis* helleborines (*pp. 112–136*). HYBRID × Sword-leaved Helleborine (*p. 250*).

IN BUD *p. 76* | IN HABITAT *p. 40*

VU VU Sword-leaved Helleborine *Cephalanthera longifolia*

Narrow-leaved Helleborine

Scattered and rare

up to 60 cm

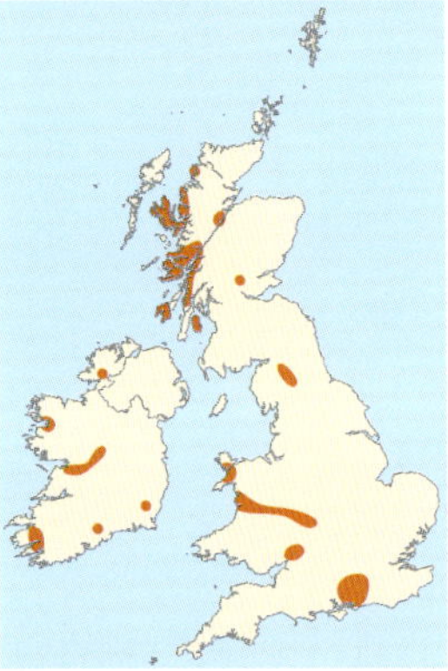

Clean white flowers face outwards and often open widely, clustered at top of stem separately from leaves.
Very short bract, which may be absent on flowers towards the top.
Long, narrow, heavily ridged leaves, usually arranged alternately up the stem below flower spike.
Base of stem whitish.

IN BUD

HABITAT: Essentially woodland but thrives best in glades, rides and woodland edges, in particular in dappled light conditions. Should an area become too shaded, can lie dormant for many years and reappear when light conditions become suitable. In southern England, found in and around Beech woods on chalk and limestone; in central and northern England, Wales and Scotland in more acidic oak woods; and in Ireland in rather wet birch, Alder and oak woodlands and also in scrub.

The large, clean white flowers and numerous long, pointed leaves are distinctive. Generally rare but widely scattered with strongholds in Hampshire and Argyll where there are clusters of sites, some of which hold thousands of plants. Elsewhere a scattering of isolated sites across southern and central England and Wales, with two in northern England. In Ireland the species is widespread but currently recorded from just 11 locations.

IN LEAF p. 57
IN FLOWER p. 85
Jan
Feb
Mar
Apr
May
Jun
Jul
Aug
Sep
Oct
Nov
Dec

In Ireland, sometimes occurs in wet oak and Alder woods.

CONFUSION SPECIES: IN FLOWER **White Helleborine** (*p. 106*). IN LEAF White and Red (*p. 110*) Helleborines; *Epipactis* helleborines (*pp. 112–136*). HYBRID × White Helleborine (*p. 250*).

IN BUD *p. 76* | IN HABITAT *p. 40*

CR Red Helleborine *Cephalanthera rubra*

Extremely rare; 3 sites

up to 60 cm

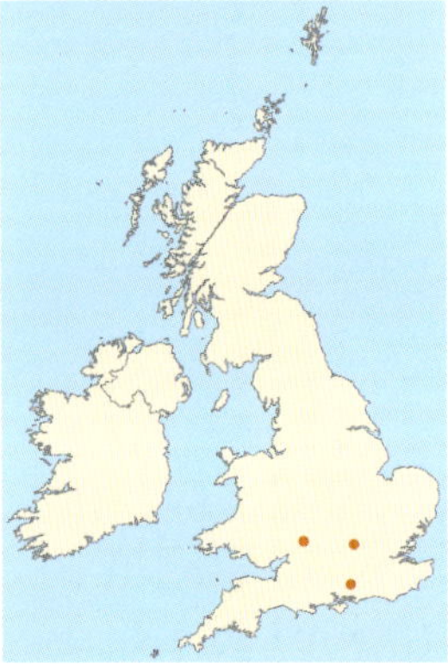

IN BUD

Large rose-pink flowers spaced around top of stem, pointing upwards at an angle.
Graceful stature, with large, dark green leaves arranged alternately up the stem.
Small basal leaf with dark veins.

HABITAT: Favours sloping Beech woods on chalk and limestone. Requires well-lit glades and can tolerate some ground vegetation, but will not withstand too much competition. Can remain dormant for long periods if conditions become too shady.

This much sought-after species, with its large, rose-pink flowers, is sadly now extremely rare and difficult to see in Britain. Previously widespread in the Cotswolds (Gloucestershire), it has mysteriously disappeared from virtually all its former locations during the last 50 years and is now confined to single sites in Gloucestershire, Buckinghamshire and Hampshire. Conservation efforts to save the species from extinction in Britain have so far proved difficult. It is only likely to be encountered on an organized visit to one of its carefully protected sites.

IN LEAF p. 57
IN FLOWER p. 85
Jan
Feb
Mar
Apr
May
Jun
Jul
Aug
Sep
Oct
Nov
Dec

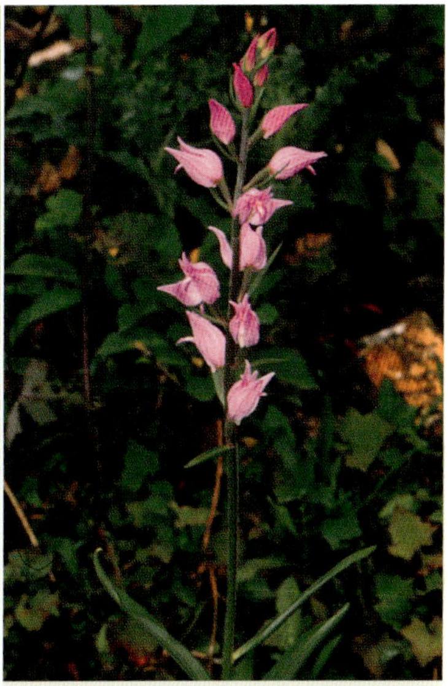

A small colony in Hampshire flowered until 2007 but no flowering plants have been seen since.

CONFUSION SPECIES: **IN FLOWER** Non-orchid lookalikes, such as bellflowers *Campanula* spp.
IN LEAF White (*p. 106*) and Sword-leaved (*p. 108*) Helleborines; *Epipactis* helleborines (*pp. 112–136*).

Epipactis helleborines

Epipactis species grow in a variety of habitats, from deeply shaded woodlands to open limestone pavement. Structurally, all species look very similar, having leaves spaced along the lower part of the stem and a narrow inflorescence above that is arced over when in bud. Each flower bears a leafy bract. This gives these plants an often narrow, tall and rather leggy appearance with comparatively small flowers. Seven species of *Epipactis* helleborine are recognized in this book.

Hybrids Four hybrid combinations are covered: two of these have been formally described; the other two are described here for the first time. *Epipactis* hybrids are very hard to identify with confidence and should only be considered when both potential parent species are present.

Primarily self-pollinated species – flowers generally rather greenish, with much less colourful flowers than the cross-pollinated species – **see *p. 115* for full identification details.**

Beware, highly variable!
SSP. *SANCTA*
'Lindisfarne Helleborine'
SSP. *HELLEBORINE*

Narrow-lipped Helleborine *p. 134*

A declining and now quite rare species, and, like Violet Helleborine, confined to dark, shady woodlands in southern Britain. The flowers have a characteristically pointed lip.

Graceful, rather 'green' plant with fairly large, widely spaced flowers that droop at 45° to the stem.

Leaves pale green, usually longer than wide; alternately and widely spaced along stem.

Green-flowered Helleborine *p. 136*

A widely distributed species with several distinct varieties; occurs in various habitats, but favours woodlands.

All-green plant with flowers drooping well below the horizontal; flowers sometimes do not open at all but ovary becomes swollen.

Leaves apple-green, arranged alternately up stem; lowest leaf often very rounded.

Dune Helleborine *p. 130*

An often-overlooked species with two subspecies: *dunensis* and *sancta* ('Lindisfarne Helleborine') and one variety: *tynensis* ('Tyne Helleborine'). It is mostly found in the north and west of Britain and often on dunes, but is regularly being discovered in new woodland locations, resulting in a much more extended range than previously thought.

Superficially similar to Broad-leaved Helleborine but paler green overall.

Insect-pollinated species – flowers generally rather colourful – **see *p. 115* for full identification details.**

Beware, highly variable!

Broad-leaved Helleborine

p. 126

The most common species, found in a wide range of habitats, and often present with other *Epipactis*. Two subspecies, *helleborine* and *neerlandica*, are recognized in this book.

Flower pink/purple and green, with white/pink lip giving a two-toned appearance.

Leaves typically dark green, usually growing spirally up the stem, lower ones broader than long; often looks very 'leafy'.

Violet Helleborine

p. 124

A scarce species confined to shady woodlands and roadsides in southern and central England, often forming densely packed groups.

Flowers large, wide-open, pale green with hints of pink; often many crowded together making plant look top-heavy.

Leaves generally quite small, narrow, dull purplish-green; arranged spirally up the stem.

Dark-red Helleborine

p. 122

A comparatively rare northern species. It is a specialist of limestone areas and typically has deep reddish flowers.

Bright crimson flowers, with obvious yellow anther cap, and frilly lip with lumpy base.

Leaves clasping, dark red, often with purplish edges; mainly on the lower half of stem, in two rows.

Marsh Helleborine

p. 120

As its name suggests, a plant of marshes and dune slacks, where it can grow in huge numbers. It is a highly distinctive species that is very easy to distinguish from any other *Epipactis* when in flower.

Large flowers with a frilly-edged, creamy-white lip, usually with pink veins.

Leaves pointed, clustered towards base of stem; arranged spirally up the stem.

IN BUD

NB In-bud **Narrow-lipped**, **Dune** and **Green-flowered Helleborines** are all very similar to **Broad-leaved Helleborine** – best identified by vegetative characters see *p. 58*.

New identities

The treatment of the genus *Epipactis* in this book is subtly different to that of other recent guides. As detailed below, genetic studies have revealed new insights into the relationships and status of the species within the group.

GREEN-FLOWERED HELLEBORINE varieties (see *p. 138*)

These forms differ in their lip and column morphology: from '*pendula*', which has a completely formed lip with a distinct hypochile and epichile, through to '*phyllanthes*', which has a lip more like a simple petal; '*vectensis*' and '*degenera*' have lip anatomies intermediate between these extremes. The limits of these 'varieties', however, are poorly defined and difficult to justify as recognizable taxa and are therefore treated in this book as part of a continuum of variation within the species. This conclusion is supported by the observations of D.P. Young (1952) who, despite originally naming most of the varieties listed above, also noted that: "*on account of the continuous and even distribution of forms, any subdivision of the aggregate species must of necessity be artificial.*"

DUNE HELLEBORINE

Previously considered endemic to Britain, genetic analysis has shown Dune Helleborine *E. dunensis* to be closely related to two continental taxa – *E. bugacensis* of Eastern Europe and *E. rhodanensis* of Central and Eastern Europe. The three are very similar in appearance and are primarily self-pollinated; they should be considered a single species (Sramko *et al.*, 2019). The most recent study shows that Dune Helleborine is likely to have evolved from Broad-leaved Helleborine relatively recently and (like some of the marsh-orchids) is still in the process of speciation. This is demonstrated by the tendency to exhibit a switch in its pollination strategies more often than other *Epipactis*.

'Tyne Helleborine' (*p. 133*)

Also categorized within Dune Helleborine is 'Tyne Helleborine' (Squirrell *et al.*, 2002), which is a greener plant than typical Dune Helleborine, with no pink or purple on the base of the stem, ovary or lip (see *p. 119*). Some plants also have a long, forward-pointing outer lip, very like Narrow-lipped Helleborine. Furthermore, 'Tyne Helleborine' occurs in a rather different habitat of river gravels and is largely restricted to the River South Tyne valley in Northumberland. Genetic testing has shown no discernible differences between 'Tyne Helleborine' and typical Dune Helleborine. On this basis, 'Tyne Helleborine' is treated here as a variety of Dune Helleborine: *E. dunensis* var. *tynensis*. Previously published references to Narrow-lipped Helleborines in Northern England will almost certainly refer to 'Tyne Helleborine'.

'Lindisfarne Helleborine' (*p. 132*)

The isolated population of *Epipactis* on Holy Island (Lindisfarne), Northumberland, was afforded species status (Lindisfarne Helleborine *E. sancta*) by Delforge & Gévaudan (2002). A single genetic study (Squirrell *et al.*, 2002) appeared to support this, affording increased conservation protection as a British endemic. This genetic evidence is regarded as insufficient to merit species status, especially when combined with minor morphological differences between 'Lindisfarne' and nominate Dune Helleborine, which is limited to the green (rather than pink/purple) ovary base (pedicel) (Bateman, 2020 Kew Bulletin). 'Lindisfarne Helleborine' is therefore treated here as a subspecies under the name *E. dunensis* ssp. *sancta*.

BROAD-LEAVED HELLEBORINE

'Dutch Helleborine' (*p. 130*)

Dutch Helleborine is found in the dune slacks of South Wales, mirroring its habitat in the Netherlands and France. It looks consistently different in appearance to typical Broad-leaved Helleborine and there has been a long-standing mystery as to whether this was just was a response to the unique local habitat conditions (*i.e.* an ecotype) or whether it is a genetically distinct taxon. Some authors treat it as a separate species, *E. neerlandica*, others as a subspecies or variety. Recent genetic studies (Sramko *et al.*, 2019) have revealed that it is indeed sufficiently distinct from Broad-leaved Helleborine to be considered a subspecies. Given its distinctiveness both morphologically and genetically, the taxon is treated here as 'Dutch Helleborine' *E. helleborine* ssp. *neerlandica*.

'Young's Helleborine'

In 1982, helleborines from Northumberland with yellowish-pink flowers, two-rowed leaves, and a tendency to convert to self-pollination were named as a new endemic species, Young's Helleborine *E. youngiana* (Richards & Porter, 1982). Subsequently, additional populations of similar plants were discovered. In 1988, based on its rarity and apparent endemic status, it was afforded legal protection under the Wildlife and Countryside Act 1981, being listed in Schedule 8 (species of highest conservation priority) (see *p. 282*), where it still resides to this day. However, subsequent genetic studies (Hollingsworth *et al.*, 2006) have revealed no differences between Young's and Broad-leaved Helleborines, proving the former to be simply a local form of the latter. While it can be reasonably distinctive, it is generally no more so than other forms within the wide range of variation for the species, and it is therefore not afforded a named rank in this book.

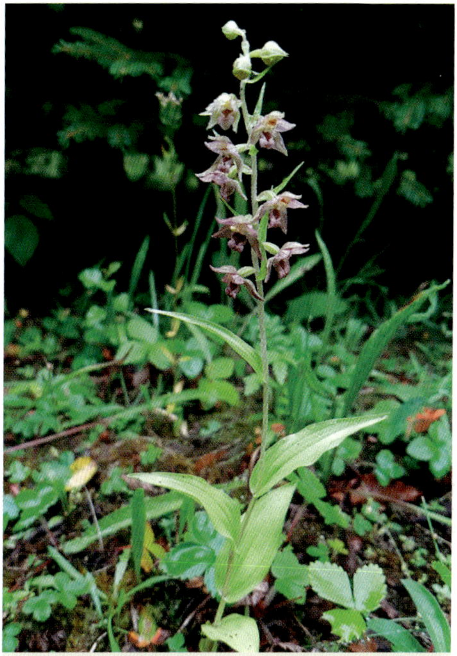

'Young's Helleborine' *E. helleborine*

Identifying *Epipactis*

FROM KEY *p. 96*

The distinctive **Marsh Helleborine** apart, *Epipactis* helleborines can be particularly difficult to separate to species level. **Broad-leaved Helleborine** is probably misidentified most often, due to its seemingly endless variability. Habitat, weather conditions and age of plants can significantly affect appearance in this species – well worth bearing in mind if faced with something unusual.

Identification within this group usually starts with determining the pollination method, so it is worth taking time to become familiar with the pollination processes and how they work. This may require more than one visit to see how plants are developing.

Botanical terms | Throughout the book some technical terms have been replaced by descriptive terms for ease of use. In this section the following apply: **'glue-blob'** for viscidium; **inner lip** for hypochile; **outer lip** for epichile.

Epipactis **flower parts**

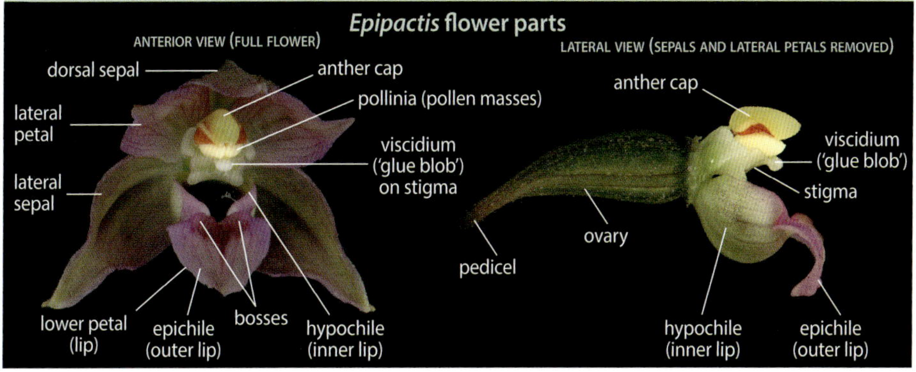
ANTERIOR VIEW (FULL FLOWER)
dorsal sepal
anther cap
pollinia (pollen masses)
lateral petal
viscidium ('glue blob') on stigma
lateral sepal
lower petal (lip)
epichile (outer lip)
bosses
hypochile (inner lip)
LATERAL VIEW (SEPALS AND LATERAL PETALS REMOVED)
anther cap
viscidium ('glue blob')
stigma
ovary
pedicel
hypochile (inner lip)
epichile (outer lip)

Epipactis pollination strategies

Insect pollination: In which an insect, typically a social wasp but also *e.g.* a hoverfly (*below*) or a carder bee (*right*), visits a flower for nectar and, in so doing, pollinates the plant. This facilitates high genetic diversity and prevents inbreeding issues. As a result, species such as Broad-leaved Helleborine exhibit a high degree of variation. This strategy can also lead to colonies of clones, as one insect can pollinate many flowers on the same plant (geitonogamy). The insect pollination strategy is not without its risks and rewards. If pollinators become scarce, the plants cannot reproduce and may consequently die out in an area. Equally, if seed sets in a new area where the preferred pollinators are already present, an insect-pollinated species can colonize quickly.

Self-pollination: In which the flower pollinates itself without the help of an insect. The form of the flower has evolved to allow pollen to fall directly down onto the stigma. This creates colonies of clones that can expand very rapidly if the habitat is suitable. While the individual plants within any one colony are all very similar, one colony can look noticeably different to the next, even though genetically they are not significantly different. Genetic evidence indicates that all self-pollinated species are descendants of insect-pollinated ones and, in the case of *Epipactis*, most often the ancestral species is Broad-leaved Helleborine (Sramko, 2019, *etc.*).

Delayed self-pollination: In which a new flower has the ability to be insect-pollinated but, if this does not take place, can revert to self-pollination, usually within 1–3 days of opening. These flowers start with the 'glue-blob' necessary for insect pollination but, in the event this does not occur, the pollen starts to crumble and falls onto the stigmas. In species that are able to self-pollinate, it is essential to look at several flowers to see if this process is happening. Delayed self-pollination can occur in locations where self-pollinated species occur with insect-pollinated ones, or where there is limited pollinator availability. It can also be an indication of hybrid origin. At first glance, this strategy seems to offer the best of both worlds. However, in a situation where a plant is already well adapted to the prevailing conditions any cross-pollination may introduce external genetic influences that make the offspring less suited to the conditions compared to the self-pollinating clones.

The insect pollination process

A visiting insect is attracted to the flower by the nectar-like substance situated in the 'bowl' of the inner lip (hypochile). When it reaches in to drink, the head or body brushes against the sticky 'glue-blob' (viscidium), which is attached to the pollinia. This 'glue-blob' attaches to the insect along with the entire pollinium, which points forward. It is common to see an insect with many pollinia attached to its head, having feasted on a large *Epipactis* helleborine.

Epipactis have no barrier to prevent an insect visiting and pollinating other flowers on the same spike, so in many cases, a single insect will pollinate a single plant several times. This is effectively self-pollination using an external agent, known as geitonogamy.

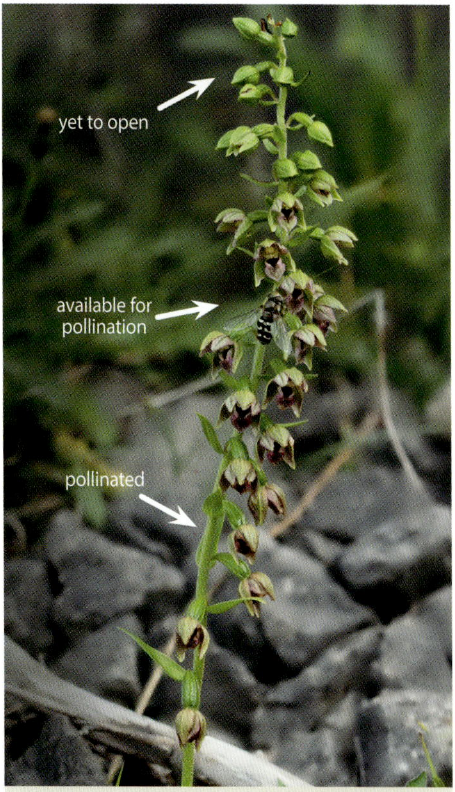
yet to open
available for pollination
pollinated

Epipactis inflorescences are pollinated from the bottom up, reflecting the order in which flowers open; newer, unpollinated flowers at the top; older, pollinated flowers lower down.

INSECT POLLINATION (Allogamy)

Broad-leaved, Violet, Dark-red and Marsh Helleborines

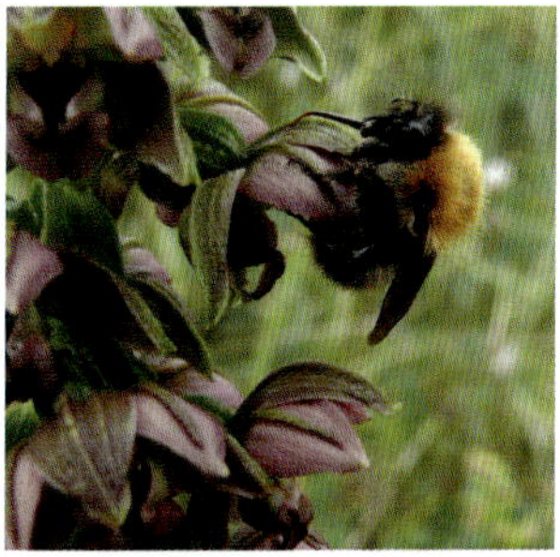

Broad-leaved Helleborine

PRE-POLLINATION: **White 'glue-blob'** visible in open flower; pollen holding together.

POST-POLLINATION: **White 'glue-blob' and pollen have gone completely**, leaving a gap under the anther cap.

SELF-POLLINATION (Autogamy)

Green-flowered (virtually all), **Narrow-lipped** (predominantly), **and Dune Helleborines** (most)

Narrow-lipped Helleborine

PRE-POLLINATION: **No white 'glue-blob'** in open flower; **pollen clearly not holding together**.

POLLINATION: **No white 'glue-blob'** in open flower; **pollen crumbles and falls onto stigma**.

UNPOLLINATED: flower open; ovary narrow
POLLINATED: flower closes; ovary oval

POST-POLLINATION: Flowers droop and start to close up; the ovaries swell and become more oval.

DELAYED SELF-POLLINATION (Facultative allogamy)

Occurs in **Narrow-lipped** (very few), **Dune** (minority), **and Green-flowered Helleborines** (extremely rare); also extremely rarely in '**Dutch Helleborine**'

Narrow-lipped Helleborine

PRE-POLLINATION: **Small white 'glue-blob'** visible in open flower; **but pollen visibly crumbly**.

PRE-POLLINATION: After 1 or 2 days, if not insect-pollinated, the **'glue-blob' shrivels and turns brown**.

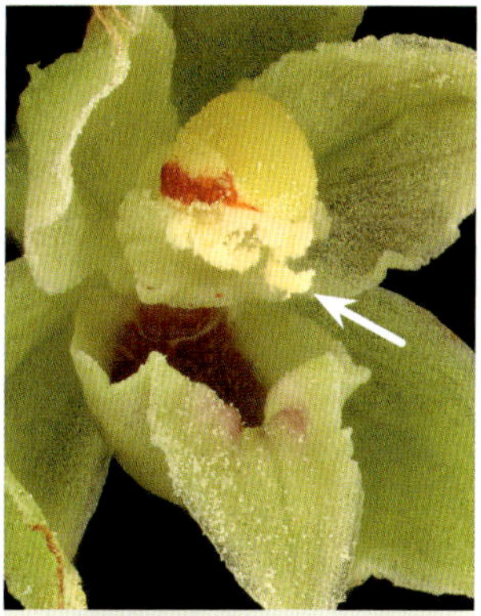

POLLINATION: **No white 'glue-blob'** visible in open flower; **pollen crumbles and falls onto stigma**.

Epipactis | detailed flower and leaf features for identification

Once the pollination method has been established (self sP, insect iP, or facultative iP+ [smaller icons = less common method]**), be aware of the habitat and check the following features:**

FLOWERS: front-on: lip colour and shape; side-on: lip straight or curled.
OVARIES: colour at the base, where it meets the stem, and whether smooth or, if hairy, how much.
LEAVES NEAR THE BASE: their shape and how they emerge from the stem.
LEAF EDGE: the pattern of 'teeth' on the edge of the **first or second large leaf from the base of the stem**. Use a hand lens; although typical examples of each species are shown here, this pattern is variable and the character should therefore only be used as a supporting feature.

NB Most individuals are fairly straightforward (see *p. 96*); on more 'difficult' plants the variability of some species and the possibility of hybridization (see *p. 250*) should always be borne in mind.

FLOWERS WITH DISTINCTIVE FRILLY LIPS

iP Marsh Helleborine *E. palustris* (*p. 120*)

FLOWER: large flowers with a frilly-edged, creamy-white lip, usually with pink veins. HABITAT: dune slacks, fens and on damp, calcareous soils.

iP Dark-red Helleborine *E. atrorubens* (*p. 122*)

FLOWER: bright crimson (to cream) flowers, with obvious yellow anther cap, and frilly lip with lumpy base. HABITAT: dry limestone, particularly limestone pavement.

Marsh Helleborine

Dark-red Helleborine

Although most of the photographs shown here are of dissected freshly opened (unpollinated) flowers, the same features can be seen in the field without removing a flower by gently folding back the petals and sepals of a freshly opened flower.

FRESH, UNPOLLINATED FLOWERS NOTICEABLY DROOPING BELOW HORIZONTAL

sP iP iP+ Narrow-lipped Helleborine *E. leptochila*

p. 134 | variation *p. 138*

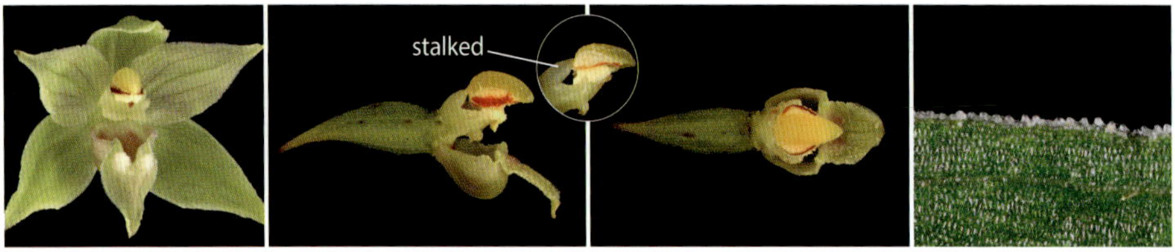
stalked

POLLINIA: a very few individuals may have a 'glue-blob' in newly opened flowers, but this is always much smaller than in Broad-leaved Helleborine and disappears quickly. FLOWER: **LIP** long, pointed, not curling under; off-white with green or sometimes pink tones; **ANTHER CAP** more pointed front than that of Broad-leaved Helleborine; anther has stalk, pushing it forward over the pollinia. OVARY: relatively long and narrow; hairy and all-green, even at base. LEAVES: pale green, usually longer than wide; opposite and widely spaced along stem; **'TEETH'** small and evenly sized along edge of lip. HABITAT: grows in dark, shady ancient woodlands on limestone or chalk in southern Britain.

sP iP iP+ Green-flowered Helleborine *E. phyllanthes*

p. 136 | variation *p. 138*

POLLINIA: flowers sometimes do not open at all but ovary becomes swollen. FLOWER: **OUTER LIP** can have pinkish tones; **INNER LIP** green or very pale brown on inside of 'cup'. OVARY: marrow-shaped, often swells before the flower has opened properly. LEAVES: apple-green, arranged alternately up stem; lowest leaf often very rounded; **'TEETH'** unique uneven serrated pattern, with occasional larger 'teeth' between regular groups of smaller ones.

FRESH, UNPOLLINATED FLOWERS ± HORIZONTAL TO STEM

iP **Violet Helleborine** *E. purpurata* — *p. 124* | variation *p. 139*

FLOWER: large, wide-open, pale green with hints of pink; often many crowded together making plant look top-heavy. OVARY: hairy; tends to be quite round and fat. LEAVES: **FORM** generally quite small, narrow, dull purplish-green; arranged spirally or alternately up the stem; **'TEETH'** small and even, running along leaf edge in a twisting line. STEM: dark, violet, especially lower half, turning dark greyish-green towards the top; rarely green along entire length. HABITAT: grows in very dark, shady parts of woods; older plants are often multi-stemmed, forming clumps.

iP **Broad-leaved Helleborine** *E. helleborine* ssp. *helleborine* — *p. 126* | variation *p. 138*

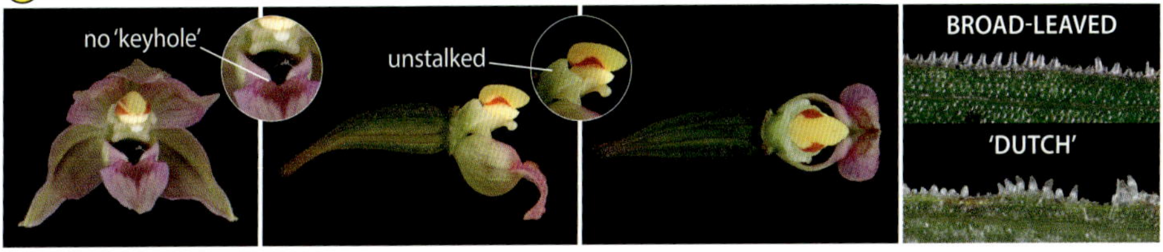
no 'keyhole'
unstalked
BROAD-LEAVED
'DUTCH'

FLOWER: **OUTER LIP** curls under; off-white with some pink; no base 'keyhole', bosses slightly bumpy; **LATERAL PETALS** pink or purple; **SEPALS** contrastingly greener, giving two-toned appearance; **ANTHER CAP** flatter-fronted than that of Narrow-lipped Helleborine. OVARY: hairy, base pink or purple. LEAVES: ovate, often as wide as long, arranged spirally up stem; **'TEETH'** variable, generally even-sized (longer than on Narrow-lipped and Violet H.), sometimes with clumps of longer ones.

iP sP iP+ 'Dutch Helleborine' *E. helleborine* ssp. *neerlandica* — *p. 128*

COMPARED TO BROAD-LEAVED: FORM: generally rather more compact and stockier; can be tiny, with just 1–4 flowers; blooms 3–4 weeks later (usually at its best in August). LEAVES: **FORM** closely grouped around base of stem, sometimes wrapping round and held at about 45° to the stem; **'TEETH'** tightly packed, triangular and lacking a hooked tip. FLOWER: not widely opening, often richly coloured, salmon-pink or purple, bosses dark; **SEPALS** often two-toned; **INFLORESCENCE** densely packed (supporting feature); **HABITAT** exclusively dunes and adjacent habitats.

sP iP iP+ **Dune Helleborine** *E. dunensis* ssp. *dunensis* — *p. 130* | variation *p. 139*

'keyhole'
folded under
pink at base
two-toned pink and green
green at base
'LINDISFARNE'
green at base
'TYNE'
not folded under

COMPARED TO BROAD-LEAVED: paler green overall; plants can be very small with just 1–4 flowers. FLOWER: **OUTER LIP** folded under, 'keyhole' at base, pinkish around 'keyhole', outer section never pink, always green with whitish margin; **LATERAL PETALS** pinkish; **SEPALS** contrastingly greener, giving two-toned appearance, especially when viewed from rear. POLLINIA: crumbling, rather messy, although regularly with 'glue-blob' in newly opened flowers. OVARY: hairy, base purple or pink. LEAVES: a dull sickly-green; ovate, longer than wide; arranged alternately up stem and often clasping it at their base, held erect at about 45°; **'TEETH'** as Narrow-lipped Helleborine, small and evenly sized along edge of lip.

sP iP iP+ 'Lindisfarne Helleborine' *E. dunensis* ssp. *sancta* — *p. 132*
'Tyne Helleborine' *E. dunensis* var. *tynensis* — *p. 133*

POLLINIA: crumbling, rather messy mass of pollen; some individuals may have a 'glue-blob' in newly opened flowers, although less often than in the nominate ssp. *dunensis* described above. FLOWER: **OUTER LIP** folded under when mature ('Lindisfarne'), or sometimes pointing forward ('Tyne'); pale green and white, with 'keyhole' at base; **INNER LIP** green inside cup. OVARY: hairy, with green at base where it meets the stem. DISTRIBUTION: confined to Northumberland – Holy Island ('Lindisfarne'); River South Tyne valley ('Tyne').

IN BUD *p. 77* | IN HABITAT *p. 41*

LC LC Marsh Helleborine *Epipactis palustris*

Scattered; locally common

up to 60 cm

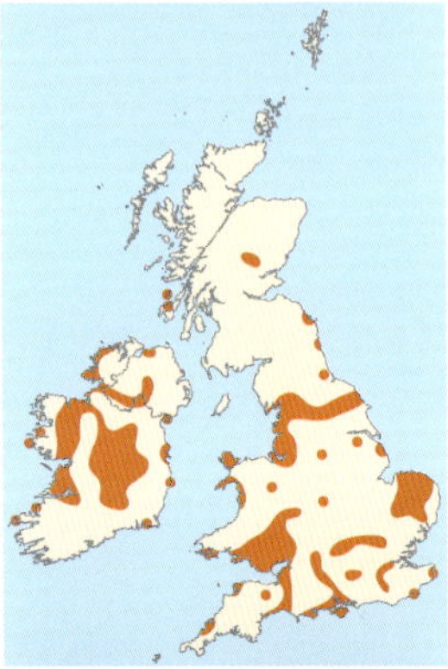

IN BUD

Buds long, teardrop-shaped and buff-coloured. Ovaries long and thin, covered in long white hairs.

Large white-and-pink flowers with broad, white frilly lip. VARIATION *p. 139*.

Leaves long, pointed and quite triangular; held erect at a greater than 45° angle; usually arranged alternately up stem.

HABITAT: Most commonly found in dune slacks and fens, and less frequently in calcium-rich marshes, flushes, seasonally flooded water meadows and old quarries. Very occasionally occurs on open chalk grassland in southern England.

The showy, pinkish-white flowers and habitat preference make this a distinctive helleborine. Colonies can be huge in dune slacks, but smaller in fens and marshes (see *p. 18*). Despite being widespread across England, Wales and Ireland, it is generally scarce, with strongholds in East Anglia, central Ireland and the large sand dune systems of Wales and northern England. It is very rare in Scotland, with a handful of sites on Colonsay and Islay, and one in Perthshire.

IN LEAF p. 61
IN FLOWER p. 89
Jan
Feb
Mar
Apr
May
Jun
Jul
Aug
Sep
Oct
Nov
Dec

Seed pods large and strongly drooping.

CONFUSION SPECIES: IN FLOWER **None.** IN LEAF Other *Epipactis* helleborines.

IN BUD *p. 77* | IN HABITAT *p. 41*

LC LC Dark-red Helleborine *Epipactis atrorubens*

Scattered and rare

up to 50 (75) cm

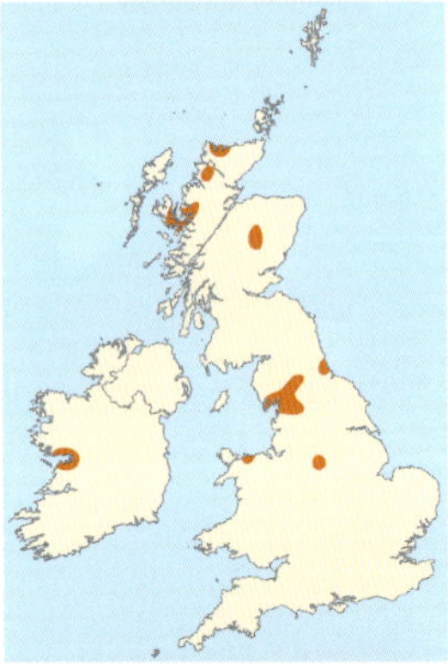

IN BUD

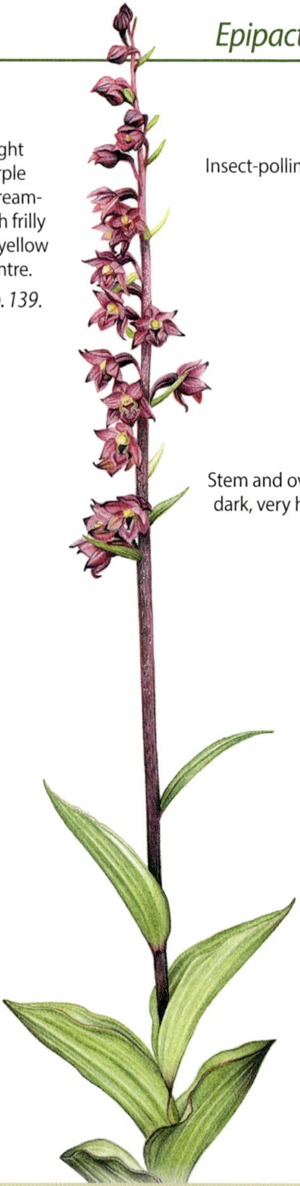

Flowers bright reddish-purple (through to cream-coloured), with frilly lip and bright yellow anther in centre.

VARIATION *p. 139*.

Insect-pollinated.

Stem and ovaries dark, very hairy.

The inflorescence in bud is usually dark (rarely green). The short bracts and squat ovaries give it a tall, narrow outline.

Leaves often with purplish tip and base, longer than wide; arranged in opposite rows and typically clustered at base of stem.

HABITAT: A limestone pavement specialist, where it can typically be found protruding from cracks and fissures in the rock ('grykes'). Also found on grasslands, scree slopes, cliff ledges, quarries and open Ash woodlands that are underlain by limestone.

A deep crimson-flowered helleborine that can be surprisingly difficult to notice as a solitary dark spike poking out of a '**gryke**', even against a pale limestone background. It grows in loose colonies and is regularly found with Broad-leaved Helleborine. Rare and sparsely distributed with a cluster of sites in North Wales, the Peak District (Derbyshire), Cumbria, Yorkshire and Co. Durham. In Scotland, scattered along the north-west coast (Ross & Cromarty and Sutherland), with a particular concentration of colonies on the Isle of Skye and a handful in the Cairngorms (Banffshire and Perthshire). In Ireland it is confined to Co. Galway and the Burren in Co. Clare.

IN LEAF p. 60
IN FLOWER p. 88
IN LEAF
Jan
Feb
Mar
Apr
May
Jun
Jul
Aug
Sep
Oct
Nov
Dec

Lip bosses are large, frilly and the same colour as the rest of the lip; ovaries rounded and densely covered in short whitish hairs.

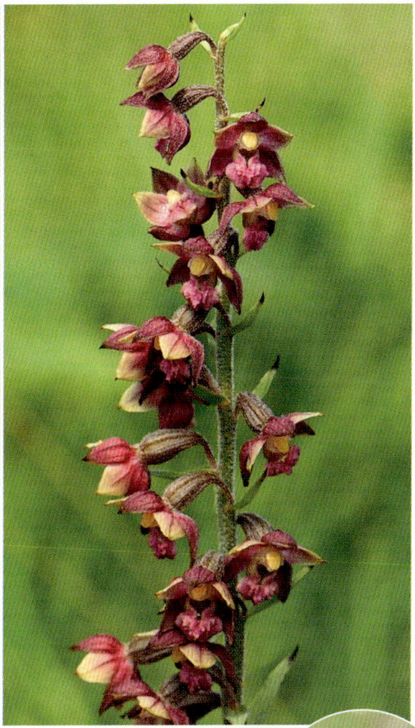

CONFUSION SPECIES: IN FLOWER **Broad-leaved Helleborine** (*p. 126*). IN LEAF Other *Epipactis* helleborines. HYBRID × Broad-leaved Helleborine (*p. 250*).

IN BUD *p. 77* | IN HABITAT *p. 41*

LC Violet Helleborine *Epipactis purpurata*

Local and scarce

up to 60 (75) cm

Flowers rather large, widely open; pale whitish-green with a pale pink wash to lip.
Insect-pollinated: shows white 'glue-blob' unless pollen has been removed.
Stem and ovaries purplish, hairy.
Can be very pale pink or purple when young, darkening as the flower spike develops.
Leaves usually small, narrow; dark green with dull purple wash along lower third of stem.

IN BUD

HABITAT: Ancient woodland, favouring deeply shaded and slightly damp conditions where little else can grow. Can also be found on wooded roadside verges and hedgebanks, sometimes among denser vegetation. Usually found under Beech *Fagus sylvatica*, oaks *Quercus* spp. or Hornbeam *Carpinus betulus*, and sometimes Hazel *Corylus avellana* coppice, underlain by chalk, limestone or clay.

Very consistent in appearance, and well known for developing large, sometimes dense clumps. Usually first noticed as pale grey-green flowers on tall spikes contrasting against a dark woodland background. Where it occurs alongside Broad-leaved Helleborine, hybrids are often present, but are very difficult to distinguish. This is a species of southern and central England, with strongholds on the North and South Downs, the Chiltern Hills, and the Midlands (particularly Worcestershire and Shropshire); it rarely reaches farther north than a line between the Wash and Anglesey.

IN LEAF *p. 61* IN FLOWER *p. 88*

Jan
Feb
Mar
Apr
May
Jun
Jul
Aug
Sep
Oct
Nov
Dec

Flowers rather uniform pale green; contrast with dark purplish-green ovaries, which are rough and covered in short whitish hairs.

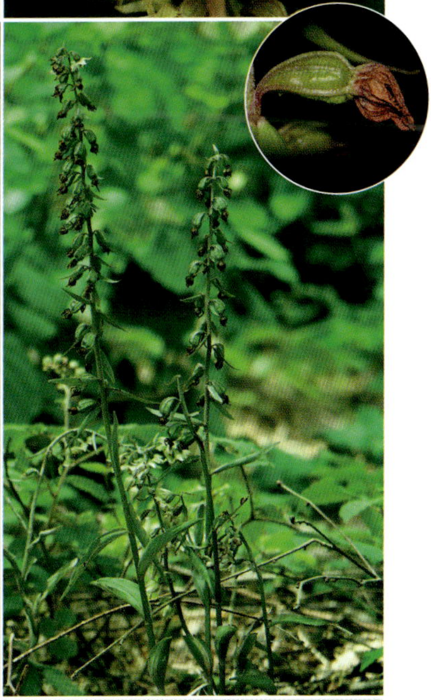

CONFUSION SPECIES: IN FLOWER **Broad-leaved Helleborine** (*p. 126*). IN LEAF Other *Epipactis* helleborines. **HYBRID** × Broad-leaved Helleborine (*p. 250*).

IN BUD p. 77 | IN HABITAT p. 41

LC LC Broad-leaved Helleborine

Epipactis helleborine

FORMER NAME: *E. latifolia*

Widespread and common

up to 90 cm

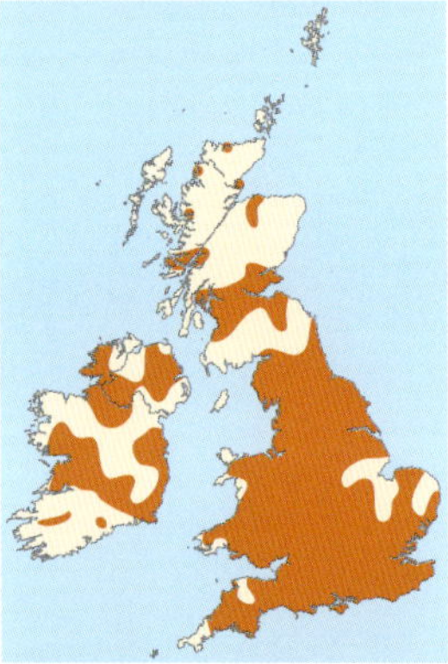

IN BUD
Inflorescence curved downwards, straightening as it develops.
Pink or purple bases to flower buds, never green.

In bud, Broad-leaved, Dune, Narrow-lipped and Green-flowered Helleborines are very similar.

Flowers very variable in colour and form but usually a mix of purplish-pink; 'dirty' bosses, which are typically a different colour to the rest of the lip; upper petals washed variably pink to purple.

Raceme often crowded with flowers; can grow to almost 1 m – the tallest of the hellborines.

TYPICAL FORM

Insect-pollinated: shows white 'glue-blob' unless pollen has been removed.

Ovaries with pink or purple base where they meet stem.

HIGHLY VARIABLE
see *p. 138*.

Stem green and hairy.

Leaves typically oval in shape, often as wide as long and arranged spirally up stem.

LAX-FLOWERED FORM

HABITAT: Essentially woodland on calcareous soils, but also grassland, dunes in South Wales (where ssp. *neerlandica* co-occurs) and Ireland, as well as a wide range of semi-natural habitats such as railway embankments, roadsides, conifer plantations, limestone pavements, quarries, spoil heaps, parks and gardens (especially around Glasgow). Within a woodland habitat, including young secondary woodland, it is usually found in clearings and along rides, although can also thrive in deep shade.

One of the most frequently encountered orchids, but highly variable in appearance and easily confused with several other *Epipactis* species. However, most plants are identifiable with practice. Widely distributed across Britain and Ireland and very common in certain areas, but notably absent from much of Scotland, central and southern Ireland and large parts of eastern England.

IN LEAF p. 58
IN FLOWER p. 89
Jan
Feb
Mar
Apr
May
Jun
Jul
Aug
Sep
Oct
Nov
Dec

Lip folded back, bosses brownish; ovaries smooth, or with a few hairs, and strongly ribbed, pink/purple at the base.

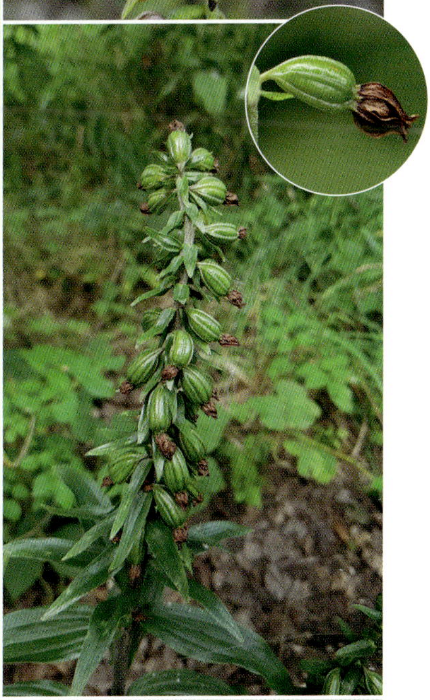

CONFUSION SPECIES: **IN FLOWER** **Other *Epipactis* helleborines**, except Marsh Helleborine.
IN LEAF Lady's-slipper (*p. 56*), other *Epipactis* helleborines, *Cephalanthera* helleborines (*p. 57*).
HYBRIDS × Dark-red, Violet, Narrow-lipped and Green-flowered Helleborines (*pp. 250–253*).

Broad-leaved Helleborine subspecies and variation

Subspecies

'Dutch Helleborine' *E. helleborine* ssp. *neerlandica*

A distinctive subspecies of Broad-leaved Helleborine, named after the Dutch dunes where it also occurs. In Britain and Ireland it is confined to the drier parts of dunes in South Wales, particularly at Kenfig and Oxwich, where it can be fairly common, flowering rather late in August. It has a squat stature, with characteristically stiff, erect leaves that are clustered near the base of the stem. The rather rounded flowers are typically on a densely packed inflorescence. The flowers are generally not widely open, although they can be, and are richly coloured salmon-pink or purple, often with two-toned sepals. They are sometimes self-pollinating. Some plants can be tiny, only a few centimetres tall.

Glamorgan, 1st August

Variation

Broad-leaved Helleborine is extremely variable in height, leaf form, inflorescence shape and flower colour. Plants range in height from 25 cm or so to almost 1 m; leaves can be arranged alternately or spirally; the inflorescence can have a few widely spaced to many densely packed flowers. Flowers vary from pale green to deep purple, with every shade in between (see *p. 138*). Despite this variability, most Broad-leaved Helleborines can be identified initially on the basis of the pollination mechanism (see *p. 116*) and then using flower details (petal and boss colour, lip shape) and leaf shape/arrangement.

IN BUD *p. 77* | IN HABITAT *p. 42*

DD NE Dune Helleborine

Epipactis dunensis

Scattered and scarce

up to 60 cm

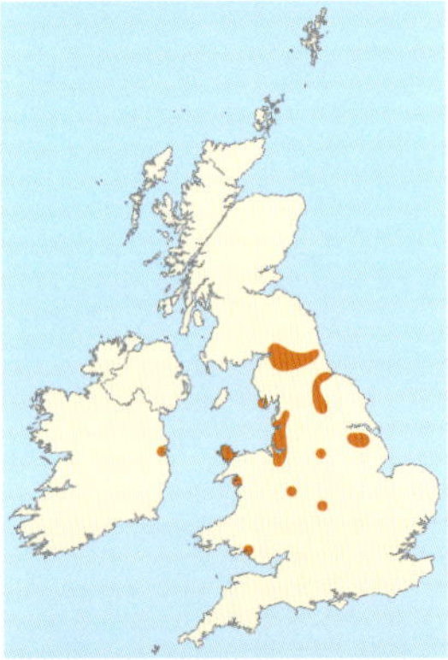

Flowers rather small, rarely open widely, giving 'box-shaped' appearance; pale greenish all over with contrasting pink on lip.

Lip almost triangular with basal 'keyhole'; pink colouring around 'keyhole', pale green near tip.

VARIATION *p. 139*.

Lip can also be green-and-white, longer, slightly twisted and pointing outwards (in 'Tyne Helleborine' *E. dunensis* var. *tynensis* – see *p. 133*).

SUBSPECIES and VARIETIES *p. 132*.

Mainly self-pollinated: crumbling, rather messy mass of pollen; many show 'glue-blob' in newly opened flowers.

Ovaries hairy with pink or purple base where they meet stem.

Base of flower stalk where it meets the stem pinkish (ssp. *dunensis*), or green ('Tyne Helleborine' ssp. *dunensis* var. *tynensis* and 'Lindisfarne Helleborine' ssp. *sancta*).

Can flower when very small.

Leaves a dull sickly-green colour; ovate, longer than wide; arranged alternately and held at approximately 45° to the stem; leaf bases often clasping stem; leaves clustered at stem base in open conditions.

IN BUD
When in bud, the **distinctive leaf-colour and structure, along with pinkish base to ovary**, are the most distinctive features.

In bud, Broad-leaved, Dune, Narrow-lipped and Green-flowered Helleborines are very similar.

HABITAT: Although Dune Helleborine does occur in dunes, it also favours pine stands established on dunes, wet birch and willow woodland (often alongside rivers) and scrubby secondary woodland in reclaimed gravel pits or on spoil heaps. It has also been recorded growing in planted flower beds.

A subtle species, often mistaken for Broad-leaved Helleborine, but it does have its own distinctive appearance. Dune Helleborine is relatively rare in Britain and Ireland, but can be quite common at sites with optimal conditions. Primarily a northern species, originally thought to occur only in dune habitats in north-west England and Wales, but more recently discovered at a variety of inland sites, to Dublin in the west and as far south as Warwickshire. Due to their similarity, Dune Helleborine may in future be discovered at sites formerly considered to be populated with Broad-leaved Helleborine.

IN LEAF *p. 59* IN FLOWER *p. 89*

Jan
Feb
Mar
Apr
May
Jun
Jul
Aug
Sep
Oct
Nov
Dec

Pale greenish-white flowers (do not open widely) with contrasting whitish-pink lip; ovaries with pink base where they meet the stem.

CONFUSION SPECIES: IN FLOWER Particularly **var. *tynensis*** ('Tyne Helleborine') (*p. 133*), but also **Broad-leaved Helleborine** (*p. 126*) and **Narrow-lipped Helleborine** (*p. 134*). IN LEAF Other *Epipactis* helleborines, *Cephalanthera* helleborines (*p. 57*). HYBRIDS × Broad-leaved Helleborine (*p. 250*).

Dune Helleborine subspecies and varieties

'Lindisfarne Helleborine' *E. dunensis* ssp. *sancta*

Considered to be a separate species by some authorities, the genetic differences between *sancta* and typical *dunensis* are slight and it is therefore best considered as a subspecies. This plant is entirely restricted to Holy Island (Lindisfarne) in Northumberland, where it occurs within the drier parts of dunes. Here, plants can characteristically be found growing directly from the bare sand, or hidden among Marram *Ammophila arenaria* or Creeping Willow *Salix repens*. Generally, 'Lindisfarne Helleborine' is rather small and greenish all over, with a pale whitish-green lip and short, sickly-green leaves. It also flowers rather early, at the beginning of July. The base of the ovary where it meets the stem is green (pink in the more widespread ssp. *dunensis*)

'Tyne Helleborine' *E. dunensis* var. *tynensis*

Helleborine populations growing on river gravels along the River South Tyne in Northumberland were previously thought to be Narrow-lipped Helleborine on account of their long, pointed lip – a feature not seen in typical Dune Helleborine. However, genetic studies have shown these plants to be a variety of Dune Helleborine. Although only certain populations display a long, pointed lip, var. *tynensis* is a much greener plant than typical Dune Helleborines, with no pinkish coloration on the lip, or on the base of the ovary where it meets the stem. Its preferred habitat of river gravels is also rather different, so its entire range is somewhat isolated from typical Dune Helleborine populations.

IN BUD *p. 77* | IN HABITAT *p. 41*

DD WL Narrow-lipped Helleborine *Epipactis leptochila*

Local and rare

up to 70 cm

IN BUD
Inflorescence curved downwards, straightening as it develops. Bases to flower buds green, never pink or purple.

In bud, Broad-leaved, Dune, Narrow-lipped and Green-flowered Helleborines are very similar.

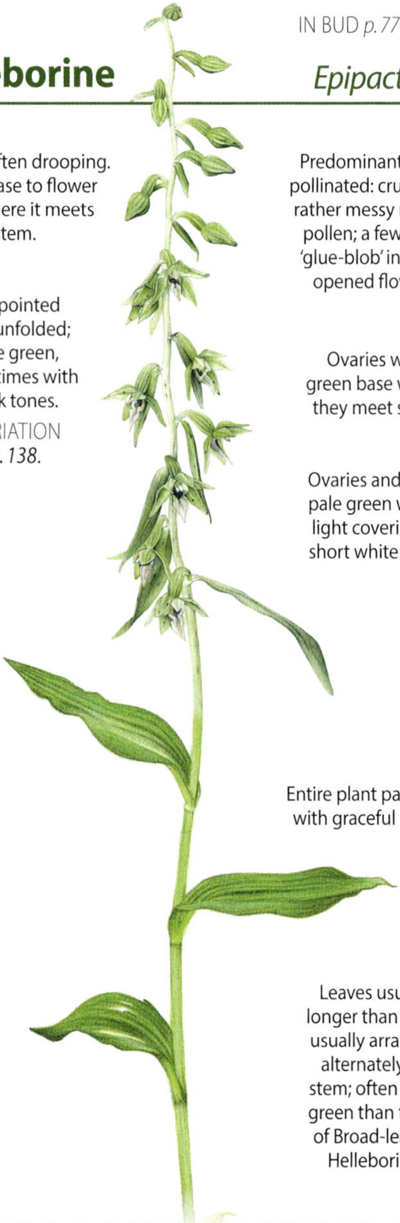

Flowers often drooping. Green base to flower stalk where it meets stem.

Lip pointed and unfolded; pale green, sometimes with pink tones.

VARIATION *p. 138.*

Predominantly self-pollinated: crumbling, rather messy mass of pollen; a few show 'glue-blob' in newly opened flowers.

Ovaries with green base where they meet stem.

Ovaries and stem pale green with a light covering of short white hairs.

Entire plant pale green with graceful stature.

Leaves usually longer than wide; usually arranged alternately up stem; often paler green than those of Broad-leaved Helleborine.

HABITAT: A specialist of dark, ancient Beech woods, including some with a Hazel *Corylus avellana* understorey, but where there is little or no herb layer on the woodland floor. It occasionally appears on road banks that pass through woodlands in which it occurs, but is intolerant of direct sunlight.

A subtle orchid that can be difficult to spot in dark woodlands. It is a scarce and declining species that is entirely confined to southern England and South Wales, with the main distribution in the Cotswolds and Chilterns, plus a large population in Surrey. Elsewhere, there are a handful of small populations in other southern counties, and one near Cardiff. In most colonies, only a small number of plants flower each year – smaller colonies may only rarely have flowering plants. Misidentification of similar-looking Broad-leaved, Green-flowered and, most notably, 'Tyne Helleborine', has confused the true range of this species. It is now clear that Narrow-lipped Helleborine is far less widespread than previously thought.

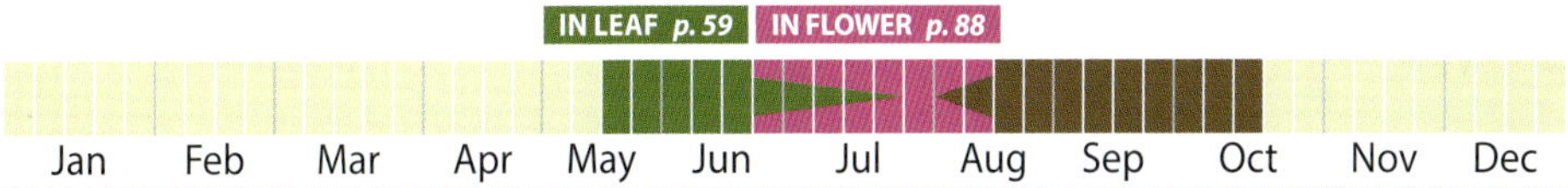
IN LEAF p. 59
IN FLOWER p. 88
Jan
Feb
Mar
Apr
May
Jun
Jul
Aug
Sep
Oct
Nov
Dec

The front of the anther cap is pointed and usually hangs low over the hypochile (*cf.* Broad-leaved Helleborine).

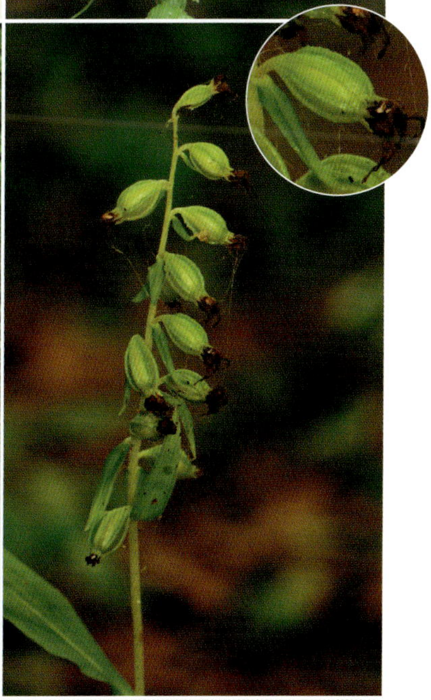

CONFUSION SPECIES: IN FLOWER **Broad-leaved** (*p. 126*), **Green-flowered** (*p. 136*) and **Dune Helleborines** (especially 'Tyne Helleborine' var. *tynensis*) (*pp. 130–133*). IN LEAF Other *Epipactis* helleborines, *Cephalanthera* helleborines (*p. 57*). HYBRIDS × Broad-leaved Helleborine (*p. 250*).

IN BUD *p. 77* | IN HABITAT *p. 42*

LC EN Green-flowered Helleborine

Epipactis phyllanthes

Pendulous-flowered Helleborine

FORMER NAMES: *E. vectensis, E. pendula*

Widespread and scarce

up to 60 cm

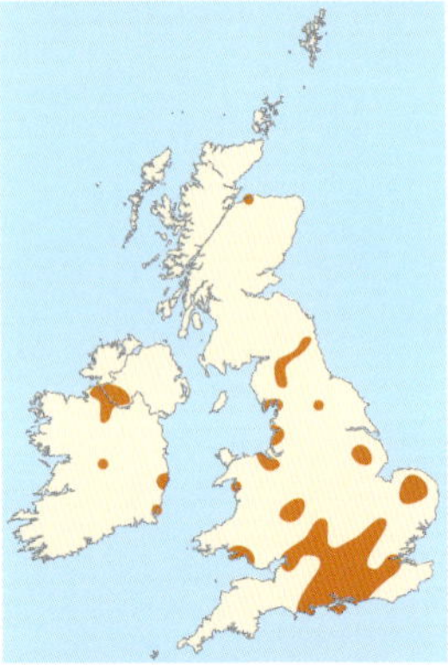

IN BUD
Inflorescence curved downwards, straightening as it develops. Can be very pale pink or purple when young, darkening as the flower spike develops.

Flowers usually green all over, often remaining closed and strongly drooping. Inside of hypochile (lip cup) always pale green.

Almost all self-pollinated: messy mass of pollen; very rarely has a 'glue-blob'.

Ovaries hairless, shiny, with green base where they meet stem; thin and marrow-shaped before swelling – often when still in flower

Very green all over.

Leaves usually small and round.

Unique pattern of 'teeth' on leaf edge (see inset *opposite*).

HABITAT: Found in a variety of habitats, although primarily a woodland species, particularly damp woodlands (often smaller tracts), beside streams, lakes and rivers. Often seen sticking up through Bramble *Rubus* spp. and Common Ivy *Hedera helix*, and even among Himalayan Balsam *Impatiens glandulifera*. Also regularly occurs in scrubby areas on open dunes, and in adjacent pine plantations. In southern England also associated with Beech woods on chalk and limestone, where it can sometimes appear on dry road verges and banks.

Rather nondescript and often weedy-looking, but distinctive in its all-green appearance with strongly drooping flowers. Generally scarce, but most common in the central chalk regions of southern England. There is a single site in northern Scotland (Moray) and several scattered sites in Ireland. It regularly occurs with other helleborines, and probable hybrids have been found in Hampshire and North Wales.

IN LEAF p. 60
IN FLOWER p. 84
Jan
Feb
Mar
Apr
May
Jun
Jul
Aug
Sep
Oct
Nov
Dec

The inside of the hypochile is always pale green and the ovaries are hairless.

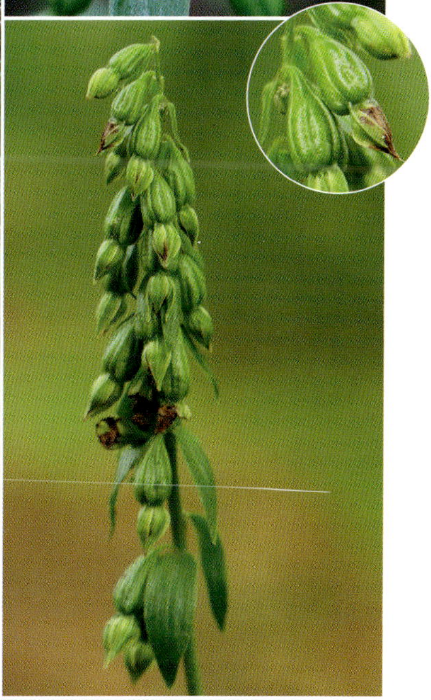

CONFUSION SPECIES: **IN FLOWER** Other *Epipactis* helleborines. **IN LEAF** Other *Epipactis* helleborines, *Cephalanthera* helleborines (*p. 57*). **HYBRIDS** × Broad-leaved Helleborine (*p. 250*).

Epipactis flower variation

Broad-leaved Helleborine *p. 126* | Extremely variable in shape, size and colour but usually some purplish-pink on upper petals; boss is a different colour to the rest of the lip, which is usually blunt-ended and curled back, although some plants (very rarely) have a pointed lip (above middle) similar to Narrow-lipped Helleborine.

Narrow-lipped Helleborine *p. 134* | Relatively consistent; individual populations may differ from one another but long, pointed lip is always apparent. Bosses may or may not be present and vary in intensity of pink coloration.

Green-flowered Helleborine *p. 136* | Flower shape highly variable – from well-formed hypochile and epichile (*left*) to sepal-like 'degenerate' lip form (*right*). Inner hypochile is always pale green in colour.

ssp. *sancta*
var. *tynensis*

Dune Helleborine *p. 130* | Distinctive and usually rather consistent in appearance with pale greenish flowers and the lip pinkish (ssp. *dunensis*) or green and white (ssp. *sancta* and var. *tynensis*).

Violet Helleborine *p. 124* | Consistent and distinctive, widely opening pale greenish flowers; bosses vary from whitish to pale pink, lateral petals typically pale green but may be pink in chlorophyll-deficient forms (*right*).

Dark-red Helleborine *p. 122* | Flowers deep crimson, contrasting with yellow anther cap, although some can have buff, pinkish or yellowish flowers. Bosses are large and frilly and always the same colour as the lip.

Marsh Helleborine *p. 120* | Unlike any other *Epipactis*; the colour of the lateral sepals ranges from deep reddish through to pale green. Plants occurring in fens often have flowers opening more widely (*centre*) than those in dune slacks (*right*).

IN BUD *p. 77* | IN HABITAT *p. 42*

LC LC Common Twayblade *Neottia ovata*

FORMER NAME: *Listera ovata*

Widespread and common

up to 75 cm

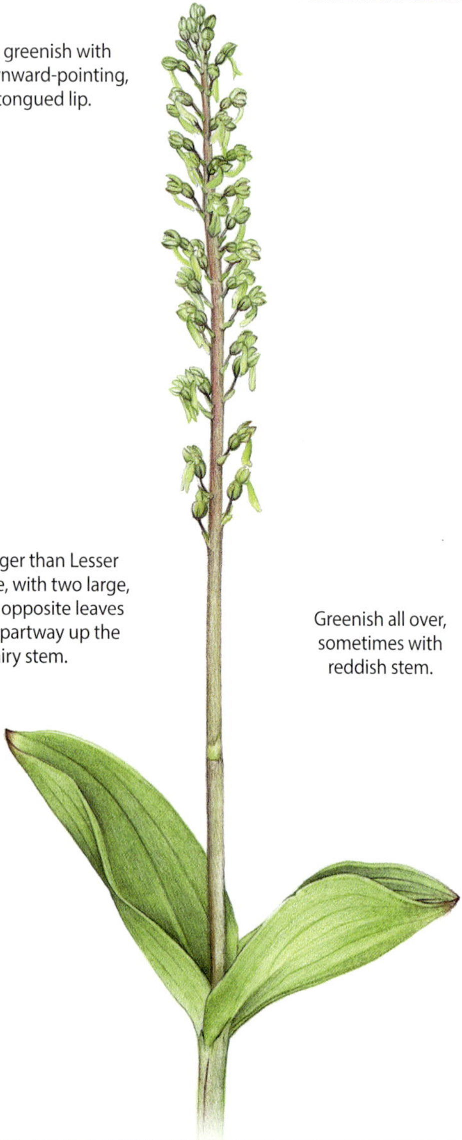
Flowers greenish with long, downward-pointing, fork-tongued lip.
Much larger than Lesser Twayblade, with two large, rounded, opposite leaves growing partway up the hairy stem.
Greenish all over, sometimes with reddish stem.

IN BUD
The budding inflorescence (looking like a bunch of grapes) emerges from the base of the broad, rounded leaves. The buds are not covered by bracts and the stem is covered in short whitish hairs.

HABITAT: Occurs primarily in the lowlands, occupying a very diverse range of undisturbed habitats, including woodland, scrub, chalk and limestone grasslands, hay meadows, churchyards, dunes, quarries, old chalk pits, road verges, fens, hedgebanks and even limestone pavements. Most common on calcareous soils, but will also tolerate mildly acidic soils.

Not immediately obvious, but very distinctive with its large, paired leaves and narrow green inflorescence. It is one of the most common and widespread orchids in Britain and Ireland, occurring in all areas except for parts of coastal Ireland, the Scottish Highlands and Shetland.

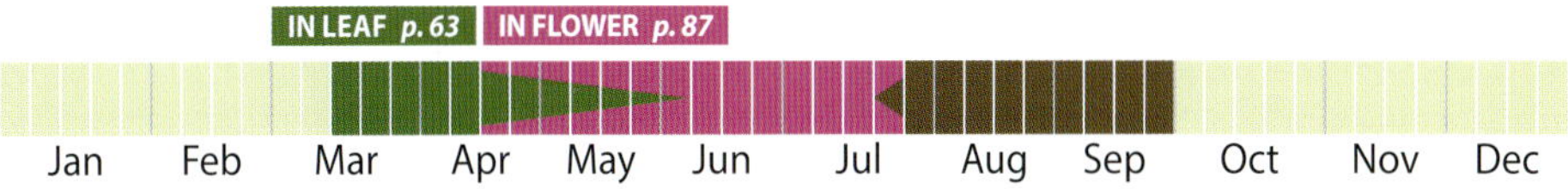
IN LEAF p. 63
IN FLOWER p. 87
Jan
Feb
Mar
Apr
May
Jun
Jul
Aug
Sep
Oct
Nov
Dec

After pollination (as indicated by swollen ovaries) flowers may persist, giving the illusion of an extended flowering period.

CONFUSION SPECIES: **IN FLOWER** **Frog Orchid** (*p. 188*). **IN LEAF** Greater Butterfly-orchid, Lesser Butterfly-orchid (both *p. 62*).

LC LC Lesser Twayblade *Neottia cordata*

FORMER NAME: *Listera cordata*

Widespread; locally common

up to 10 (25) cm

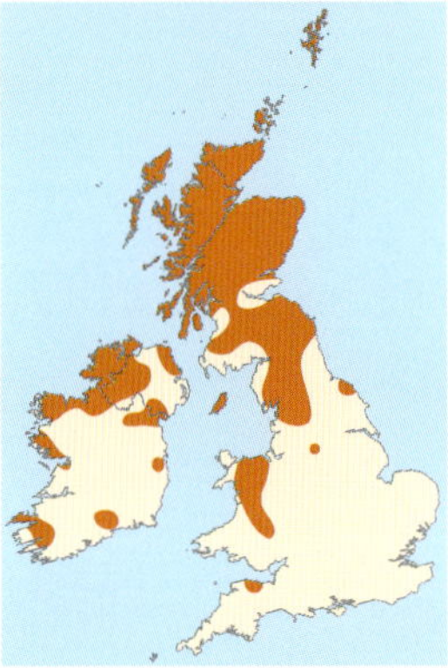

Loose cluster of spiky flowers at top of stem.

Tiny, and very difficult to spot; stem and flowers dark wine-coloured to greenish-buff.

Two (very occasionally three) heart-shaped, opposite leaves growing partway up hairy stem.

IN BUD
Inflorescence looks like a bunch of tiny grapes emerging from the twin, heart-shaped leaves.

HABITAT: Very different to that of Common Twayblade: always on boggy, acid soils and particularly wet upland moorlands, where it grows on beds of *Sphagnum* moss under the shelter of mature Heather *Calluna vulgaris* or Bilberry *Vaccinium myrtillus*. Also occurs among mosses in mature pine woods, including plantations, and in wet willow, birch and Alder woodland.

One of the most difficult species to spot, due to its size, colour and tendency to be hidden among vegetation. It is often easier to spot the leaves than the flowers, and familiarity with its habitat preferences is helpful in locating plants. Primarily a species of northern and western uplands, and therefore most common in Scotland, northern England, North Wales and in the north of Ireland, where it is also found at scattered sites mostly in the west and south-west. There are also small populations in Somerset (Exmoor), Herefordshire and Derbyshire – relicts from a period of cooler climate. The species' diminutive stature and habitat means it is undoubtedly under-recorded.

IN LEAF *p. 63* **IN FLOWER** *p. 87*

Jan
Feb
Mar
Apr
May
Jun
Jul
Aug
Sep
Oct
Nov
Dec

After pollination (as indicated by swollen ovaries) flowers may persist, giving the illusion of an extended flowering period.

CONFUSION SPECIES: **IN FLOWER** None. **IN LEAF** Seedlings of Bilberry *Vaccinium myrtillus* and other non-orchid species.

IN BUD p. 77 | IN HABITAT p. 42

NT LC Bird's-nest Orchid *Neottia nidus-avis* N

Widespread; locally common

up to 50 cm

Entire plant creamy yellowish- and pinkish-brown in colour, with no green.

No obvious leaves, just sheaths on the stem.

IN BUD

HABITAT: Found in a variety of dark woodlands, but especially Beech, on calcareous soils with little or no other vegetation on the woodland floor. In northern England, the species often occurs in more open situations and sometimes strays into grassy glades and on to hedgebanks, but cannot survive in areas that are too dry.

Distinctive and rather other-worldly on bare, sun-dappled woodland floors, often growing next to the previous years' dead spikes. Scattered across the whole of Britain and Ireland where there is suitable habitat, although more common in southern England. Emerges in larger numbers when the ground is damper, particularly during wet springs.

IN FLOWER p. 84
Jan
Feb
Mar
Apr
May
Jun
Jul
Aug
Sep
Oct
Nov
Dec

Previous years' dead inflorescences often persist close to the current flowering plants.

CONFUSION SPECIES: IN FLOWER **Ghost Orchid** (*p. 146*), the parasitic non-orchid species Yellow Bird's-nest *Hypopitys monotropa* and broomrapes *Orobanche* spp. (see *p. 81*).

IN BUD p. 77 | IN HABITAT p. 43

CR Ghost Orchid *Epipogium aphyllum*

Spurred Coralroot Orchid

Last recorded 2009

up to 15 (25) cm

IN BUD

Pink-and-white 'nodding' hood, formed by the lip and spur, above a creamy-white four-pointed, finger-like lower half.

One to four large flowers on a thin stem, making the plant look top-heavy.

Very small, leafless and pale all over; whitish at a distance; may even be partly or wholly obscured by surrounding leaf-litter.

HABITAT: Restricted to very dark ancient Beech and oak woodland in southern and central England, although has been recorded from a largely coniferous woodland in Herefordshire (occurs under spruce and pine in continental Europe). Associated with larger woodland tracts in old, botanically-rich landscapes, such as the Teme, Wye and Thames valleys. Most often on calcareous soils, but has been recorded in more acidic conditions. Usually favours damp areas of deep leaf-litter that collects in shallow hollows, ditches, paths and old cart tracks.

The most difficult orchid to see in Britain, due to its extreme rarity, infrequent flowering, small size and tendency to be hidden in deep leaf-litter, camouflaged against sun-dappled leaves. The potential flowering period is very long, primarily mid-July to the end of September, with the earliest recorded in late May and the latest mid-October. Historically, this species appeared occasionally at seven sites in the Chilterns and Teme and Wye Valleys. At its most reliable site, which was in Buckinghamshire, it flowered almost annually between 1953 and 1987 but has not been seen there since. There has been only one confirmed British record subsequently: in Herefordshire in 2009. The lack of more recent records could indicate a genuine decline but Ghost Orchid has often been found by chance in the past, so it is possible it will reappear spontaneously wherever the habitat and conditions are suitable.

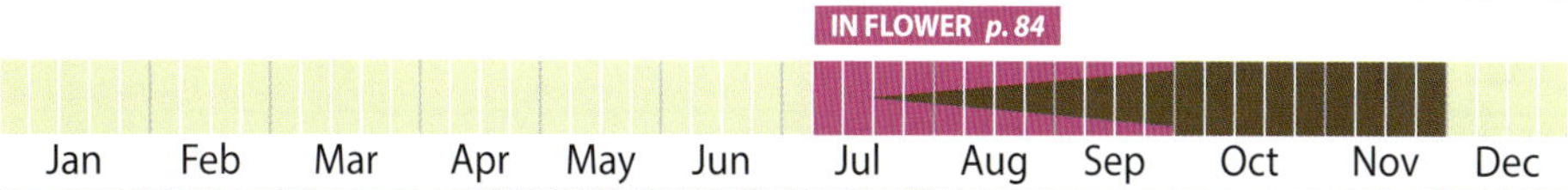
IN FLOWER p. 84
Jan
Feb
Mar
Apr
May
Jun
Jul
Aug
Sep
Oct
Nov
Dec

This was the penultimate year that Ghost Orchid was recorded flowering in the Chilterns, when six plants were found. Buckinghamshire, 4th August 1986.

CONFUSION SPECIES: **IN FLOWER** Bird's-nest Orchid – also in seed (*p. 144*), the parasitic non-orchid species Yellow Bird's-nest *Hypopitys monotropa* (*p. 81*), headless fungus stems (which have no sheathing leafy scales on the stem) and dead Bluebell *Hyacinthoides non-scripta* racemes (*p. 81*).

VU Coralroot Orchid *Corallorhiza trifida*

Scattered and scarce

up to 20 (30) cm

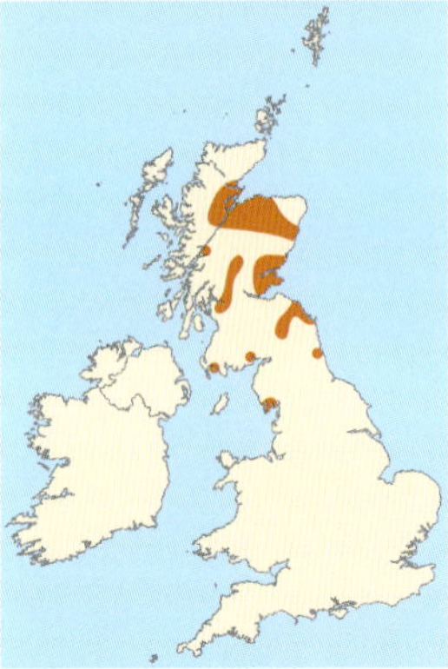

IN BUD

Very small; flowers tiny with some red markings on the white lip.
Leafless, with loosely spaced yellowish-green flowers clustered at the top of the thin, greenish or reddish stem.

HABITAT: Found in two distinct habitats: boggy willow, birch or pine woodlands; and open dune slacks. Often occurs in areas that are seasonally flooded, flourishing best when moisture levels are optimum for growth during early spring.

A small, yellowish-green species that can be difficult to spot, especially in its dune slack habitat where its colours blend into surrounding vegetation. In woodland habitats, it is often taller and paler, and therefore more obvious among carpets of moss. Strictly northern in its distribution, it is most common in eastern Scotland and the Cairngorms, and also along the Borders. In northern England it is largely restricted to the coastal sand dune systems of Cumbria and Northumberland, and two inland woodland sites. Until the 1990s, it also occurred regularly at a site in the Yorkshire Dales.

IN FLOWER p. 87

Jan
Feb
Mar
Apr
May
Jun
Jul
Aug
Sep
Oct
Nov
Dec

CONFUSION SPECIES: IN FLOWER None.

IN BUD *p. 76* | IN HABITAT *p. 43*

EN Fen Orchid *Liparis loeselii* G

Very rare; fewer than 10 sites

up to 20 cm

IN BUD

DUNE FORM

Spiky yellowish-green flowers face upwards to catch rain that enables pollination.

FEN FORM

Two erect basal leaves with strong central rib; these sheathe the base of the stem and are folded along their length into a shallow trough.

HABITAT: Occurs in two distinct habitats: newly formed wet dune slacks in South Wales; and fens in East Anglia, where it is often found among reeds *Phragmites australis* in areas traditionally cut for peat. Both habitats offer a similar combination of bare, wet earth and limited competition from other plants.

Small and rarely obvious, the dense spike of bright yellowish-green flowers often being the first noticeable feature. This is one of the rarest British orchids, now confined to Kenfig Dunes in South Wales and a handful of fens in Norfolk and Suffolk, following a rapid decline at the turn of this century. The fall in numbers was primarily due to a lack of active management, resulting in the invasion of scrub and trees at the remaining sites, and the consequential general drying of the soils. Significant conservation action in recent years has been successful in reintroducing the species to former sites and massively increasing the populations at existing sites.

IN LEAF p. 64
IN FLOWER p. 87
Jan
Feb
Mar
Apr
May
Jun
Jul
Aug
Sep
Oct
Nov
Dec

FEN FORM

DUNE FORM

FEN FORM
Plants in East Anglia have longer leaves and are often taller.

DUNE FORM

DUNE FORM

CONFUSION SPECIES: **IN FLOWER** **Bog Orchid** (*p. 152*), **Musk Orchid** (*p. 154*).
IN LEAF Butterfly-orchids (*p. 62*).

IN BUD *p. 76* | IN HABITAT *p. 43*

LC NT Bog Orchid *Hammarbya paludosa*

Scattered and scarce

up to 6 (12) cm

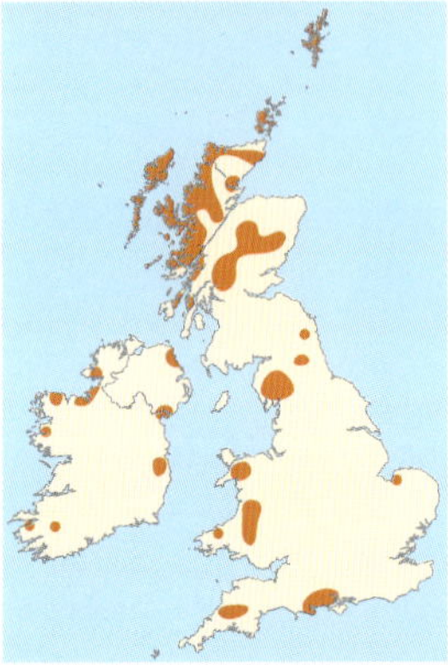

IN BUD

Flowers tiny, with small shield-shaped lip at top of flower.
Looks top-heavy at a distance.
Very small, yellowish-green all over.
Round or oval leaves at base of stem, with small 'teeth' (bulbils) around the rim.

HABITAT: A species of permanently wet bogs, where it perches precariously on bare peat and carpets of *Sphagnum* moss. It requires areas where there is some water movement, so is often found along the edges and sometimes even in the middle of small streams and flushes.

The smallest species of orchid in Britain and Ireland, typically around 6 cm tall. Usually very difficult to spot among the surrounding vegetation, although the pale green spikes of flowers and sickly-green leaves often give it away. Once familiar with its preferred micro-habitat, searches can be narrowed to areas of bog where the water is flowing. Nowhere common, this species' range is limited by its specialist habitat requirements, the strongholds being: Scotland, including the Hebrides, Orkney and Shetland; northern England, particularly the Lake District; and southern England, where it occurs in the New Forest (Hampshire), Purbeck (Dorset) and Dartmoor (Devon). In Wales, there are scattered sites throughout the mountainous regions. It is rare in Ireland, with only a handful of sites clustered in Co. Antrim, another cluster of sites south of Dublin, and a few scattered along the west coast. Bog Orchid is very susceptible to trampling and to its habitat drying out.

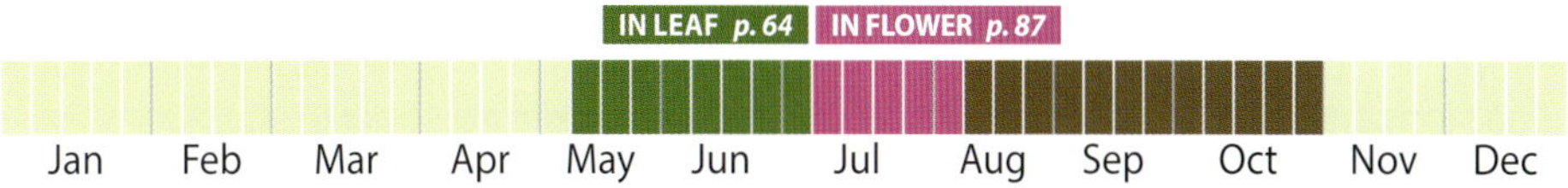
IN LEAF p. 64
IN FLOWER p. 87
Jan
Feb
Mar
Apr
May
Jun
Jul
Aug
Sep
Oct
Nov
Dec

CONFUSION SPECIES: IN FLOWER **Fen Orchid** (*p. 150*). IN LEAF None.

IN BUD p. 78 | IN HABITAT p. 43

VU Musk Orchid

Herminium monorchis

Local and rare

up to 15 (25) cm

IN BUD

Untidy flower spike of drooping, spiky, yellowish-green flowers that become more widely spaced as the plant develops.

Very small and difficult to spot; usually grows in groups.

Two (sometimes three) opposite, triangular leaves at base of stem.

HABITAT: A specialist of botanically-rich chalk and limestone grassland with long continuity in southern England. It favours areas where the turf is short, and can be rather numerous in particular spots on downland, ancient hilltop earthworks and in old chalk pits.

Diminutive and dainty, Musk Orchid forms large colonies where conditions are suitable. A tiny spike of greenish-yellow, drooping flowers among sparse grasses is usually the first indication of its presence. It is entirely restricted to southern England, with strongholds in Hampshire, Surrey, Buckinghamshire, the Cotswolds and the North and South Downs, with a few scattered sites in adjacent counties. It formerly occurred at one or two sites in South Wales but has not been seen there for decades. This species is very susceptible to drought and can disappear for years, or even permanently, after particularly long dry spells. Its smell is more akin to honey than musk.

IN LEAF p. 65
IN FLOWER p. 87
Jan
Feb
Mar
Apr
May
Jun
Jul
Aug
Sep
Oct
Nov
Dec

CONFUSION SPECIES: IN FLOWER **Small-white Orchid** (*p. 156*), **Fen Orchid** (*p. 150*), **Dense-flowered Orchid** (*p. 158*). IN LEAF Small-white Orchid (*p. 64*).

 IN BUD p. 76 | IN HABITAT p. 45

VU VU Small-white Orchid *Pseudorchis albida*

Scattered and scarce

up to 40 cm

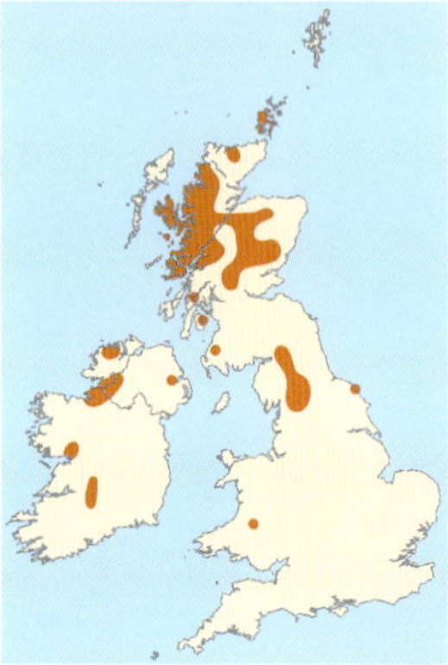

IN BUD

Flowers unmarked, with pointed central lobe and much shorter side lobes; face forward or droop slightly.

Thin narrow flower spike, 'tidier' looking than Musk Orchid's; flowers whiter.

Quite small plant, with tiny bulbous greenish-and-white flowers that resemble berries at a distance.

Leaves longish, oval to elliptical, with 'pinched', keeled tips.

HABITAT: A species of the uplands, where it can be found in hay meadows, short grassy heathland and grazed hill pastures on both calcareous and acid soils.

A delicate species with tiny, scented flowers. Unfortunately, it has disappeared from much of its former range, and is now found primarily in Scotland. In northern England, it is largely restricted to Northumberland, Cumbria and Yorkshire. It is patchily distributed across Ireland, with a concentration of records in Co. Sligo and Co. Leitrim and Co. Fermanagh. Populations recently collapsed in Wales, where there is now only one reliable site, and it is extinct in southern England.

IN LEAF p. 64
IN FLOWER p. 86
IN LEAF
Jan
Feb
Mar
Apr
May
Jun
Jul
Aug
Sep
Oct
Nov
Dec

CONFUSION SPECIES: IN FLOWER **Musk Orchid** (*p. 154*). IN LEAF Fragrant-orchids (*p. 67*) and marsh-orchids (*p. 69*). HYBRIDS × Heath Fragrant-orchid (*p. 260*), Heath Spotted-orchid (*p. 260*), Greater Butterfly-orchid (*p. 249*).

IN BUD *p. 76* | IN HABITAT *p. 45*

NT Dense-flowered Orchid *Neotinea maculata*

FORMER NAME: *N. intacta*

Local and rare

up to 20 (30) cm

IN BUD

Small and difficult to spot, with tiny flowers, either plain creamy-white or marked with pink.
Flowers twisted, facing in all directions.
Ovaries often swollen while still in flower.
Leaves oval to strap-shaped, either spotted or unspotted, and often yellowing by flowering time; basal leaves often lying flat on the ground.

HABITAT: Restricted to botanically-rich limestone grasslands in Ireland. Favours areas where the turf is particularly short. Also recorded (rarely) from Ash and Hazel woodlands and sand dunes. Interestingly, the species is most common in the warmer, drier regions of the Mediterranean, but in Ireland it is unique in co-occurring with Arctic species, such as Mountain Avens *Dryas octopetala*.

An Irish speciality and one of the characteristic species of the limestone pavements and grasslands of western Ireland. Famously difficult to spot, it is small and rather compact with self-pollinating flowers that quickly brown and 'go over'. Although its stronghold is the Burren (Co. Clare), there are also a handful of sites in neighbouring Co. Galway and Co. Mayo, with single sites in each of Counties Roscommon, Offaly, Limerick and Donegal. In addition, there are two large populations in Co. Fermanagh and a single record from coastal Co. Antrim. It previously occurred on the Isle of Man but has not been recorded there since 1985.

IN LEAF *p. 64* IN FLOWER *p. 86*

Jan
Feb
Mar
Apr
May
Jun
Jul
Aug
Sep
Oct
Nov
Dec

'WHITE' FORM

'PINK' FORM

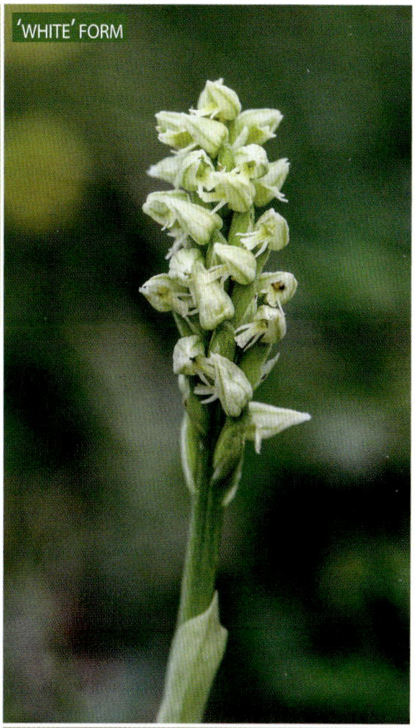
'WHITE' FORM

Two forms: one with pinkish flowers and spotted leaves and another with creamy-white flowers and unspotted leaves. Although both forms occur throughout, the white form is more prevalent in the Burren and only the pink form is present at one of the Co. Fermanagh sites.

'PINK' FORM

CONFUSION SPECIES: IN FLOWER **Small-white Orchid** (*p. 156*), **Musk Orchid** (*p. 154*).
IN LEAF Bee Orchid (*p. 75*).

IN BUD *p. 78* | IN HABITAT *p. 45*

EN Burnt Orchid *Neotinea ustulata*

Burnt-tip Orchid

FORMER NAME: *Orchis ustulata*

Scattered and scarce

up to 15 (30) cm

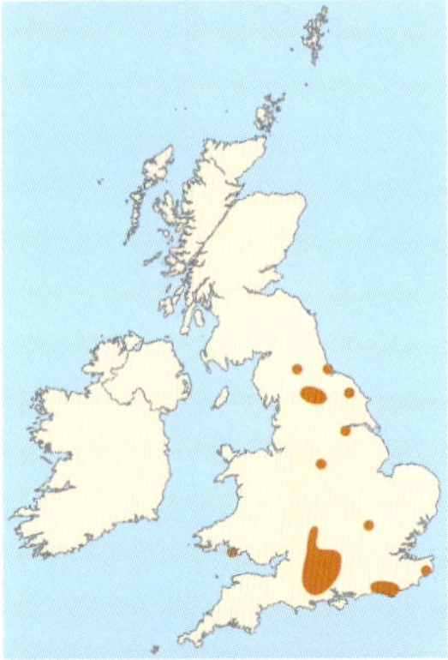

IN BUD

Two-tone flower spike: dark purple buds at top, fading to small white flowers with crimson spots on forked lip, rarely much paler or even all-white.
Small, sometimes quite difficult to spot.
Leaves unspotted.

HABITAT: Botanically rich chalk and limestone grassland is the most common habitat, especially old hilltop earthworks, always where the turf is short. Also occurs in riverside pastures in Yorkshire, and on the roughs of a golf course near the coast in County Durham. At one unique site in Lincolnshire, it thrives in a water meadow where chalky silt is regularly deposited by the nearby river.

An often surprisingly tiny orchid with uniquely contrasting deep crimson buds and whitish flowers on a densely packed inflorescence. There are two varieties that have distinctly separate flowering periods (see *p. 162*), and which are rarely at the same locality. It has suffered a severe decline across much of its range in the Midlands, East Anglia and northern England, and is now rare. There are still large populations in its stronghold of Wiltshire, and also in Hampshire, East Sussex and Derbyshire, with small colonies in Lincolnshire, Kent, Gloucestershire, Bedfordshire, Yorkshire and Co. Durham. There is a single site in Wales (Gower Peninsula), which was discovered in 1993.

IN LEAF p. 65 IN FLOWER p. 91

Jan
Feb
Mar
Apr
May
Jun
Jul
Aug
Sep
Oct
Nov
Dec

CONFUSION SPECIES: **IN FLOWER** **Lady Orchid** (although this is much larger) (*p. 234*).
IN LEAF Military Orchid (*p. 72*), Lady Orchid (*p. 73*), Green-winged Orchid (*p. 66*), Early-purple Orchid (*p. 71*), Bee Orchid (*p. 75*), Early Spider-orchid (*p. 74*).

Burnt Orchid varieties

N. ustulata var. *aestivalis*

This variety flowers from late June to mid-July, later than the nominate *ustulata* (which flowers from mid-May to early June), and is restricted to East Sussex, Hampshire and Wiltshire. It is generally taller than var. *ustulata*, with darker-coloured flowers, although the differences are often exaggerated. The two varieties rarely occur at the same site but, where they do, they form discrete populations.

TYPICAL FORM

Jan
Feb
Mar
Apr
May
Jun
Jul
Aug
Sep
Oct
Nov
Dec

VAR. *AESTIVALIS*

Jan
Feb
Mar
Apr
May
Jun
Jul
Aug
Sep
Oct
Nov
Dec

The nominate variety *ustulata* flowers during May and June, usually peaking in late May. Gloucestershire, 30th May.

The late-flowering var. *aestivalis* flowers during June and July, usually peaking in early July, over one month later than the nominate variety. Hampshire, 8th July.

Lady's-tresses

The lady's-tresses comprise three species in two genera – *Goodyera* and *Spiranthes*. The three species differ not only in appearance but also occur in very different habitats; since there is limited overlap in their respective distributions, misidentification is unlikely. All are rather late-flowering, from mid-July onwards, with Autumn Lady's-tresses appearing in late August and September, after most other orchid species have long gone-over.

Creeping Lady's-tresses *p. 164*

White, furry, 'spiky' flowers around the stem (but not in a spiral).

Very hairy all over.

Leaves triangular or oval in a rosette; pale veins giving marbled effect.

Autumn Lady's-tresses *p. 166*

Tubular ice-white flowers spiralling up upper half of thin stem.

Stem with a greyish, furry appearance.

Leaves oval or triangular, in a flat rosette.

Irish Lady's-tresses *p. 168*

Large, tubular creamy-white flowers arranged in three rows at top of stem.

Stem green.

Leaves erect, thin and grass-like.

IN BUD

IN LEAF

The three lady's-tresses have very different rosettes and occur in different habitats.

IN BUD *p. 76* | IN HABITAT *p. 44*

LC Creeping Lady's-tresses *Goodyera repens*

Locally common

up to 25 (35) cm

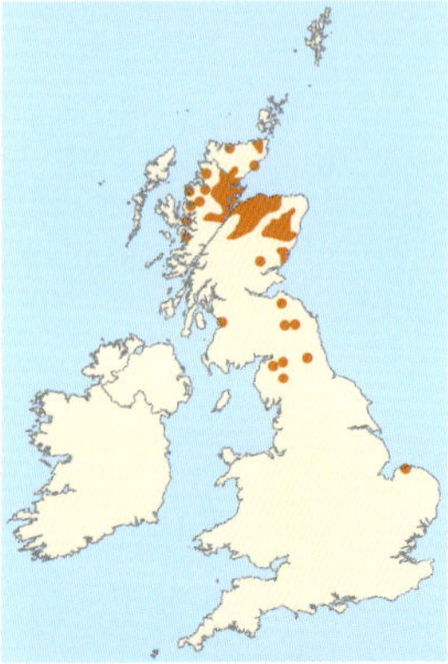

White, furry, 'spiky' flowers around the stem (but not in a spiral as Autumn Lady's-tresses (*p. 166*)).

Very hairy all over.

Leaves triangular or oval in a rosette at base of stem, with pale veins giving marbled effect.

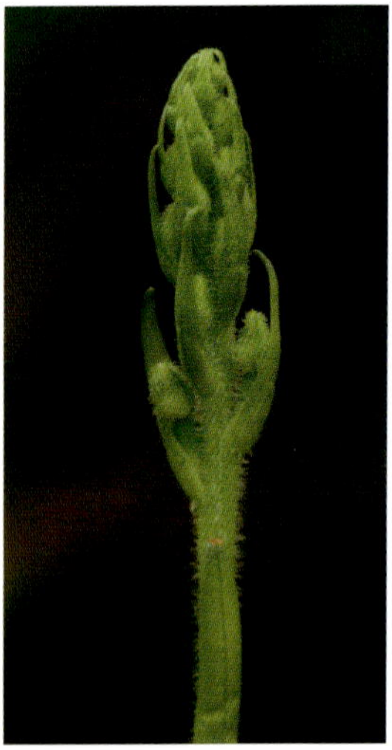

IN BUD
The buds are covered in thick white hairs, making them easy to distiunguish from other orchids and wintergreen (*Pyrola* and *Orthiliaa*) species.

HABITAT: Damp or boggy mature pine woods, often among Heather *Calluna vulgaris*, Bilberry *Vaccinium myrtillus* and Bracken *Pteridium aquilinum* with a good layer of moss.

Delicate and relatively small but usually rather conspicuous as its compact, furry white flowers contrast with dark pine bark. It can be very common within the Caledonian pinewoods of northern and eastern Scotland, which are its stronghold. There are also small populations in Cumbria, Northumberland, County Durham and north Norfolk.

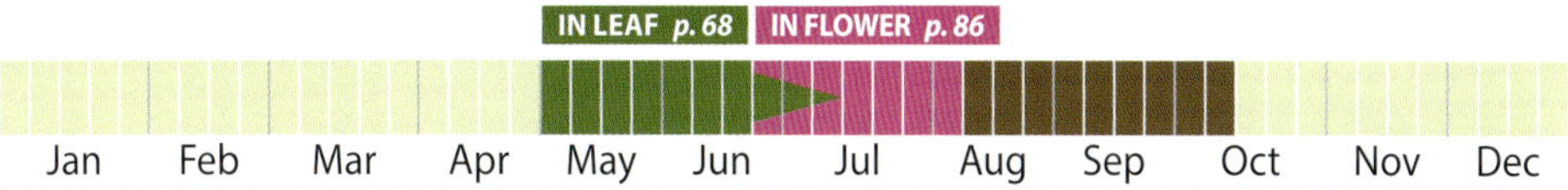
IN LEAF p. 68
IN FLOWER p. 86
Jan
Feb
Mar
Apr
May
Jun
Jul
Aug
Sep
Oct
Nov
Dec

CONFUSION SPECIES: IN FLOWER **Autumn Lady's-tresses** (*p. 166*), **Irish Lady's-tresses** (*p. 168*), **Summer Lady's-tresses** [extinct] (*p. 274*). IN LEAF Wintergreens (*Pyrola* (*p. 68*) and *Orthilia* spp.).

IN BUD p. 76 | IN HABITAT p. 44

NT NT Autumn Lady's-tresses *Spiranthes spiralis*

Widespread; locally common

up to 20 cm

Tubular ice-white flowers spiralling up upper half of thin stem.
Stem covered with pale hairs, giving it a greyish, furry appearance.
Leaves oval or triangular, in a flat rosette at stem base.

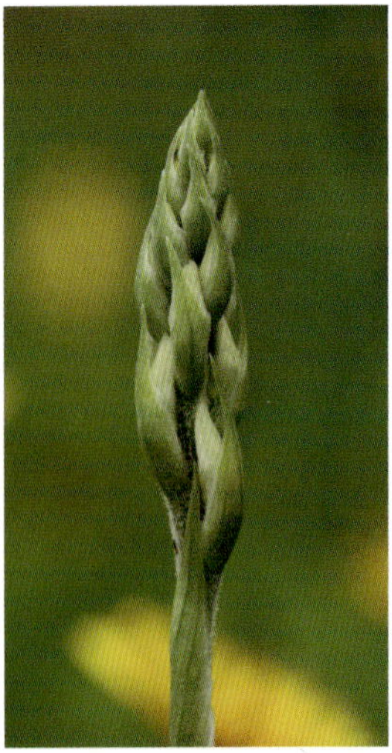

IN BUD

HABITAT: Favours a variety of undisturbed dry, calcareous grasslands, but is most common on chalk and limestone, and in dunes where the turf is very short. It can also be found on cliff tops, lawns, embankments, golf courses, old commons, limestone pavements, and even derelict tennis courts.

Often growing in groups and clumps on short turf, this species is usually spotted by its delicate spike of spiralling white flowers, which, on first encounter, can be smaller than expected. Can be very common at favourable locations, sometimes numbering in the tens of thousands. Most frequent in southern England, coastal northern and southern Wales and coasts of western and southern Ireland, it occurs as far north as the Morecambe Bay area of Cumbria and, in Ireland, the coastal dunes of Co. Sligo.

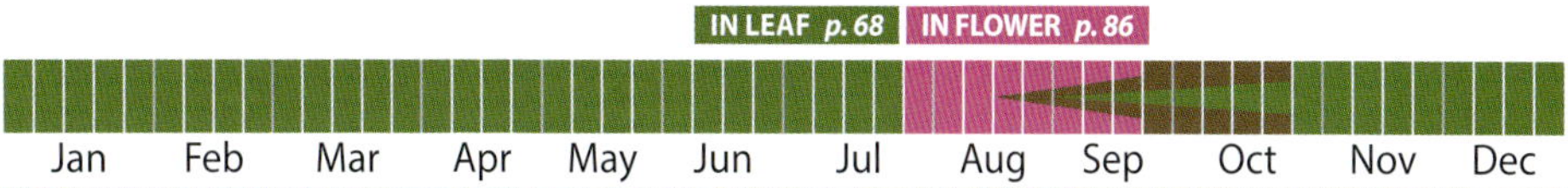
IN LEAF p. 68
IN FLOWER p. 86
Jan
Feb
Mar
Apr
May
Jun
Jul
Aug
Sep
Oct
Nov
Dec

CONFUSION SPECIES: IN FLOWER **Creeping Lady's-tresses** (*p. 164*), **Irish Lady's-tresses** (*p. 168*), **Summer Lady's-tresses** [extinct] (*p. 274*). IN LEAF Burnt Orchid (*p. 65*), Bee Orchid (*p. 75*).

IN BUD *p. 76* | IN HABITAT *p. 44*

LC NT Irish Lady's-tresses *Spiranthes romanzoffiana*

Hooded Lady's-tresses

Scattered and scarce

up to 30 cm

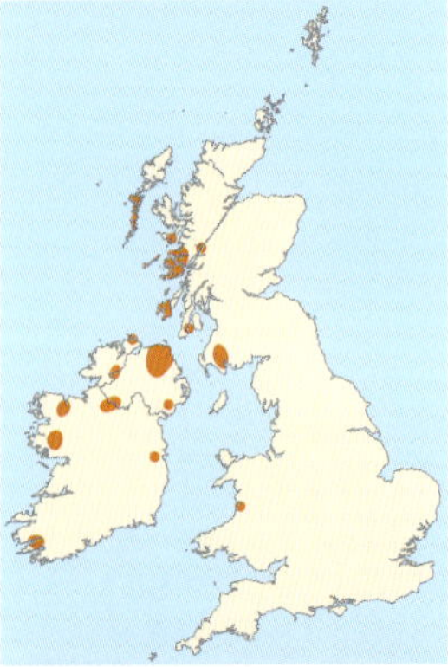

IN BUD

Large, tubular, greenish-white flowers packed at the top of the stem, arranged spirally in three distinct rows.
Generally white-and-green in overall appearance.
Leaves erect and thin; often very difficult to distinguish from surrounding grasses.

HABITAT: Usually found in marshes and grasslands that are seasonally flooded, particularly along lake shores, boggy flushes, damp rush pastures and wet meadows. Like Coralroot Orchid (*p. 148*), it flourishes best when spring water levels drop at the optimum time for growth. There is some evidence to suggest that it responds well to ground that is heavily 'poached' by grazing cattle, which may act as a stimulus to flowering.

Distinctive, with white tubular flowers and long, grass-like leaves. Flowering numbers vary considerably from year to year, possibly linked to soil moisture levels in spring. Although never common, some populations can number several hundred in good years. It is essentially a North American species that, in Europe, occurs only in Britain and Ireland, where the distribution is very much westerly. The main strongholds are in Ireland, particularly around the larger loughs. In Ireland, there are a number of colonies around the shores of Lough Neagh with a scattering of sites farther north and west. There are also sizeable populations on the Hebrides, with a handful of small colonies on mainland Scotland. In England, it formerly occurred at a single location on Dartmoor (Devon) but has not seen there since 1993. Several new sites have been discovered in recent years, including the first record for Wales in 2019, suggesting it could appear elsewhere and is probably under-recorded.

IN LEAF p. 68 IN FLOWER p. 86

Jan Feb Mar Apr May Jun Jul Aug Sep Oct Nov Dec

CONFUSION SPECIES: IN FLOWER **Creeping Lady's-tresses** (*p. 164*), **Autumn Lady's-tresses** (*p. 166*), **Summer Lady's-tresses** [extinct] (*p. 274*). IN LEAF Grasses and sedges.

Butterfly-orchids

The two *Platanthera* species are very similar and identifed by subtle details of the pollinia. However, and although not absolute, Lesser Butterfly-orchid is often smaller and appears more 'delicate' than Greater Butterfly-orchid.

Identifying butterfly-orchids in bud

The buds are concealed by large bracts until approximately one week prior to flowering – unlike Common Twayblade, in which the buds are clearly visible from very early emergence (see *pp. 62–63*). The stem is distinctly ridged and has small bract-like leaves spaced widely along it. When close to flowering, the very long, nectar-filled spurs are clearly visible.

Identifying butterfly-orchids in flower

The lip usually points straight down in Lesser Butterfly-orchid and usually curves backwards in Greater Butterfly-orchid. However, there are exceptions and the safest way to distinguish the two is in details of the pollinia: widely spaced and angled in Greater Butterfly-orchid and close together and parallel in Lesser Butterfly-orchid.

Greater Butterfly-orchid

angled
typically curved back

Lesser Butterfly-orchid

parallel
typically straight

Hybrids (see *p. 253*)
The hybrid between the two butterfly-orchids is rare but, in the areas they co-occur, an individual with pollinia characteristics that are intermediate between the two species is worth a closer look.

IN LEAF (*p. 62*), BUD and SEED

Although the long, usually paired leaves of vegetative butterfly-orchids are distinctive, the species are effectively identical when not in flower. The slight differences in habitat may provide some clue but they can only be identified safely when in flower.

IN BUD

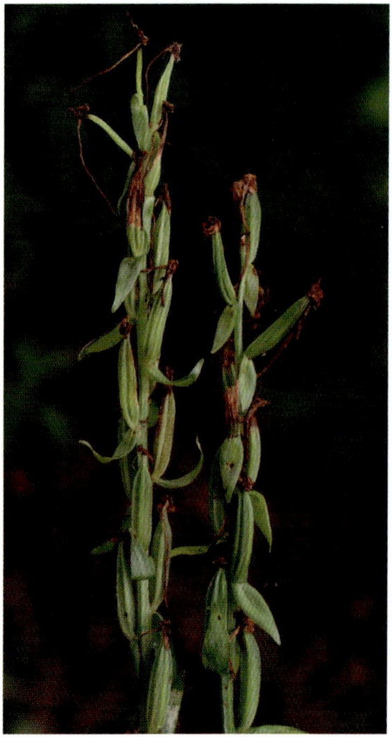

IN SEED

IN LEAF p. 62 IN FLOWER p. 87

GREATER

Jan
Feb
Mar
Apr
May
Jun
Jul
Aug
Sep
Oct
Nov
Dec

LESSER

Jan
Feb
Mar
Apr
May
Jun
Jul
Aug
Sep
Oct
Nov
Dec

Greater Butterfly-orchid
p. 172

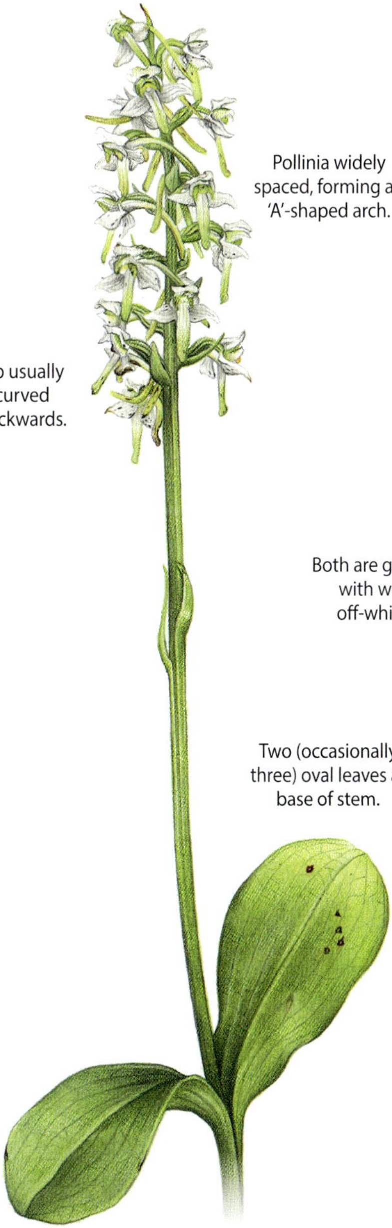

Pollinia widely spaced, forming an 'A'-shaped arch.

Lip usually curved backwards.

Two (occasionally three) oval leaves at base of stem.

Both are graceful plants with well-spaced off-white flowers.

Lesser Butterfly-orchid
p. 173

Pollinia very close together and parallel to each other.

Lip usually straight, pointing downwards.

Two (occasionally three, or even four) oval, blunt-ended leaves at base of stem.

NT LC Greater Butterfly-orchid *Platanthera chlorantha*

Widespread; locally common

up to 60 cm

HABITAT: Favours calcareous soils in ancient and coppiced woodlands, but is equally common on open rough downland, old commons, hay meadows and grazed hill pastures.

An orchid that is usually quite obvious, especially in grasslands, due its large whitish flowers and often tall stature. The scent is strongest in the evening and attracts pollinating night-flying moths. It is subtly different from its closest relative, Lesser Butterfly-orchid, with which it rarely co-occurs. Quite common and widely distributed across Britain and Ireland, with strongholds in the limestone and chalk regions of southern, central and northern England. In Scotland it has a mainly western distribution, with numerous sites around Glasgow and the Isle of Skye. Very scarce and widely scattered in Ireland, more common in the north. There is one record (1980) of a hybrid with Small-white Orchid (*p. 156*).

CONFUSION SPECIES: IN FLOWER **Lesser Butterfly-orchid.** IN LEAF Lesser Butterfly-orchid (*p. 62*), Common Twayblade (*p. 63*). HYBRIDS × Lesser Butterfly-orchid (*p. 253*), Small-white orchid (*p. 249*).

LC Lesser Butterfly-orchid *Platanthera bifolia*

Widespread; locally common

up to 55 cm

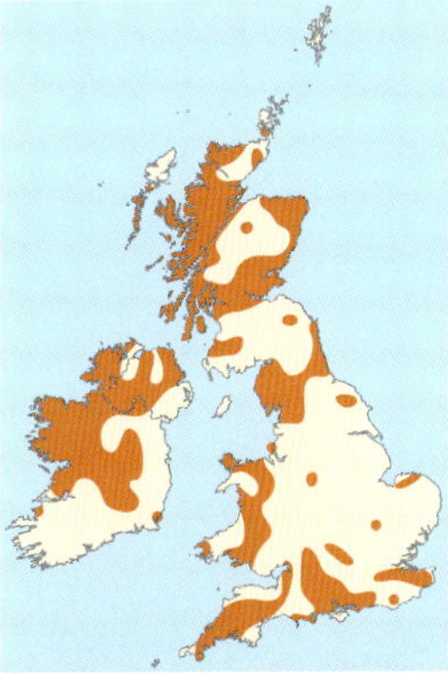

HABITAT: Although found in the same habitat types as Greater Butterfly-orchid, the two species rarely occur together. Lesser Butterfly-orchid is much more tolerant of damp, acid soils and is far less frequent on calcareous grasslands and in woodlands, although there are sizeable populations in such habitats in Kent and Wiltshire. This species is more regularly found on moorland, heathland, hill flushes and tussocks in bogs and damp acid grasslands in the west and north of Britain. It also occurs occasionally in hay meadows and, albeit infrequently, in fens in Ireland and Anglesey.

Often smaller and more delicate than Greater Butterfly-orchid. Like that species, the scent is strongest in the evenings to attract pollinating moths, especially Small Elephant Hawk-moth *Deilephila porcellus*. Fairly common across Britain and Ireland although with a rather westerly bias, with strongholds in western Scotland and the Hebrides, western Wales, western and central Ireland and coastal northern Ireland. There are also significant populations in southern England, particularly in the New Forest (Hampshire), Wiltshire, Devon and Cornwall.

CONFUSION SPECIES: IN FLOWER **Greater Butterfly-orchid.** IN LEAF Greater Butterfly-orchid (*p. 62*), Common Twayblade (*p. 63*). HYBRIDS × Greater Butterfly-orchid (*p. 253*).

Fragrant-orchids

The genus *Gymnadenia* has undergone repeated studies to establish its intrageneric relationships. The latest molecular study (Stark *et al.*, 2011) supports the theory that they are three distinct species, rather than one species with three subspecies. Although not all plants are separable due to their variability, they do each have a distinct ecology, morphology and subtle differences in fragrance and, as in the case of Marsh Fragrant-orchid, a different flowering period.

FROM KEY *p. 100*

Identifying fragrant-orchids in flower

There is significant overlap in morphology between the three fragrant-orchid species, meaning it will not always be possible to identify every individual specimen. Examining a single plant in isolation can be misleading and it is therefore important to examine several plants in a population to get a feel for the average appearance.

Check the consistency of the following features in combination:

- Lip shape and proportions.
- Colour tone (rather than depth).
- The general stature of plants, as well as the most common spike shape and its density of flowers.
- Habitat type.
- Scent character (sweet, sharp, *etc.*)

Fortunately, although more than one species may occur in the same broad area, they very rarely occupy the same specific habitat type, and so are usually found in clearly separated populations. When average appearance and habitat type are considered together, the identification of a given population is usually clear-cut.

FRAGRANT-ORCHIDS COMPARED – *p. 178*.
FRAGRANT-ORCHID VARIATION – *p. 179*.

Hybrids (see *p. 254*)
The fragrant-orchids, despite their genetic similarity, do not seemingly hybridize between themselves, probably due to their occurrence in different habitats. However, hybrids of all three with a range of *Dactylorhiza* orchids have been recorded relatively frequently; in addition, Heath Fragrant-orchid × Small-white Orchid and Chalk Fragrant-orchid × Pyramidal Orchid have also been recorded.

IN LEAF (*p. 67*), BUD and SEED

Fragrant-orchid rosettes are formed of narrow leaves, typically folded along their length but the three species are effectively identical when not flowering and, as such, a 'most-likely' approach based on habitat is the most practical solution. However, an in-leaf fragrant-orchid seen on chalk before late April will almost certainly be Chalk Fragrant-orchid.

IN BUD

IN SEED
Chalk (*left*) and Marsh Fragrant-orchids (*right*)

Fragrant-orchids are distinctive, with a pink or purple, torpedo-shaped flower spike that is generally taller than it is wide. They have long, narrow, arching leaves arranged oppositely up the stem. As the name implies, they have a strong scent – sometimes noticeable from some distance – and produce large amounts of nectar, which is stored in very long, curved spurs. **The flowers and leaves are never marked with spots, stripes or loops.**

Chalk Fragrant-orchid

p. 176

Spike cylindrical and often lax.

Widespread, locally common

up to 50 cm

Heath Fragrant-orchid

p. 176

Spike short, conical and often densely packed.

Widespread; locally common

up to 30 cm

Marsh Fragrant-orchid

p. 177

Spike tall and densely packed.

Scattered, locally common

up to 90 cm

IN BUD *p. 78* | IN HABITAT *p. 45*

LC LC Chalk Fragrant-orchid *Gymnadenia conopsea*

HABITAT: Primarily **dry chalk and limestone grassland**, particularly downland, old quarries and chalk or lime pits (NB Marsh Fragrant-orchid can also occur in these habitats). Most common in southern Britain.

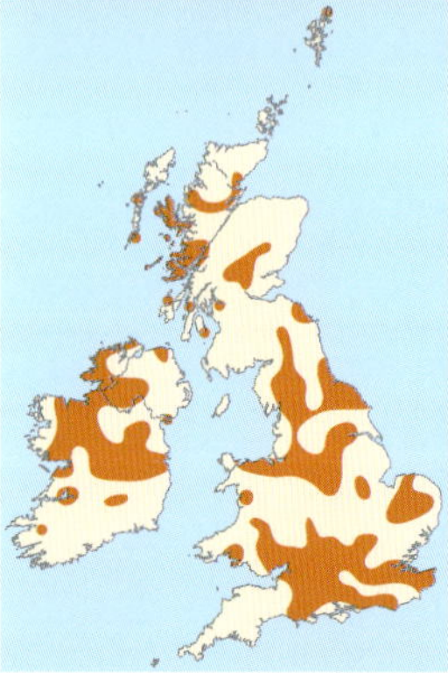

LC LC Heath Fragrant-orchid *Gymnadenia borealis*

HABITAT: Typically **heathland, hill pastures, upland hay meadows, and tussocks within damp acidic grasslands and bogs**. Most common in northern and western Britain, and probably endemic.

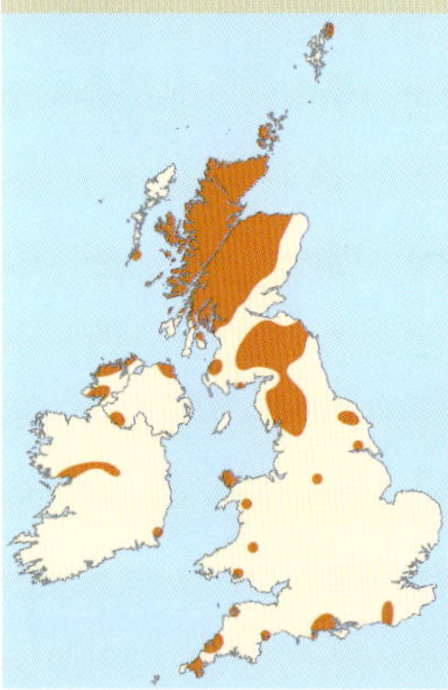

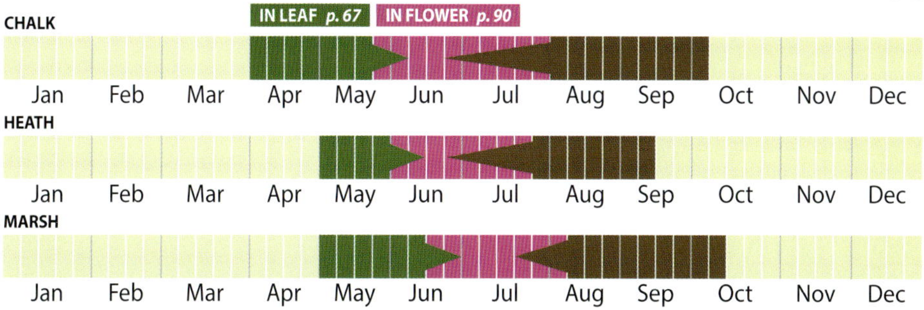
IN LEAF p. 67
IN FLOWER p. 90
CHALK
Jan Feb Mar Apr May Jun Jul Aug Sep Oct Nov Dec
HEATH
Jan Feb Mar Apr May Jun Jul Aug Sep Oct Nov Dec
MARSH
Jan Feb Mar Apr May Jun Jul Aug Sep Oct Nov Dec

CONFUSION SPECIES: IN FLOWER **Other fragrant-orchids.** IN LEAF Green-winged Orchid, Pyramidal Orchid (both *p.* 66). **HYBRIDS** ALL | × Common Spotted-orchid (*p.* 256); HEATH, MARSH | Northern and Southern Marsh-orchids (*p.* 258); HEATH | Small-white Orchid (*p.* 260), Heath Spotted-orchid (*p.* 255), Early and Pugsley's Marsh-orchids (*p.* 258); CHALK | Frog (*p.* 258) and Pyramidal Orchids (*p.* 249).

LC Marsh Fragrant-orchid *Gymnadenia densiflora*

HABITAT: Typically **fens and marshy calcareous meadows and flushes.** Rarely also on road verges, dune slacks, chalk and limestone grassland, slumped clay cliffs and in old limestone quarries. Widely distributed across Britain and Ireland.

NB There are also some confusing populations in Sussex and South Wales that look similar to orchids sometimes known as var. *friesica* on the Dutch Frisian Islands. No meaningful genetic study has been done on any of these plants, so these populations are not afforded varietal status in this book.

IN BUD *p.78* | IN HABITAT *p.45*

Fragrant-orchids compared

	Chalk [up to 50 cm]	**Heath** [up to 30 cm]	**Marsh** [up to 90 cm]
HABITAT	dry chalk and limestone grassland	heathland, acid grasslands, hill pastures and bogs	fens, damp calcareous meadows, flushes (rarely also chalk and limestone grassland and dune slacks)
LIP SHAPE	**about as long as wide**; lobes clearly 3-lobed	**longer than wide**; lobes not very obvious	**wider than long**; lobes obvious
LATERAL SEPALS	rolled and often angled downwards	pale lilac to pink – more variable than the other two spp.	unrolled and held out straight
FLOWER COLOUR	pale lilac to pink – more variable than the other two spp.	pale pink to deep pink	pale pink to deep pink with whitish lip base
SPIKE	cylindrical and often lax	short, conical and often densely packed	tall and densely packed
SCENT	strong, sweet; not clove-like	clove-like; sweet	clove-like; spicy

Examples of inflorescence and flower variation

Chalk Fragrant-orchid *G. conopsea*	Heath Fragrant-orchid *G. borealis*	Marsh Fragrant-orchid *G. densiflora*

Dactylorhiza orchids

The *Dactylorhiza* orchids, commonly known as the marsh-orchids and spotted-orchids, are some of the most distinctive and widespread orchids in Britain and Ireland. All species have whitish-lilac through to deep purple flowers. They favour damp grasslands and other wet habitats, particularly fens and marshes, where they can be abundant. However, *Dactylorhiza* also represents the most challenging orchid genus to identify to species level on account of their variability, close relationships and propensity for hybridization.

Species

Eight species of *Dactylorhiza* in Britain and Ireland are recognized in this book.

With a roughly north–south divide, **Northern Marsh-orchid** *D. purpurella* and **Southern Marsh-orchid** *D. praetermissa* are the two most commonly encountered marsh-orchid species. Equally common are the spotted-orchids – **Common Spotted-orchid** *D. fuchsii* and **Heath Spotted-orchid** *D. maculata* – which can be abundant in favoured locations although each species generally has quite different habitat preferences.

Less common, but widely distributed, is **Early Marsh-orchid** *D. incarnata,* which encompasses several varieties, from the Critically Endangered cream-coloured **'Fen' Early Marsh-orchid var. *ochroleuca*** to the squat, brick-red **'Dune' Early Marsh-orchid var. *coccinea***, which is often ubiquitous in the damp slacks of many sand dune systems.

Having been repeatedly reclassified, the next two species have a muddled history, so carry with them a long list of former names.

Irish Marsh-orchid *D. kerryensis* is squat and, as the name suggests, found only in Ireland, where it is the most common marsh-orchid in a wide range of habitats.

By far the rarest *Dactylorhiza* species is **Pugsley's Marsh-orchid** *D. traunsteinerioides*, which is restricted to fens and hill flushes across western and northern Britain, and found at scattered sites across Ireland. It is a cryptic species that can be a challenge to identify conclusively.

The final species, **Frog Orchid** *D. viridis*, is quite different in appearance to the rest and has only recently been placed in the *Dactylorhiza* genus. It was previously known as *Coeloglossum viride* and, indeed, some authorities still prefer to use this name. Identifying this species is straightforward because of its habitat preferences, size, colour and very different flower structure.

Hybrids (see *p. 261*)

Most of the *Dactylorhiza* species in Britain and Ireland are closely related genetically and, as a result, hybridize freely. Such rampant cross-fertilization causes problems when trying to identify plants or even determine whether a particular population is a *bona fide* species or a hybrid swarm. This section aims to outline clearly the most consistent features of each species, to help you to navigate this complex genus.

Dactylorhiza, such as these Southern Marsh-orchids, can occur in large numbers.

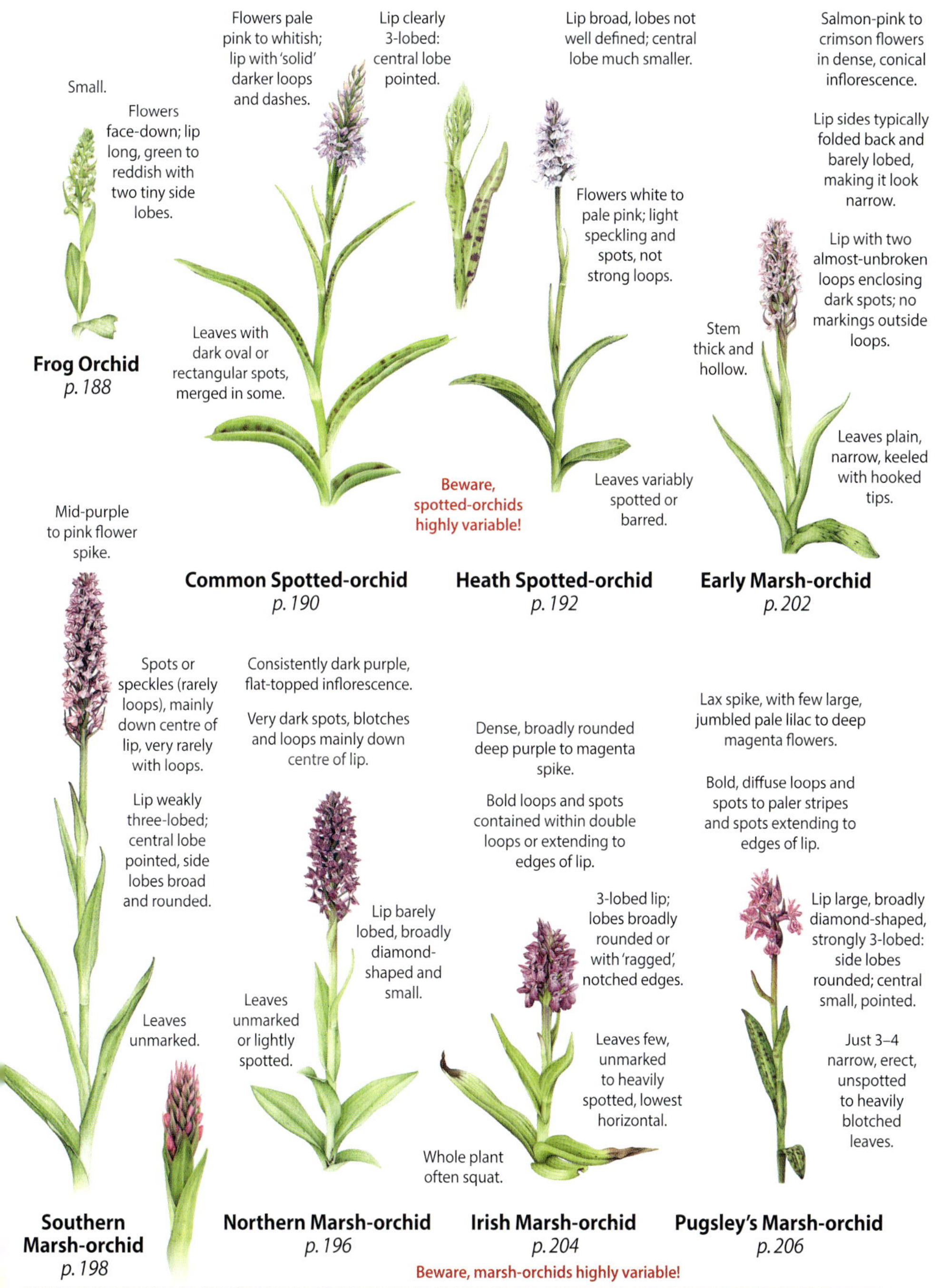
Small.
Flowers face-down; lip long, green to reddish with two tiny side lobes.
Frog Orchid
p. 188
Flowers pale pink to whitish; lip with 'solid' darker loops and dashes.
Lip clearly 3-lobed: central lobe pointed.
Leaves with dark oval or rectangular spots, merged in some.
Common Spotted-orchid
p. 190
Lip broad, lobes not well defined; central lobe much smaller.
Flowers white to pale pink; light speckling and spots, not strong loops.
Beware, spotted-orchids highly variable!
Leaves variably spotted or barred.
Heath Spotted-orchid
p. 192
Salmon-pink to crimson flowers in dense, conical inflorescence.
Lip sides typically folded back and barely lobed, making it look narrow.
Lip with two almost-unbroken loops enclosing dark spots; no markings outside loops.
Stem thick and hollow.
Leaves plain, narrow, keeled with hooked tips.
Early Marsh-orchid
p. 202
Mid-purple to pink flower spike.
Spots or speckles (rarely loops), mainly down centre of lip, very rarely with loops.
Lip weakly three-lobed; central lobe pointed, side lobes broad and rounded.
Leaves unmarked.
Southern Marsh-orchid
p. 198
Consistently dark purple, flat-topped inflorescence.
Very dark spots, blotches and loops mainly down centre of lip.
Lip barely lobed, broadly diamond-shaped and small.
Leaves unmarked or lightly spotted.
Northern Marsh-orchid
p. 196
Dense, broadly rounded deep purple to magenta spike.
Bold loops and spots contained within double loops or extending to edges of lip.
3-lobed lip; lobes broadly rounded or with 'ragged', notched edges.
Leaves few, unmarked to heavily spotted, lowest horizontal.
Whole plant often squat.
Irish Marsh-orchid
p. 204
Lax spike, with few large, jumbled pale lilac to deep magenta flowers.
Bold, diffuse loops and spots to paler stripes and spots extending to edges of lip.
Lip large, broadly diamond-shaped, strongly 3-lobed: side lobes rounded; central small, pointed.
Just 3–4 narrow, erect, unspotted to heavily blotched leaves.
Pugsley's Marsh-orchid
p. 206
Beware, marsh-orchids highly variable!

IN LEAF AND IN BUD

In-bud **spotted-orchids** are effectively identical to one another, as are in-bud **marsh-orchids**. Frog Orchid is similar but identifiable by its broader leaves and lack of pink or purple colour in the buds.

Species boundaries

Hybridization can eventually lead to the formation of new species; indeed, most of the currently accepted *Dactylorhiza* 'species' are of hybrid origin. Apart from **Early Marsh-orchid**, all the marsh-orchid species of Britain and Ireland are the product of hybridization events during the last 10,000 years.

Northern, **Southern** and **Pugsley's Marsh-orchids** are descendants from multiple hybridization events between Common Spotted-orchid and Early Marsh-orchid, with Irish Marsh-orchid similarly descended from Heath Spotted-orchid and Early Marsh-orchid hybrids. It is now known that Common Spotted-orchid and Early Marsh-orchid are much 'older' species that formed several million years ago and that these are also the ancestors of most other *Dactylorhiza* species in Europe. Indeed, some authorities consider all the British and Irish marsh-orchids to be subspecies of a single pan-European species – *Dactylorhiza majalis* (Western Marsh-orchid) – and in this book the species' alternative status as subspecies of *D. majalis* is recognized for completeness.

The *Dactylorhiza* genus therefore provides a glimpse of evolution in action, raising some interesting questions about how botanists define a species. Traditionally, *Dactylorhiza* species were determined by morphological features alone, often with an excessive focus on the extent of spotting on the leaves. This has given rise to a long list of names, as botanists have attempted to classify different colour forms and ecotypes.

In recent years, genetic analysis, combined with morphometric data, has provided new insights into the more confusing *Dactylorhiza* populations. This has resulted in multiple revisions, where some populations have been described as 'new' species, while others have been reclassified from species to mere varieties. In this book, an attempt has been made to provide a clear and logical rationale on the validity and status of all native *Dactylorhiza* types and populations, including the most controversial. However, it is recognized that these classifications could change again as the result of more sophisticated genetic analysis methods becoming available.

New identities

Pugsley's Marsh-orchid reclassifications, 1988–2012

The species that has undoubtedly seen the most revision is Pugsley's Marsh-orchid *D. traunsteinerioides*, also referred to as Narrow-leaved Marsh-orchid. The most comprehensive recent analysis of Pugsley's Marsh Orchid is Bateman (2012), the conclusions of which are broadly followed here, with explanations of any differences. This reflects the precautionary approach adopted in this book regarding the treatment of some of the more controversial populations.

'ssp. *francis-drucei*'

Bateman (2012) named small-flowered populations of Pugsley's Marsh-orchid in northern Scotland (and possibly northern Ireland) as a new subspecies, *D. traunsteinerioides* 'ssp. *francis-drucei*'. Some of these populations include richly coloured plants with heavy leaf spotting, which were identified in 1988 as a European species, Lapland Marsh-orchid *D. lapponica*. Based on field experience, there is very little difference between these Scottish populations of Pugsley's Marsh-orchid and those elsewhere. The minor differences used to describe this taxon do not appear to merit subspecies status, but instead appear to sit at one end of the overall spectrum of variation for Pugsley's Marsh-orchid. This is therefore how it is treated in this book.

'Hebridean Marsh-orchid *D. ebudensis*'

In 2000, a small population of stocky, richly coloured marsh-orchids on the machair of North Uist (Outer Hebrides) were assigned species rank as 'Hebridean Marsh-orchid *D. ebudensis*'. However, Bateman (2012) reclassified these orchids as Pugsley's Marsh-orchid *D. traunsteinerioides* 'ssp. *francis-drucei* var. *ebudensis*'. The confusion surrounding the identity of this population is likely due to significant hybridization with other *Dactylorhiza* species occurring in the same area – particularly Northern Marsh-orchid, Early Marsh-orchid and Common Spotted-orchid – resulting in misleading genetic results, and a somewhat different appearance to the typical form. Similar populations of Pugsley's Marsh-orchid occur in machair habitat on nearby Hebridean islands and the north-west coast of Scotland. This suggests the North Uist colony is part of a wider, if slightly genetically mixed, population of squat Pugsley's Marsh-orchids adapted to the short, wind-blasted turf. In view of this, the varietal name '*ebudensis*' is not recognized in this book, these Scottish populations instead being treated as coastal ecotypes of Pugsley's Marsh-orchid.

East Anglian fenland marsh-orchids

Bateman (2012) reclassified Pugsley's Marsh-orchid more strictly as a northern and western species, with all populations in southern and eastern England being reclassified as a fenland subspecies of Southern Marsh-orchid under the name *D. praetermissa* ssp. *schoenophila*. However, not all East Anglian populations were sampled in the 2012 study and there are examples from East Anglia that closely conform to Pugsley's Marsh-orchid in appearance. Furthermore, based on the close similarity of the habitats compared to those of undisputed populations of Pugsley's Marsh-orchid, it is difficult to state categorically that the species is not present in East Anglia. In this book it is therefore suggested that both Pugsley's and Southern Marsh-orchid ssp. *schoenophila* occur in East Anglia, but that extensive hybridization means that it is near impossible to separate the two in many cases. Similarly, *schoenophila* is considered here as a variety of Southern Marsh-orchid pending further studies to confirm whether it is sufficiently genetically distinct to warrant subspecies status.

'Hebridean Marsh-orchid'

Other *Dactylorhiza* taxa

Early Marsh-orchid 'subspecies'

The widely accepted subspecies of Early Marsh-orchid *D. incarnata* (sspp. *ochroleuca*, *coccinea*, *cruenta* and *pulchella*) are broadly allied to different habitat types or regions and frequently show colour and, in some cases, morphological differences. However, these visible differences are often exaggerated and have not yet been supported by genetic studies. This situation is exemplified by the uncertain status of purple-flowered Early Marsh-orchids that sometimes occur in fens and other habitats (often alongside the nominate type) but which look very similar to *pulchella* – a taxon supposedly restricted to acidic bogs.

Genetic studies have failed to resolve clearly the differences between these Early Marsh-orchid types and they are therefore treated as varieties in this book (see *p. 212*). However, it is recognized that further genetic studies may provide new evidence to support elevation to subspecies status for one or more of these taxa in the future.

Two other Early Marsh-orchid taxa – '*gemmana*' and '*lobelii*' – are also not included in this book. The status of *gemmana* is considered uncertain and is not recognized by some authorities. The recently described *lobelii* appears to represent nothing more than robust, squat examples of var. *incarnata* and var. *coccinea* – well within the typical range of variation for both taxa.

Southern Marsh-orchid
var. *schoenophila*

'Leopard Marsh-orchid' [Southern Marsh-orchid]
***'D. praetermissa* var. *junialis*'**

For decades, Southern Marsh-orchids with bold, dark ring markings on the leaves and a dark, solid loop pattern on the lip have caused considerable confusion. Appearing as small groups among colonies of typical Southern Marsh-orchid or (rarely) forming larger populations of their own, these plants have been named as 'Leopard Marsh-orchid' – *D. pardalina*, *D. praetermissa* 'var. *junialis*', or the lower-ranking forma, 'f. *junialis*'. These plants are rare and appear to be restricted to southern England, where they are virtually indistinguishable from the common and widespread hybrid between Southern Marsh-orchid and Common Spotted-orchid (*D.* × *grandis*). Identification therefore relies mostly on the consistency in appearance of the whole population and whether Common Spotted-orchid is present. However, bona fide '*junialis*'-type Southern Marsh-orchids show no genetic differences from unmarked Southern Marsh orchids and often occur admixed with 'normal' unmarked plants. For these reasons, '*junialis*' is not recognized here as a named taxon.

'Leopard Marsh-orchid'

Northern Marsh-orchid *D. purpurella* 'ssp. *cambrensis*'

Repeatedly reclassified over the decades – most notably as 'Western Marsh-orchid' – marsh-orchids with heavily blotched leaves from coastal Wales and northern Britain have most recently been treated as a subspecies or variety of Northern Marsh-orchid called '*cambrensis*'. However, as explained previously, the presence or absence of leaf markings does not correlate with genetic or ecological distinctiveness and is therefore a rather weak rationale for assigning a new subspecific or varietal rank. Furthermore, the size and intensity of the leaf markings is not consistent and, indeed, some '*cambrensis*' populations contain a mixture of individuals with different levels of leaf marking, ranging from unmarked through to heavily marked without any clear division. These heavily marked plants are therefore best considered as a part of the variability of Northern Marsh-orchid, but can be easily confused with hybrids involving one or both of the spotted-orchids. It is perhaps worth noting that Northern Marsh-orchid plants with fine leaf markings, which are common in northern England, are universally accepted as part of the variation within the species.

Dark- and pale-flowered Common Spotted-orchid *D. fuchsii* populations from western and northern Britain and Ireland

'hebridensis' and ***'cornubiensis'*** Richly coloured with large, differently shaped flowers occur on coastal grasslands in Cornwall, Ireland and western Scotland. These populations have variously been given subspecies and varietal ranks under the names '*cornubiensis*' and '*hebridensis*'. Based on their strong morphological and ecological similarity, they are treated here as a single taxon under the name var. *hebridensis*.

'alpina' Richly coloured plants from upland and coastal northern Britain, but with small flowers, have often been known as 'var. *alpina*.' Plants of this type seem poorly defined, and regularly occur admixed with the nominate form. There appears, therefore, to be no logical reason why this taxon should be recognized as anything other than a local colour form.

'o'kellyi' Similarly, pale-flowered populations from Ireland and Scotland have long been referred to as var. or ssp. '*o'kellyi*'. As with '*alpina*' types, these appear admixed with populations of the normal type and would appear to represent simply a local colour form.

Common Spotted-orchid
'ssp. *cornubiensis*'

Identifying *Dactylorhiza*

Identifying *Dactylorhiza* to species level can be straightforward when the whole population is broadly uniform. But where two or more species grow together, hybridization will often occur. Observing specific populations over several seasons generally makes it easier to distinguish between 'pure' and hybrid individuals, although this requires time, experience and patience. Nonetheless, a first-generation hybrid should be fairly easy to spot – a halfway house, sharing features of both parents. Mixed colours will often be evident in hybrid populations, while 'pure' populations tend to look much more uniform overall.

There are a few key points to remember before trying to identify *Dactylorhiza*:

- Get to know the key features of each species (see *p. 186*) and the breadth of variability within them. Individuals within a population that look different could just be within the typical range of variation.
- Habitat and location can be helpful in narrowing down the number of potential species.
- Flowering times vary according to latitude, altitude, recent weather and other habitat conditions, so should be used only as a supporting feature.
- If possible, visit a site with confusing plants a week later to see how they have developed, and if anything else has appeared.
- Identification is much easier in context, so for second opinions encourage others to see the plants in the field for themselves instead of sending photographs. However, if the latter is the only option, follow the *Photographic advice* on *p. 37*.

Southern Marsh-orchids with Early Marsh Orchids and the hybrid between the two.

Southern Marsh-orchids
hybrid
Early Marsh-orchids

On approach, colonies of *Dactylorhiza* containing more than one species (in this case Common Spotted-orchids and Southern Marsh-orchids), plus their hybrids, will show plants with various colour tones.

Typical spotted-orchids and marsh-orchids at-a-glance

	Common Spotted-orchid *p. 190*	Heath Spotted-orchid *p. 192*	Early Marsh-orchid *p. 202*
TYPICAL LIP All variable in lip and spike characters – variation may be simply within the normal range expected, or could be indicative of some degree of hybridization – see *p. 261*.			
	LIP: strongly three-lobed, with thick central lobe. **COLOUR + PATTERN:** whitish flower with obvious loops.	**LIP:** broad, blousy, with less obvious central lobe, overlapped by side lobes. **COLOUR + PATTERN:** whitish flowers, markings generally spotty or looped.	**LIP:** small, often folded back at the side along a vertical line, large 'mouth' at base. **COLOUR + PATTERN:** white–brick-red with double loops that contain dots and dashes.
TYPICAL SPIKE A larger-than-usual spike in a mixed colony could be indicative of some degree of hybridization – see *p. 261*.			
	SPIKE: starts pyramidal-shaped, developing to torpedo-shaped and quite tall when fully mature; pale pinkish-white from a distance.	**SPIKE:** squat, rounded at top; flowers generally appearing quite large and crowded together; pale pinkish-white from a distance.	**SPIKE:** torpedo-shaped; flowers look small and often crowded together; variable in colour depending on variety and habitat.
LEAF DETAILS	Relatively broad, usually with dark spots and blotches.	Spots generally lacking or light; darker plants have blotches similar to Common Spotted-Orchid	Typically unmarked, folded-in slightly along length, with a hooded tip

Spotted-orchid and marsh-orchid ranges of colour variation

The table opposite shows the normal and possible colour ranges found in each spotted-orchid and marsh-orchid species. The table is simplifed as it is not possible to indicate the full range of colour depth and saturation.

Key: **CSO** Common Spotted-orchid; **HSO** Heath Spotted-orchid; **EMO** Early Marsh-orchid; **SMO** Southern Marsh-orchid; **NMO** Northern Marsh-orchid; **PMO** Pugsley's Marsh-orchid; **IMO** Irish Marsh-orchid.

▬ = typical range; ⊢⊣ = possible range

NB Frog Orchid (*p. 188*) not included as looks very different from other *Dactylorhiza*.

Southern Marsh-orchid *p. 198*	Northern Marsh-orchid *p. 196*	Pugsley's Marsh-orchid *p. 206*	Irish Marsh-orchid *p. 204*
		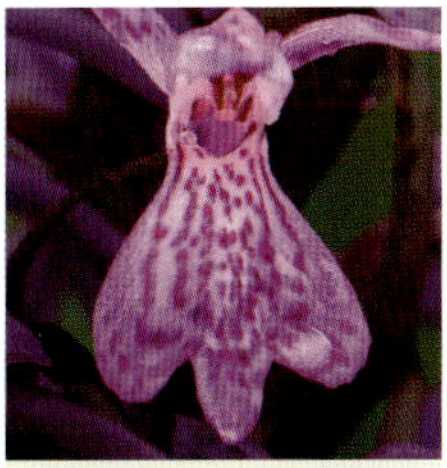	
LIP: weakly three-lobed. **COLOUR + PATTERN:** mid-pink-purple; pattern usually mainly vertical and down the centre, usually with dashes rather than solid lines.	**LIP:** usually diamond-shaped, but sometimes weakly lobed. **COLOUR + PATTERN:** generally looks dark purple, especially at a distance, with extremely dark dashes and/or loops.	**LIP:** drawn-out, widest near bottom, strongly three-lobed. **COLOUR + PATTERN:** very variable but often dark pinkish-purple. **FLOWER:** large spur and hood overhangs pollinia.	**LIP:** usually quite broad, weakly three-lobed. **COLOUR + PATTERN:** purplish, but variable in colour with variable dots, dashes and loops.

SPIKE: often quite tall, torpedo-shaped (can be small and weedy); flowers medium-sized, pinkish-purple (can be darker). Populations can look uniform on approach.	**SPIKE:** shorter, rounder-topped; flowers much darker purple, slightly smaller-looking, and more densely packed (*cf.* Southern Marsh-orchid). Populations can look uniform on approach.	**SPIKE:** loose, untidy appearance; large-looking, usually purple, flowers giving a 'top-heavy' look to the plant.	**SPIKE:** round-topped, short; usually purple/pink; flowers, medium-sized, blousy.
Always unmarked, can be quite broad	Usually unmarked, occasionally with small, faint spots. Quite broad and relatively short	Always longer than wide, usually only two or three, unmarked to heavily blotched, appear small compared to inflorescence	Quite broad, unmarked to heavily blotched

Identification of Pugsley's *p.* 208

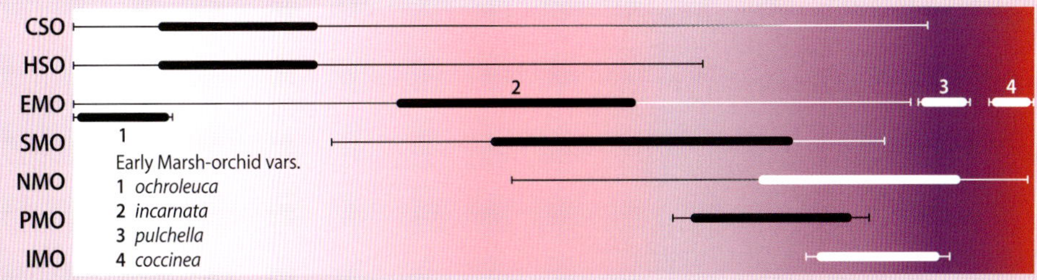
CSO
HSO
EMO
SMO
NMO
PMO
IMO
1
2
3
4
Early Marsh-orchid vars.
1 *ochroleuca*
2 *incarnata*
3 *pulchella*
4 *coccinea*

IN BUD *p. 79* | IN HABITAT *p. 49*

VU NT Frog Orchid

Dactylorhiza viridis

FORMER NAME: *Coeloglossum viride*

Widespread; locally common

up to 15 (35) cm

IN BUD

Downward-facing flowers with rounded hood; long, green to reddish lip with two side lobes and a tiny central one.
Leafy bract of varying length at base of each flower.
Small, well-camouflaged in long grass.
Unmarked, oval to blade-shaped leaves.

HABITAT: Found in a wide variety of calcareous habitats. In the south of Britain its favoured habitat is chalk and limestone grassland, and so can also be found in quarries and lime or chalk pits. In the north and west it grows in hay meadows, damp pastures, rocky ledges, old quarries, road verges, railway embankments, stabilized dunes and especially machair.

A relatively small, unassuming orchid that can be very difficult to spot. However, with experience the distinctive shape and colour of the flower spike help when locating this otherwise well-camouflaged species among the surrounding vegetation. It can appear in a variety of colours and sizes. Usually scarce, although can be common in optimal habitat, it has a wide distribution across Britain and Ireland, but largely restricted to chalk and limestone, with strongholds in the Chilterns, South Downs, Derbyshire, Yorkshire, the Western Isles, the Burren (Co. Clare), and the north-west coast of Ireland. It has been lost from large parts of its former range due to changes in farming practices. It regularly hybridizes with marsh-orchids and spotted-orchids, reflecting its position within *Dactylorhiza* despite looking very different to the other species within the genus.

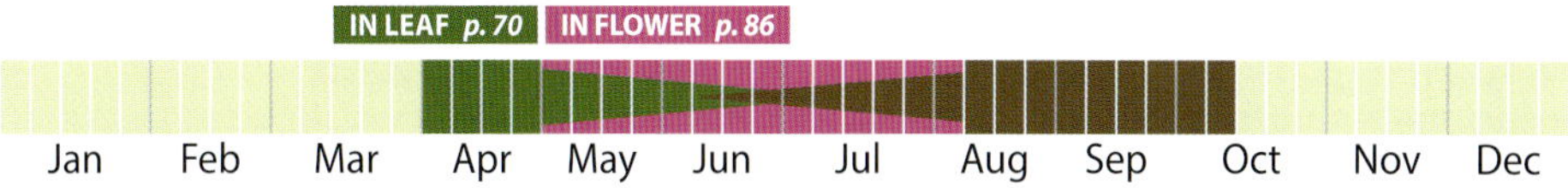
IN LEAF p. 70
IN FLOWER p. 86
Jan
Feb
Mar
Apr
May
Jun
Jul
Aug
Sep
Oct
Nov
Dec

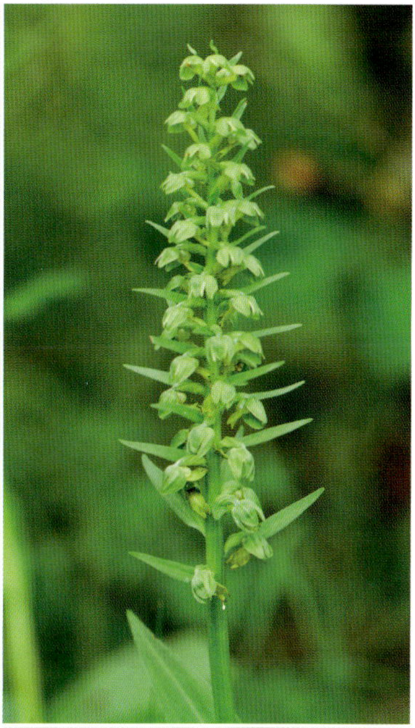

CONFUSION SPECIES: **IN FLOWER** **Common Twayblade** (*p. 140*). **IN LEAF** marsh-orchids (*pp. 196–213*). **HYBRIDS** × Heath Fragrant-orchid (*p. 176*), Common Spotted-orchid (*p. 262*), Northern Marsh-orchid (*p. 262*).

IN BUD *p. 79* | IN HABITAT *p. 47* | SPOTTED-ORCHIDS COMPARED *p. 194*

LC LC Common Spotted-orchid *Dactylorhiza fuchsii*

Widespread; often abundant

up to 70 cm

IN BUD
In-bud Common and Heath Spotted-orchids are virtually identical.

Lip split clearly into three lobes: the central one pointed and narrow, the side ones wider and often quite square-shaped.

Flowers pale pink to whitish; lip with two 'solid' darker loops and dashes that are typically deep lilac to purple.

HIGHLY VARIABLE see *Spotted-orchids compared (p. 194)*.

Flower spike conical at first, gradually filling out to a torpedo shape; compared to Heath Spotted-orchid often taller, slightly more 'open' as flower lips are not as broad and overlapping.

Leaves almost always have dark oval or rectangular spots, merged in some individuals.

HABITAT: Favours calcareous or neutral soils in a wide variety of habitats. The most common are chalk and limestone grassland, damp meadows, marshes, fens, dune slacks, machair, industrial waste ground, roadside verges, parks, woodland edges, hay meadows and railway embankments.

The most common and widespread orchid in Britain and Ireland, being absent only from parts of eastern and northern Scotland, southern Ireland and much of Cornwall. Its pale lilac, boldly marked flowers and narrow, spotted leaves are distinctive. Despite this, the sheer range of variability often means it is confused with other species in the genus, particularly Heath Spotted-orchid. In western Scotland, northern Ireland and north Cornwall, var. *hebridensis* (*p. 184*) occurs on coastal grasslands and machair. These populations have larger, deep pink flowers, but are otherwise very similar to nominate *fuchsii*, with which it only occasionally co-occurs.

IN LEAF p. 70
IN FLOWER p. 92
Jan
Feb
Mar
Apr
May
Jun
Jul
Aug
Sep
Oct
Nov
Dec

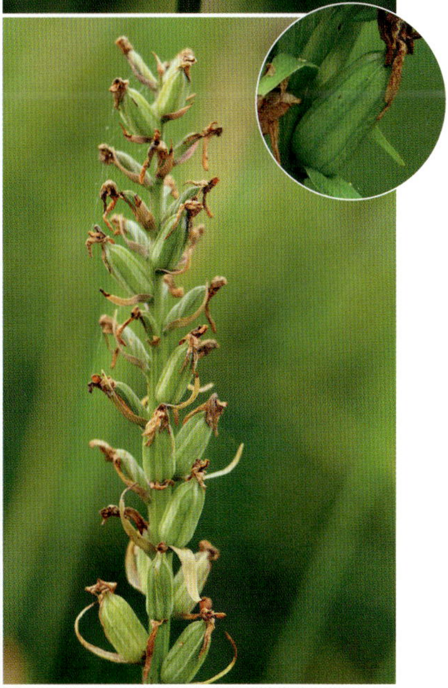

CONFUSION SPECIES: IN FLOWER **Heath Spotted-orchid** (*p. 192*), marsh-orchids (*pp. 196–213*). IN LEAF Heath Spotted-orchid, marsh-orchids, Early-purple Orchid (*p. 71*). **HYBRIDS** × Frog Orchid (*p. 262*), Heath Spotted-orchid (*p. 267*), Northern (*p. 264*), Southern (*p. 265*), Pugsley's (*p. 266*), Irish (*p. 265*) and Early Marsh-orchids (*p. 267*).

 IN BUD *p. 79* | IN HABITAT *p. 47* | SPOTTED-ORCHIDS COMPARED *p. 194*

LC LC Heath Spotted-orchid *Dactylorhiza maculata*

Widespread; often abundant

up to 40 (70) cm

IN BUD
In-bud Heath and Common Spotted-orchids are virtually identical.

Lip broad and blousy, with central lobe much smaller and less well defined than larger side lobes.

Flowers typically white to pale pink; markings very variable, but more often light speckling and spots, rather than strong loops (as typically shown by Common Spotted-orchid).

HIGHLY VARIABLE see *Spotted-orchids compared* (*p. 194*).

Flower spike conical at first, gradually filling out to a torpedo shape; compared to Common Spotted-orchid often more rounded, and fuller-looking due to overlapping broad flower lips.

Leaves variably spotted or barred; markings often smaller and paler than in Common Spotted-orchid.

HABITAT: Favours damp acidic soils and therefore very common on heathland, bogs and upland pastures and meadows, although can also be found in fens and marshes. Due to its fondness for these habitats, it is often found at high elevations (up to 900 m above sea level) in upland regions.

Widespread and common, but can be difficult to separate from Common Spotted-orchid, and hybrids appear to occur in the rare instances where the two species occur together. It is very variable in appearance, even within single populations. It also readily hybridizes with marsh-orchids, although such hybrids are usually relatively easy to recognize. Heath Spotted-orchid has a much stronger western and northern bias than Common Spotted-orchid, and can be ubiquitous in much of Wales, south-west England, northern England, the whole of Scotland and much of Ireland.

IN LEAF p. 70
IN FLOWER p. 92
Jan
Feb
Mar
Apr
May
Jun
Jul
Aug
Sep
Oct
Nov
Dec

CONFUSION SPECIES: IN FLOWER **Common Spotted-orchid** (*p. 190*), **marsh-orchids** (*pp. 196–213*). IN LEAF Marsh-orchids, Common Spotted-orchid. **HYBRIDS** × Small-white Orchid (*p. 260*), fragrant-orchids (*p. 255*), Common Spotted-orchid (*p. 267*), marsh-orchids (*pp. 268–269*).

Common and Heath Spotted-orchids compared

Strong dark 'loops' and dashes.

Lip with three distinct lobes; central lobe pointed and ±½ width of side lobes.

COMMON SPOTTED- *p. 190*

HEATH SPOTTED- *p. 192*

No strong 'loops'; light speckling and spots.

Lip lobes not well-defined; central lobe much smaller.

Common Spotted-orchid
Heath Spotted-orchid

Both species are highly variable and readily hybridize with other species in the genus (*p. 261*), producing plants with a bewildering range of intermediate features. However, typical examples, as above, are straightforward to identify. In addition, the leaves of Common Spotted-orchid typically have dark spots or blotches; those of Heath Spotted-orchid often being smaller, paler and less rounded.

Common Spotted-orchid

Heath Spotted-orchid

Common Spotted-orchid

Heath Spotted-orchid

IN BUD *p. 79* | IN HABITAT *p. 48*

LC LC Northern Marsh-orchid *Dactylorhiza purpurella*

FORMER NAME: Western Marsh-orchid *D. majalis* ssp. *purpurella*

Widespread; often abundant

up to 30 (45) cm

IN BUD
All pre-flowering marsh-orchids look very similar, but habitat type/associated species are clues to their identity.

Inflorescence flat-topped, consistently coloured dark purple.

Very dark spots, blotches and loops mainly down centre of lip.

VARIABLE – see *Northern and Southern Marsh-orchids compared (p. 200)*.

Lip barely lobed, broadly diamond-shaped but can be more deeply three-lobed in some areas.

Lip small in relation to spur mouth.

Leaves unmarked, lightly marked with fine spots or (rarely) heavily blotched in coastal Wales and northern Britain.

HABITAT: Occurs in a wide range of habitats, but usually where it is damp or marshy. Most common in hay meadows, unimproved pastures, golf courses, roadside verges, landscaped spoil heaps, quarries, old industrial sites, dune slacks and flushes. Can be very common in urban environments in Scotland.

A common orchid of northern Britain, where it replaces Southern Marsh-orchid (*p. 198*). Seen from a distance, it is usually distinguishable from that species by its typically darker colour. Northern Marsh-orchid often occurs in large colonies and hybridizes freely with any other *Dactylorhiza* species nearby. As its name suggests, this is a northern species that occurs primarily north and west of a line between Cardiff and the Humber, being most common in Scotland; the southernmost location is at Kenfig Dunes, South Wales. It has a scattered distribution in Ireland but is most widespread in the north, with more southern sites in Co. Wexford, Co. Clare and on Cape Clear Island (Co. Cork).

IN LEAF p. 69
IN FLOWER p. 93
Jan
Feb
Mar
Apr
May
Jun
Jul
Aug
Sep
Oct
Nov
Dec

CONFUSION SPECIES: IN FLOWER **Other marsh-orchids** (*pp. 196–213*), **spotted-orchids** (*pp. 190–192*). IN LEAF Other marsh-orchids, spotted-orchids. HYBRIDS × Frog Orchid (*p. 262*), Common (*p. 264*) and Heath Spotted-orchids (*p. 268*), Southern (*p. 266*), Pugsley's (*p. 266*), Irish (*p. 264*) and Early Marsh-orchids (*p. 266*).

IN BUD *p. 79* | IN HABITAT *p. 48*

LC NE Southern Marsh-orchid *Dactylorhiza praetermissa*

Widespread; often abundant

up to 50 (90) cm

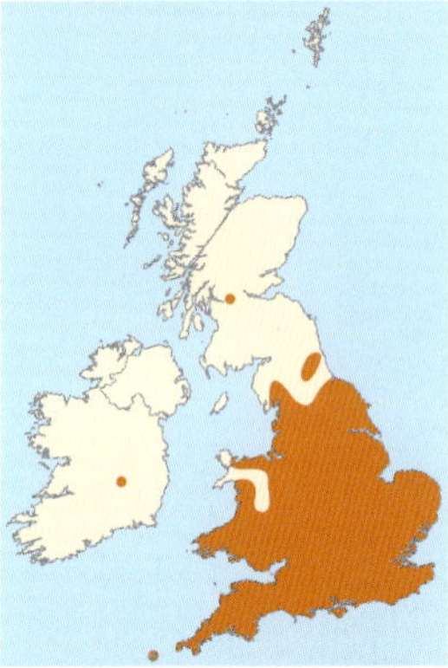

FORMER NAMES:
Western Marsh-orchid
D. majalis ssp. *praetermissa*
and *D. majalis* ssp. *integrata*

Mid-purple to pink flower spike.
Flowers with pattern confined largely to the centre of lip, from top to bottom.
Lip pattern a series of spots and speckles, only very rarely surrounded by solid loops.
VARIABLE – see *Northern and Southern Marsh-orchids compared (p. 200).*
Lip typically three-lobed, sometimes not very obviously: central lobe usually pointed; side lobes broad and rounded.
Lip large in relation to spur mouth.
Leaves unmarked but a few colonies in southern England show ring-shaped markings ('Leopard Marsh-orchid') similar to hybrid with Common Spotted-orchid.

IN BUD
All pre-flowering marsh-orchids look very similar, but habitat type/associated species are clues to their identity.

HABITAT: Can be encountered in a variety of habitats, but usually where it is damp or marshy. Occurs in hay meadows, unimproved pastures, golf courses, parks, roadside verges, landscaped spoil heaps, old industrial sites and gravel workings, fens (var. *schoenophila* (*p. 211*)), dune slacks, slumped cliffs, water meadows and lakesides.

The southern counterpart of Northern Marsh-orchid (*p. 196*). From a distance, it is usually distinguishable from that species by its paler colour. Southern Marsh-orchid regularly forms large colonies where conditions are favourable – plants are taller in wetter areas but shorter and lax-flowered in drier conditions. Hybridizes freely with with any other *Dactylorhiza* species nearby. Common in England and Wales north to a line between Lancaster and Scarborough, beyond which it becomes less frequent, although it is rapidly spreading northwards. One of very few orchid species to occur on the Isles of Scilly. Discovered in 2020 both in Ireland (Co. Laois) and in Scotland (near Glasgow).

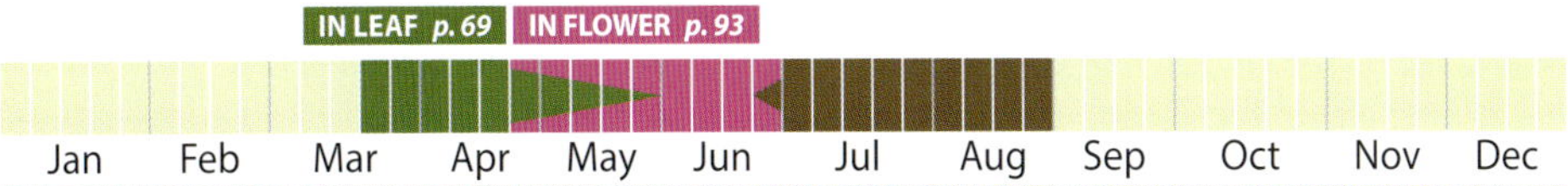
IN LEAF p. 69
IN FLOWER p. 93
Jan
Feb
Mar
Apr
May
Jun
Jul
Aug
Sep
Oct
Nov
Dec

CONFUSION SPECIES: IN FLOWER **Other marsh-orchids** (*pp. 196–213*), **spotted-orchids** (*pp. 190–192*). IN LEAF Other marsh-orchids, spotted-orchids. HYBRIDS × Heath Fragrant-orchid (*p. 255*), Common (*p. 265*) and Heath Spotted-orchids (*p. 268*), Northern (*p. 266*) and Early Marsh-orchids (*p. 263*).

Northern and Southern Marsh-orchids compared

Flowers dark purple with dark spots, blotches and loops, usually extending over most of lip.

NORTHERN MARSH-

Lip weakly lobed and broadly diamond-shaped (rarely three-lobed). Lip small in proportion to spur mouth.

SOUTHERN MARSH-

Lip three-lobed or more saucer-shaped: central lobe pointed; side lobes broad, rounded. Lip large in proportion to spur mouth.

Flowers pink to mid-purple with spots or speckles along centre of lip, sometimes forming faint, thin loops.

■ Northern Marsh-orchid
■ Southern Marsh-orchid

Typical Northern Marsh-orchid has a round-topped inflorescence of dark purple flowers, Southern Marsh-orchid a more pointed spike of pink to mid-purple flowers. The leaves of both species are typically unmarked, although those of Northern Marsh-orchid can be lightly spotted or heavily marked with blotches at a few sites in coastal Wales and northern Britain. Hybrids between the two appear to be scarce but could be under-recorded (*p. 266*) possibly due to the difficulties of identifying definite hybrids from the huge range of variation found in both species. Hybrids may become more common in the future as Southern Marsh-orchid continues to spread northwards and the range overlap zone increases.

Northern Marsh-orchid

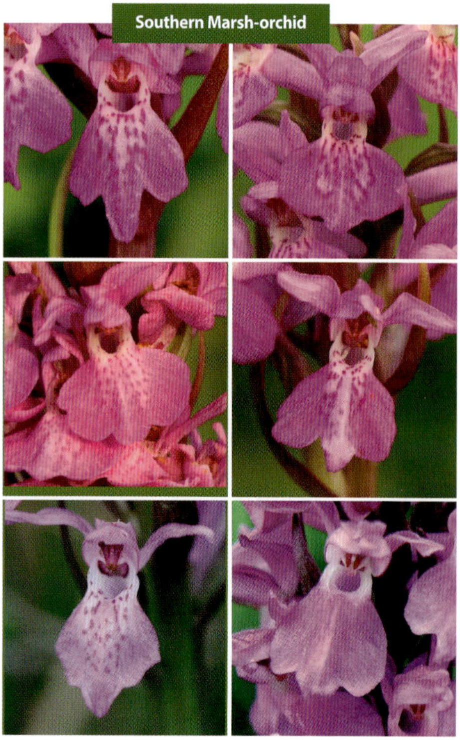
Southern Marsh-orchid

Beware: some Northern Marsh-orchids can have a more three-lobed lip

Beware: some Southern Marsh-orchids can have a more diamond-shaped lip

Northern Marsh-orchid

Southern Marsh-orchid

IN BUD *p. 79* | IN HABITAT *p. 48*

LC LC Early Marsh-orchid *Dactylorhiza incarnata*

Widespread; locally common

up to 40 (80) cm

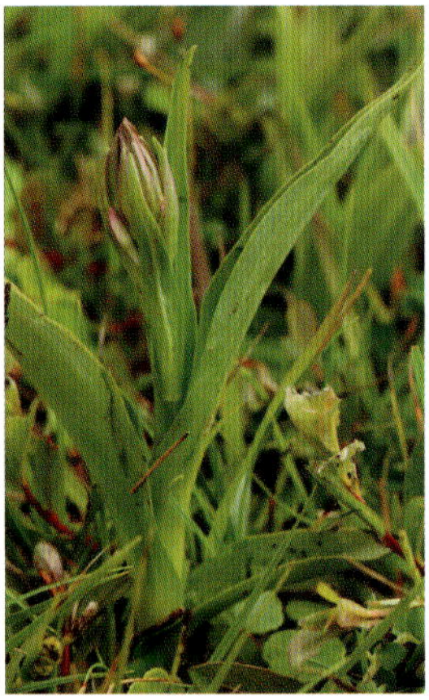

IN BUD
All pre-flowering marsh-orchids look very similar, but habitat type/associated species are clues to their identity. In Early Marsh-orchid the often strongly keeled, hook-tipped leaves are an additional pointer.

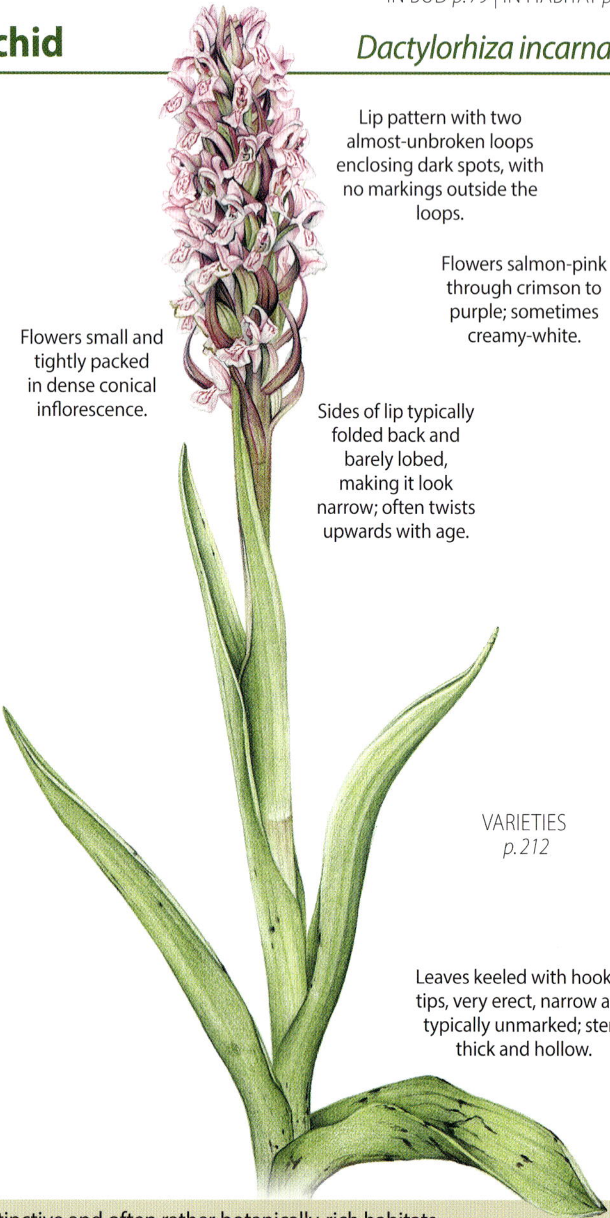
Lip pattern with two almost-unbroken loops enclosing dark spots, with no markings outside the loops.
Flowers salmon-pink through crimson to purple; sometimes creamy-white.
Flowers small and tightly packed in dense conical inflorescence.
Sides of lip typically folded back and barely lobed, making it look narrow; often twists upwards with age.
Leaves keeled with hooked tips, very erect, narrow and typically unmarked; stem thick and hollow.

VARIETIES *p. 212*

HABITAT: Occurs in several distinctive and often rather botanically-rich habitats. Individual varieties occupy specific habitat types, including water meadows, damp pastures, flushes, fens, dune slacks, slumped cliffs and acidic peat bogs.

A variable species consisting of four varieties, each usually linked to a specific habitat. Each variety, has consistent characteristics, although they look quite different from each other. However, as a species, Early Marsh-orchid is distinctive in overall appearance, having a densely packed spike of small, strongly marked flowers atop a thick stem, and erect, often hook-tipped leaves. This species is the most widely distributed of the marsh-orchids, being scattered across Britain and Ireland from Cornwall to Shetland, but is generally rather scarce.

IN LEAF p. 69
IN FLOWER p. 93
Jan
Feb
Mar
Apr
May
Jun
Jul
Aug
Sep
Oct
Nov
Dec

Typical form (LEFT) and purple form (RIGHT) of the nominate var. *incarnata*.

CONFUSION SPECIES: IN FLOWER **Other marsh-orchids** (*pp. 196–213*), **spotted-orchids** (*pp. 190–192*). IN LEAF Other marsh-orchids, spotted-orchids. HYBRIDS × Heath Fragrant-orchid (*p. 259*), Common (*p. 267*) and Heath Spotted-orchids (*p. 268*), Northern (*p. 266*), Southern and Pugsley's Marsh-orchids (both *p. 263*).

 IN BUD *p. 79* | IN HABITAT *p. 49*

LC Irish Marsh-orchid *Dactylorhiza kerryensis*

Widespread; locally common

up to 30 (50) cm

FORMER NAMES: Western Marsh-orchid *D. occidentalis*, *D. majalis* ssp. *occidentalis* and *D. majalis* ssp. *kerryensis*

IN BUD
All pre-flowering marsh-orchids look very similar, but habitat type/associated species are clues to their identity.

Flower spike densely packed and broadly rounded.

Broad, deep purple to magenta flowers with three-lobed lip; all lobes broadly rounded or with 'ragged', notched edges.

Whole plant often squat.

Lip with bold loops and spots contained within double loops or extending to edges.

Leaves few, unmarked to heavily spotted; lowest held horizontally.

HABITAT: Occurs in a similar range of habitats to the other common marsh-orchids, including hay meadows, unimproved pastures, roadside verges, landscaped spoil heaps, old industrial sites, fens, dune slacks, flushes, water meadows, lakesides and limestone grassland.

Unlike the other marsh-orchids of hybrid origin, this distinctive species has Heath Spotted-orchid (*p. 192*), rather than Common Spotted-orchid (*p. 190*), as one of its ancestral parents. This gives it a different overall appearance, including a rather 'ragged-edged' lip and generally large flowers. It is also often rather squat, with a short, rounded inflorescence. The readiness of other species of *Dactylorhiza* to hybridize, producing progeny that look similar to Irish Marsh-orchid, may have caused confusion and led to possible misinterpretations of its true range. Endemic to Ireland, it is most common in the west and south, particularly Counties Mayo, Galway, Kerry, Cork and Waterford. It is rather rare in the north, with only a handful of scattered sites.

IN LEAF p. 69
IN FLOWER p. 93
Jan
Feb
Mar
Apr
May
Jun
Jul
Aug
Sep
Oct
Nov
Dec

CONFUSION SPECIES: **IN FLOWER** **Other marsh-orchids** (*pp. 196–213*), **spotted-orchids** (*pp. 190–192*). **IN LEAF** Other marsh-orchids, spotted-orchids. **HYBRIDS** × Common Spotted-orchid (*p. 265*), Heath Spotted-orchid (*p. 268*), Northern Marsh-orchid (*p. 264*).

IN BUD *p. 79* | IN HABITAT *p. 49*

LC LC Pugsley's Marsh-orchid *Dactylorhiza traunsteinerioides* N

Narrow-leaved Marsh-orchid

FORMER NAMES: Western Marsh-orchid *D. majalis* ssp. *traunsteineri* and *D. majalis* ssp. *lapponica*

Scattered and scarce

up to 30 (50) cm

?

Rather long and broad-based, triangular spur.

Hood long and arching; often hanging forward over lip

Upper half of stem usually washed reddish-purple.

Spike with few, large-looking, widely-spaced flowers, often in messy jumbled arrangement, giving the plant a top-heavy appearance.

VARIATION *p. 208*.

Lip often large, long and usually widest towards the tip. The side lobes are typically folded back along their length. Pointed central lobe often protrudes beyond the side lobes.

Leaves few (usually two to four), often narrow and erect, unspotted, lightly spotted or heavily blotched, rarely blackish-purple.

IN BUD
All pre-flowering marsh-orchids look very similar, but habitat type/associated species are clues to their identity.

HABITAT: Restricted to botanically-rich fens, calcareous flushes and damp machair where it often co-occurs with Black Bog-rush *Schoenus nigricans* (see *p. 208*).

A subtle species that has been repeatedly reclassified under several different names during the last 50 years. Although it can be distinctive, this near-cryptic species is possibly the most difficult to identify due to its wide variability and similarity to other *Dactylorhiza* species and hybrids. Pugsley's Marsh-orchid is a relatively newly formed species and is by far the rarest of the *Dactylorhiza*, with scattered colonies in North Wales, northern England, western Scotland and – very sparsely – across central and coastal north-west Ireland and northern Ireland. It may possibly occur in East Anglia, but the identity of the plants there is uncertain (see *East Anglian fenland marsh-orchids* in *Dactylorhiza* introduction, *p. 183*).

IN LEAF p. 69 IN FLOWER p. 93

Jan
Feb
Mar
Apr
May
Jun
Jul
Aug
Sep
Oct
Nov
Dec

CONFUSION SPECIES: IN FLOWER **Other marsh-orchids** (*pp. 196–213*), **spotted-orchids** (*pp. 190–192*). IN LEAF Other marsh-orchids, spotted-orchids. **HYBRIDS** × Heath Spotted-Orchid (*p. 268*), Northern (*p. 266*) and Early Marsh-orchids (*p. 263*).

Pugsley's Marsh-orchid identification and variation

FORM: looks 'top-heavy'

Typically a short, slender marsh-orchid with long, narrow leaves (*left*) but can be stockier with short, broad leaves in machair habitats (*right*).

Co. Donegal

Inverness-shire

Anglesey

Cumbria

Form

- Lax flower spike of large-looking flowers with a thin stem and few narrow leaves gives a 'top-heavy' appearance.
- Often rather short and delicate in comparison to other *Dactylorhiza*.

Leaves

- Rather narrow and often short; typically two (sometimes three) lower leaves and one, erect bract-like leaf below the inflorescence.
- Unmarked, lightly spotted or heavily marked with blotches/bars.

Inflorescence

- Messy, jumbled appearance with flowers often facing at different angles.
- Inflorescence stem (rachis) and flower bracts usually washed purplish-red.

Flowers

- Entire hood usually long and arching forward over lip such that pollinia are usually hidden when viewed head-on.
- Angle between lip base and hood typically acute (less than 90°) when viewed side-on.
- Lip usually longer than wide; side lobes often folded back lengthways; central lobe protrudes beyond side lobes.
- Lip markings varied, from light speckles to strong loops, typically covering most of the lip surface.
- Lateral sepals usually held very erect, often marked with spots or rings in heavily pigmented plants.
- Widest point of lip is usually near the lower (distal) end of the lip.
- Large, broad-based spur, giving a large 'gaping mouth' to the flower when viewed front-on.

An additional pointer is that Pugsley's Marsh-orchid often grows in areas with Black Bog-rush *Schoenus nigricans*.

Pugsley's vs. other marsh-orchids

Small stature, a lax-flowered inflorescence and narrow leaves are, alone, **not diagnostic features** of Pugsley's Marsh-orchid. Weak individuals of other marsh-orchid species, particularly those subject to environmental stress, such as strong wind or drought, naturally have fewer flowers and narrower leaves, and can be common within large, variable populations. **In addition to the consistent flower morphology outlined here, it is vital that context is considered: Pugsley's Marsh-orchid only occurs in flushes, fens and on machair, where it forms discrete populations of plants with a similar stature and general appearance.**

Northern Marsh-orchid

Early Marsh-orchid

Most Northern and Southern Marsh-orchids (Southern Marsh-orchid)
POLLINIA: showing
widest point of lip
HOOD: curved
ANGLE: >90°

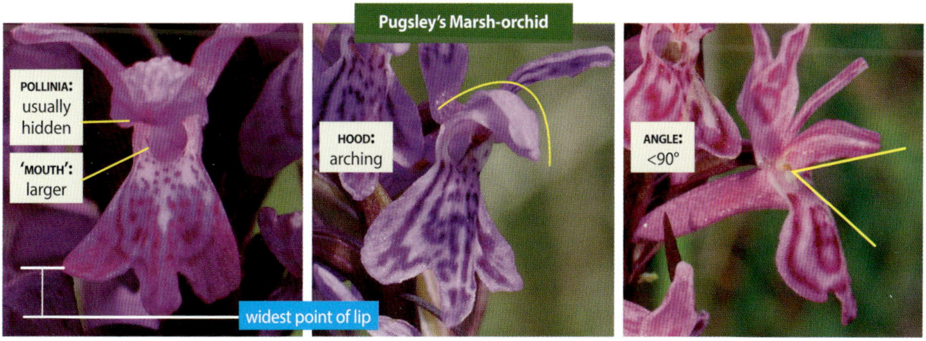
Pugsley's Marsh-orchid
POLLINIA: usually hidden
'MOUTH': larger
widest point of lip
HOOD: arching
ANGLE: <90°

Variation

Despite the variety of lip shape, size, colour and markings found in Pugsley's Marsh-orchid, the characters outlined above, such as the angle between the lip base and the hood, the size of the spur and the number of leaves, are relatively consistent.

Spotted-orchid and marsh-orchid varieties

Common Spotted-orchid *D. fuchsii* var. *hebridensis*

A characteristic orchid of Cornish coastal grasslands and machair of northern Ireland and Scotland, where it can form large populations, flowering in mid-summer. The flowers are, on average, larger and darker (sometimes as dark as the co-occurring Southern or Northern Marsh-orchids) than typical Common Spotted-orchid (var. *fuchsii*), with a contrasting whitish base to the lip. The side lobes are usually rather broad and rounded with distinctive 'frilly' edges, unlike typical Common Spotted-orchid. The leaves are regularly unmarked, despite the strong coloration of the flowers.

'typical' *fuchsii*

var. *hebridensis*

Southern Marsh-orchid *D. praetermissa* var. *schoenophila*

First described in 2012, this taxon was, for many years, overlooked as Pugsley's Marsh-orchid (*p. 206*), since the two can look very similar indeed. Southern Marsh-orchid var. *schoenophila* is restricted to fens in southern and eastern England, where it does not, in theory, overlap in range with Pugsley's Marsh-orchid. However, the possibility that these two taxa may occur together in East Anglia could explain some of the ongoing confusion, although this is difficult to confirm (see *East Anglian fenland marsh-orchids* in *Dactylorhiza* introduction, *p. 183*). Southern Marsh-orchid var. *schoenophila* is much more delicate than typical *D. praetermissa* (var. *praetermissa*), with fewer, narrower leaves, sometimes larger flowers with bolder lip markings, and a lax-flowered inflorescence. However, the limits of this taxon are poorly understood and it is unclear what separates var. *schoenophila* from small, weak examples of var. *praetermissa*. Furthermore, this taxon appears to be extremely variable and most colonies contain a mixed range of forms intermediate in stature between var. *praetermissa* and 'typical' var. *schoenophila*. This casts doubt on the validity of var. *schoenophila* as a distinct taxon, which may yet, for example, turn out to be an ecotype with varying levels of introgression from other marsh-orchid species.

var. praetermissa
var. schoenophila
Pugsley's Marsh-orchid

Early Marsh-orchid varieties

Early Marsh-orchid *D. incarnata* var. *incarnata*

The nominate variety, with flowers that are usually a distinctive salmon-pink colour, although can be purplish and sometimes white. Purple-flowered plants of this species occurring alongside typical pale pink ones will be nominate *incarnata*, rather than var. *pulchella*, which is a plant of peat bogs. In western Ireland and one or two sites in Scotland, populations consist of plants with variably marked leaves and stems (formerly 'ssp. *cruenta*' – see *New identities: Other Dactylorhiza taxa p. 183*). It is distributed across Britain and Ireland, favouring wet calcareous habitats, such as water meadows, flushes and fens.

D. incarnata var. *cruenta*

A rare variety with pinkish-purple flowers characterized by variable dark spots or blotches on the leaves, stem and bracts. Restricted to western Ireland and one or two sites in Scotland, where it favours lough shores, fens, dune slacks and flushes. Populations usually contain only a handful of plants. Genetic studies have indicated that although British and Irish populations look similar to European *cruenta*, they are not closely related and may therefore be a distinct taxon.

D. incarnata var. coccinea
This variety has unique brick-red flowers. It is usually rather squat, as a response to the open, wind-blasted nature of its habitats – dune slack, machair and, less frequently, slumped cliff. It is distributed widely across Britain and Ireland, although restricted to the stretches of coast where these habitats occur.

D. incarnata var. pulchella
This variety has deep purple flowers that are tightly clustered in a dense spike atop a rather long, lime-green stem that has very narrow, erect leaves. Notably, it always occurs in the slightly more botanically-rich areas of peat bogs, usually growing on beds of *Sphagnum* moss. It is widely distributed across Britain and Ireland.

D. incarnata var. ochroleuca
By far the rarest variety, and one of the most threatened orchid taxa in Britain. It is a tall plant, with creamy-white flowers that have a distinctively three-lobed lip. Now restricted to a handful of botanically-rich fens in Suffolk and Norfolk, but formerly much more widespread in East Anglia; it is currently the subject of concerted conservation efforts.

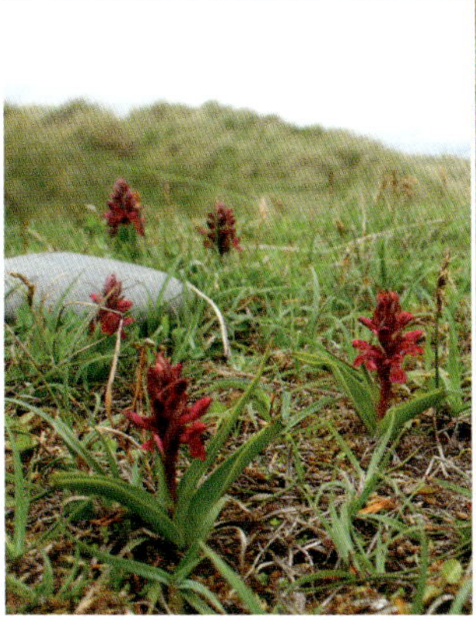

IN BUD p. 78 | IN HABITAT p. 50

LC Lizard Orchid *Himantoglossum hircinum* G

Scattered and rare

up to 90 cm

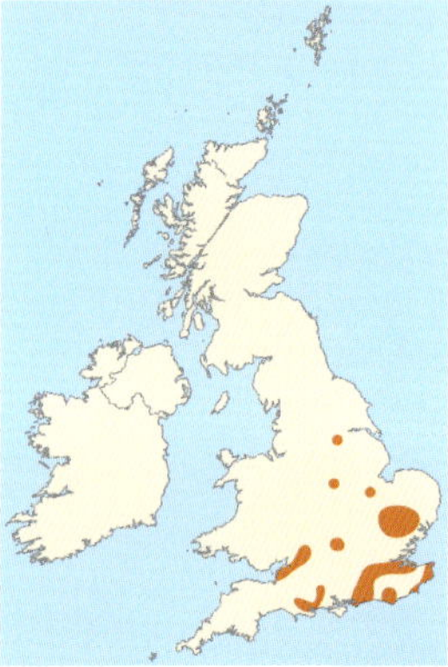

IN BUD

Unmistakable: tall with messy, often bent or kinked flower spike of greenish to wine-coloured flowers with long, wavy lip.

Leaves large and very shiny, but always yellow or blackened when in flower.

HABITAT: Usually occurs on calcareous soils among quite tall grasses, particularly on stabilized sand dunes, the edges of golf courses and occasionally open chalk and limestone grassland. Single plants can appear spontaneously in rather nondescript patches of grassland along field margins, railway embankments and roadside verges – sometimes in surprisingly urban locations.

This grand species is unique both in its appearance and pungent, somewhat unpleasant smell, and is the sole representative of the genus in Britain. It is primarily a southern English species, with strongholds in Kent (especially around Sandwich), Cambridgeshire and Somerset. There are also scattered, intermittent colonies in several other southern counties and one outlier near Doncaster in Yorkshire. New sites are being discovered almost annually, so this is definitely a plant to look out for in unexpected places, especially as the overwintering rosette is distinctive.

IN LEAF p. 67
IN FLOWER p. 84
Jan
Feb
Mar
Apr
May
Jun
Jul
Aug
Sep
Oct
Nov
Dec

CONFUSION SPECIES: IN FLOWER **None.** IN LEAF Lady Orchid (*p. 73*).

IN BUD *p. 78*

NE Tongue-orchid *Serapias lingua*

Greater Tongue-orchid

Extremely rare; 2 sites

up to 40 cm

IN BUD

Large-looking pink-purple flowers with large pink lip and cowled, veined hood.
Lip relatively large and tongue-like: broad at base, pointed at tip; hairy in centre of base with quite a large spur entrance.
Hood protrudes beyond rest of flower; vertical bract protrudes above flower.
Leaves long, narrow and erect.

HABITAT: Occurs in damp, calcareous grasslands at both its known sites.

A continental species that has occurred several times in southern England and the Channel Isles. It is the most widespread of its genus in Europe, where it is relatively common, raising the possibility that it has arrived here naturally via wind-blown seed. As well as plants flourishing at Wakehurst Place in Sussex, a colony of 60+ spikes was discovered in a rough meadow in Essex in 2017. The presence of such a large number of spikes in a relatively small area suggests they had spread by vegetative reproduction, and had therefore been established for some time. The species also previously occurred in a meadow near Kingsbridge in South Devon (see *p. 275*). Seeing this species in Britain would mean visiting one of its known sites, although there is a possibility it could be found in new locations.

IN LEAF p. 65
IN FLOWER p. 94
Jan
Feb
Mar
Apr
May
Jun
Jul
Aug
Sep
Oct
Nov
Dec

CONFUSION SPECIES: **IN FLOWER** **Other tongue-orchids** (*p. 276*). **IN LEAF** Pyramidal Orchid (*p. 66*).

IN BUD *p. 78* | IN HABITAT *p. 46*

LC LC Pyramidal Orchid

Anacamptis pyramidalis

Widespread; often abundant

up to 60 cm

IN BUD

Pyramidal, spherical, conical or torpedo-shaped flower spike; flowers usually pink to magenta and densely packed at top of stem.

Flowers have three-lobed lip that is always unmarked and with two lumps, or 'guide rails' at the base in the 'mouth'.

Sheathing leaves all the way up stem; papery, with strong veins.

Long, narrow leaves, with delicate black tip, at base of stem; usually blackened or yellowed during flowering.

HABITAT: Common on dry calcareous grasslands. Particularly favours sand dunes (the drier upper sections), chalk and limestone grassland, roadside verges, motorway embankments, meadows, industrial waste ground, spoil heaps, quarries and railway embankments, where it can grow among quite tall vegetation.

This striking orchid is a frequent sight in early to mid-summer and often abundant where it occurs. Distinctive even from a distance, it is generally bright pink with a conical to rounded, densely packed flower spike. It is mostly a southern species, with a coastal bias towards the north of its range. Strongholds are the limestone and chalk regions of southern England, and major dune systems as far north as the Hebrides. It is common in central and coastal Ireland, but is rather scarce in the north away from the coast. The species is absent from much of mainland Scotland, as well as from inland Wales and northern and south-west England. It is one of the few species that has not contracted in range considerably in recent years, and may indeed be expanding in response to the warming climate.

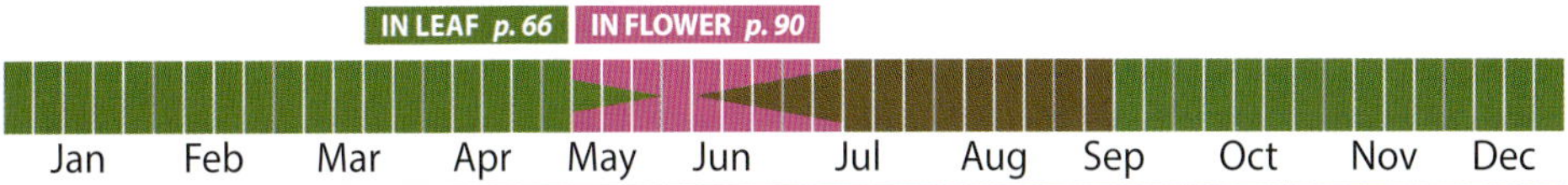
IN LEAF p. 66
IN FLOWER p. 90
Jan
Feb
Mar
Apr
May
Jun
Jul
Aug
Sep
Oct
Nov
Dec

CONFUSION SPECIES: IN FLOWER **Chalk Fragrant-orchid** (*p. 176*). IN LEAF Green-winged Orchid (*p. 66*), Chalk Fragrant-orchid (*p. 67*), Tongue-orchid (*p. 65*), Fly Orchid (*p. 75*).

NT VU Green-winged Orchid *Anacamptis morio* N

Green-veined Orchid

FORMER NAME: *Orchis morio*

Widespread; locally common

up to 20 (40) cm

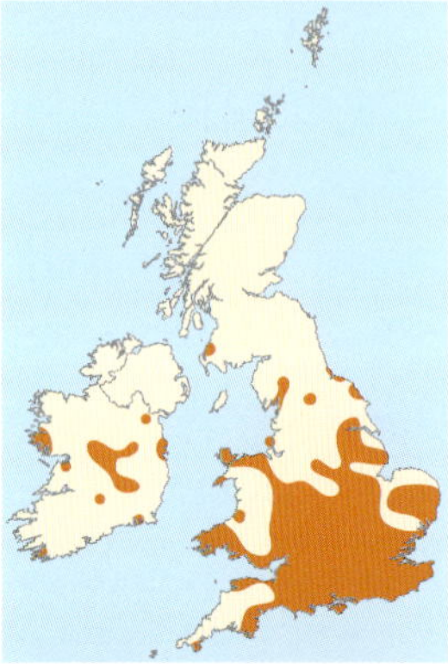

IN BUD

Generally quite short with few large, usually deep purple flowers, but colour variable, from white to pinkish/purple.
VARIATION p. 222.
Flowers always have dark veins on hood.
Lip often folded backwards along length, marked variably with spots or blotches down centre, usually wider than deep.
Leaves always unspotted.

HABITAT: Most abundant in damp, unimproved pastures and hay meadows on calcareous or neutral soils (especially clay), where it often occurs *en masse*. It particularly favours village greens, old commons, churchyards and golf courses. Smaller numbers may also appear on chalk and limestone grasslands, but plants in such habitats are often rather small. In recent years, small colonies have appeared on green roofs in highly urban locations.

A joyful little spring-flowering orchid that can occur in tens of thousands in favoured meadows. Most have dark purple flowers, but single colonies can contain a huge variety of colour forms. Generally shorter in stature and a subtly different colour compared to the similar-looking Early-purple Orchid, as well as always having unmarked leaves and distinctive dark greenish veins on the hood or 'wings' – hence the common name. Mostly a species of southern Britain, it ranges as far north as southern Scotland, but is largely absent from south-west, central and northern England. In Wales it is primarily coastal, and in Ireland is scattered across the central limestone areas. Over the past century, this species has suffered severe declines across Britain and Ireland due to habitat loss.

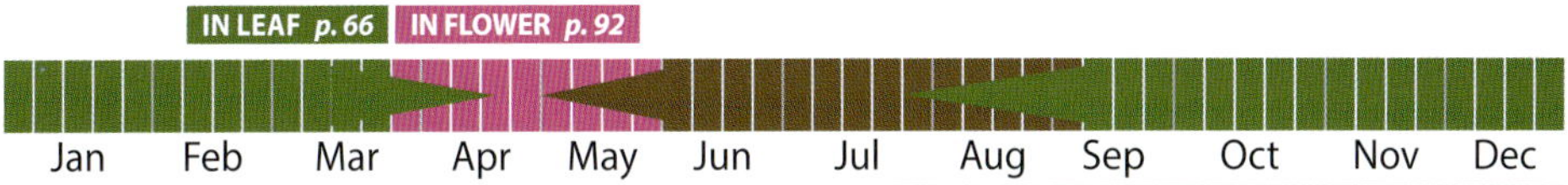
IN LEAF *p. 66*
IN FLOWER *p. 92*
Jan
Feb
Mar
Apr
May
Jun
Jul
Aug
Sep
Oct
Nov
Dec

CONFUSION SPECIES: **IN FLOWER** **Early-purple Orchid** (*p. 226*), **marsh-orchids** (*pp. 196–213*).
IN LEAF Early-purple Orchid (*p. 71*), Pyramidal Orchid (*p. 66*), Chalk Fragrant-orchid (*p. 67*), *Orchis* orchids (*pp. 72–73*).

Green-winged and Early-purple Orchid identification and variation

Identification The flower colour in both species ranges from white to purple. However, the lateral sepals of Green-winged Orchid are held tightly together to form a hood that has prominent dark veins, while the lateral sepals of Early-purple Orchid are held erect and lack veins. The spur of Early-purple Orchid is longer and more upcurved. In addition, the leaves of Green-winged Orchid are never spotted; Early-purple Orchid typically has dark spots or blotches, but regularly shows unmarked leaves.

veins
plain
GREEN-WINGED
EARLY-PURPLE

Green-winged Orchid

	Green-winged Orchid *Anacamptis morio*	**Early-purple Orchid** *Orchis mascula*
FORM	Spike often looks wider than tall at a distance, almost rectangular-shaped when fully mature. Flowers appear to point outwards due to angle of lip.	Spike tends to be taller than wide, flowers more densely packed/overlapping, appear to point downward due to angle of lip, slightly 'messier'-looking than Green-winged Orchid.
FLOWER	White to purple.	
LATERAL SEPALS	Held tightly together to form a hood that has prominent dark veins.	Held erect; plain.
SPUR	Shorter; slightly upcurved.	Longer; more upcurved.
LEAVES	Typically with dark spots or blotches, but regularly unmarked.	Always unspotted.

Early-purple Orchid

Orchis orchids

The *Orchis* genus comprises some of the most impressive and attractive orchids of Britain and Ireland. It is also the 'original' orchid that gave the family its name. 'Orchid' is itself based on the Greek word for testicle – from the paired, rounded tubers. This led the Victorians to assume that *Orchis* species, particularly Early-purple Orchid, were potent aphrodisiacs when consumed.

All species are adapted to either dry calcareous grassland or open woodland, and often occur in both. Some species may appear in very large numbers and in a wide variety of colour forms.

Species

Five species of *Orchis* are recognized in Britain and Ireland (although only one occurs in Ireland).

By far the most common and widespread species is the **Early-purple Orchid** *O. mascula*, which is a characteristically early flowering species and typically has spotted leaves (although a few have unspotted leaves).

All the other *Orchis* species (**Man Orchid** *O. anthropophora*, **Lady Orchid** *O. purpurea*, **Military Orchid** *O. militaris* and **Monkey Orchid** *O. simia*) are largely restricted to southern England. These are sometimes known as the **'manikin' orchids**, as their highly modified lips resemble humanoid figures. The most widespread of this group, Man Orchid, was previously classified in its own genus (*Aceras*) on the basis that it lacks a spur. However genetic study has shown the species to be within *Orchis*, despite this unique morphological difference.

Hybrids (see *p. 270*)

Although a very rare occurrence in Britain, hybrids do occur between 'manikin' orchids, which is evidence of the close genetic relationship between them. By contrast, hybrids involving Early-purple Orchid as a parent have not been confirmed, despite regularly co-occurring with all the other *Orchis* species.

'Manikin' orchids are usually in colonies, and can hybridize when two or more species grow together, as evidenced by these Monkey Orchid × Lady Orchid hybrids.

IN LEAF

Leaves oval to blade-shaped, usually quite shiny, and forming a rosette.

Flowers rich mid-purple, magenta or pink. No dark lines on hood.

Leaves glossy, long, blunt-ended, often with dark spots or blotches, less often unmarked; form a rosette around base of stem.

Early-purple Orchid
p. 226

Narrow and often tall, with slightly 'ragged-looking' flower spike of small yellow to reddish flowers.

Lip humanoid in shape, with drooping, narrow 'arms' and 'legs'.

Long, oval to elliptical, glossy leaves, yellowing during flowering.

Man Orchid
p. 228

Lip broad, whitish to lilac, often frilly, with variable dark flecks that contrast with dark crimson to purplish hood.

Large and stately, with whitish-and-purple flower spike.

Large, glossy, floppy leaves.

Lady Orchid
p. 234

Large and stately; flowers lilac-mauve to purple or pink.

Lip humanoid in shape, with rounded 'feet' and neat rows of spots along its length on a paler background colour.

Large, glossy, oval-shaped leaves arranged in a spiral at base.

Military Orchid
p. 232

Inflorescence rounded and densely packed at top of stem.

Lip humanoid in shape, with narrow, wavy 'arms' and 'legs', and tips of varying degrees of pink or purple.

Long, shiny, oval-shaped leaves.

Monkey Orchid
p. 230

 IN BUD *p. 79* | IN HABITAT *p. 49*

LC LC Early-purple Orchid *Orchis mascula*

Widespread; often abundant

up to 60 cm

Top buds change from creamy-white to purplish-magenta as they develop.
Flowers rich mid-purple, magenta or pink. No dark lines on hood.
VARIATION *p. 222*.
Lip split into three roughly equal lobes and tends to be longer than wide, with dark speckles or spots in centre; 'arms' (lateral sepals) held erect; longish spur curved upwards.
Top of stem stained purple.
Bract at base of each flower not obvious.
Leaves glossy, long, blunt-ended, often with dark spots or blotches, less often unmarked; form a rosette around base of stem.

IN BUD

HABITAT: Primarily a woodland species, particularly coppiced woods where the soil is calcareous, but often common on chalk and limestone grassland, roadside verges, hedgebanks, hay meadows, grazed hill pastures, cliff tops, limestone pavement, quarries, dunes and railway embankments.

Often growing among Bluebells *Hyacnthoides non-scripta* in woods, or Cowslips *Primula veris* on open grasslands during spring, this familiar species is one of the most recognizable. It is highly variable in colour, ranging from magenta to pale pink, with long, usually (but not always) spotted, glossy leaves. It is relatively common across Britain and Ireland, particularly in chalk and limestone regions, and is absent only from areas of extensive arable farmland and upland areas dominated by acidic soils.

IN LEAF p. 71 IN FLOWER p. 92

Jan
Feb
Mar
Apr
May
Jun
Jul
Aug
Sep
Oct
Nov
Dec

CONFUSION SPECIES: IN FLOWER **Green-winged Orchid** (*p. 220*), **marsh-orchids** (*pp. 196–213*).
IN LEAF SPOTTED-LEAVED FORM – Common Spotted-orchid (*p. 70*); UNSPOTTED-LEAVED FORM – Pyramidal Orchid (*p. 66*), Green-winged Orchid, other *Orchis* species (*pp. 72–73*).

IN BUD *p. 79* | IN HABITAT *p. 46*

EN Man Orchid

Orchis anthropophora

FORMER NAME: *Aceras anthropophorum*

Local and scarce

up to 50 cm

IN BUD

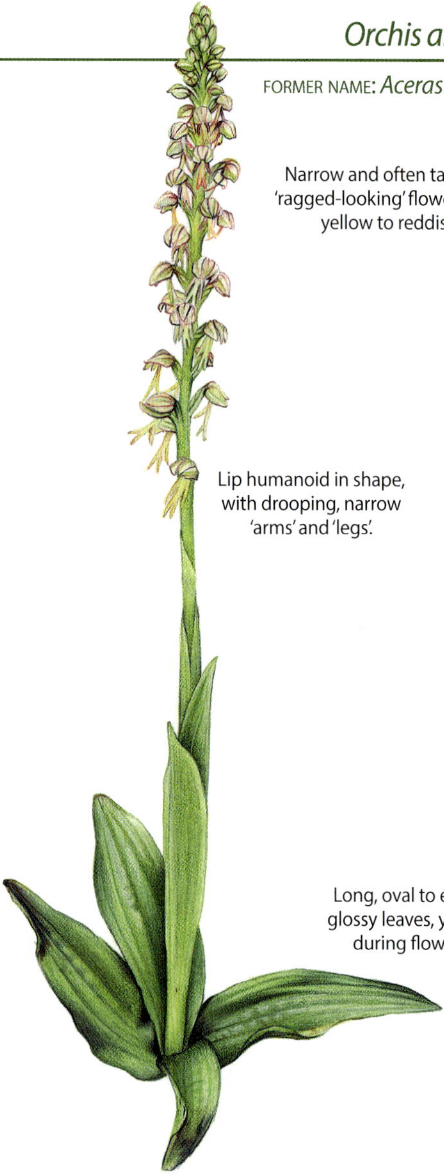
Narrow and often tall, with slightly 'ragged-looking' flower spike of small yellow to reddish flowers.
Lip humanoid in shape, with drooping, narrow 'arms' and 'legs'.
Long, oval to elliptical, glossy leaves, yellowing during flowering.

HABITAT: A specialist of chalk and limestone grassland (including areas of longer grass and scrub) but can occur on roadside verges and in old quarries. Sometimes also in open woodland in Kent, and on stabilized dunes in north Norfolk.

Rather unassuming at first glance, with a long, thin, rusty-red to yellowish spike of small humanoid flowers. It is a speciality of southern England, with strongholds on the North Downs in Kent and Surrey, although there are outlying populations in several counties – as far north as Lincolnshire and as far west as Worcestershire and Somerset. It has been lost from a large proportion of its former range across East Anglia and the southern counties but has recently been rediscovered in Buckinghamshire.

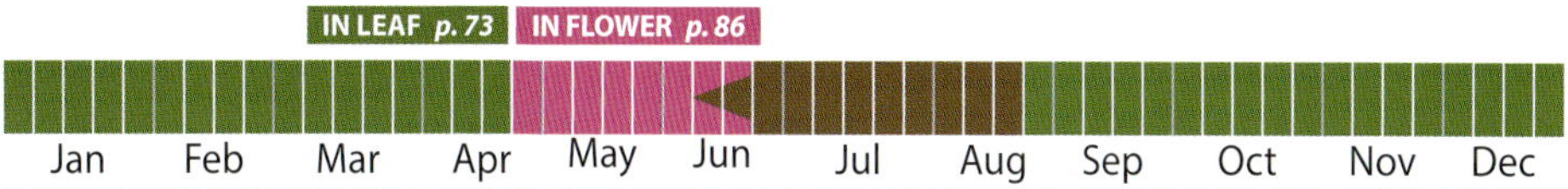
IN LEAF p. 73
IN FLOWER p. 86
Jan
Feb
Mar
Apr
May
Jun
Jul
Aug
Sep
Oct
Nov
Dec

CONFUSION SPECIES: IN FLOWER **None.** IN LEAF Military Orchid (*p. 72*), Lady Orchid (*p. 73*), Green-winged Orchid (*p. 66*), Early-purple Orchid (*p. 71*). **HYBRIDS** × Lady, Military and Monkey Orchids (*p. 270*).

IN BUD *p. 79* | IN HABITAT *p. 46*

VU Monkey Orchid *Orchis simia* G

Extremely rare; 3 sites

up to 40 cm

IN BUD

Inflorescence rounded and densely packed at top of stem.

Top flowers usually open first, giving flat-topped appearance early in season.

Large hood, often with two points at front, with varying amounts of purple flecking on inside and outside.

Lip humanoid in shape, with narrow, wavy 'arms' and 'legs', and tips of varying degrees of pink or purple.

Long, glossy, oval-shaped leaves.

HABITAT: Occurs exclusively on botanically-rich chalk grasslands with relatively short turf, although can survive in denser areas of scrub.

One of Britain's rarest and most charismatic orchids, with its dense, tangled spike of purple-and-white flowers, each with a lip that looks remarkably like a small monkey. Like Military Orchid, this species has been lost from most of its former range and is now extremely rare and confined to three nature reserves: two in Kent; and one in Oxfordshire. Relatively common in mainland Europe, this is a species that could appear at new sites where the habitat conditions are suitable.

IN LEAF p. 72
IN FLOWER p. 91
Jan
Feb
Mar
Apr
May
Jun
Jul
Aug
Sep
Oct
Nov
Dec

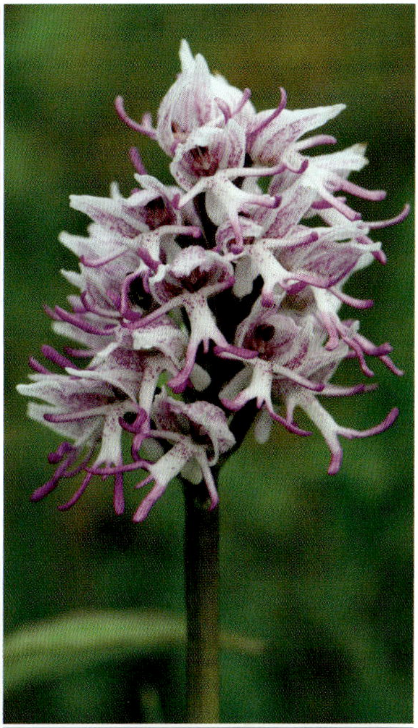

CONFUSION SPECIES: IN FLOWER **Military Orchid** (*p. 232*). IN LEAF Military Orchid (*p. 72*), Lady Orchid (*p. 73*), Lizard Orchid (*p. 67*), Green-winged Orchid (*p. 66*), Early-purple Orchid (*p. 71*).
HYBRIDS × Lady and Man Orchids (*p. 270*), Military Orchid (historical) (*p. 249*).

VU Military Orchid *Orchis militaris* G

Soldier Orchid

Extremely rare; 3 sites

up to 60 cm

IN BUD

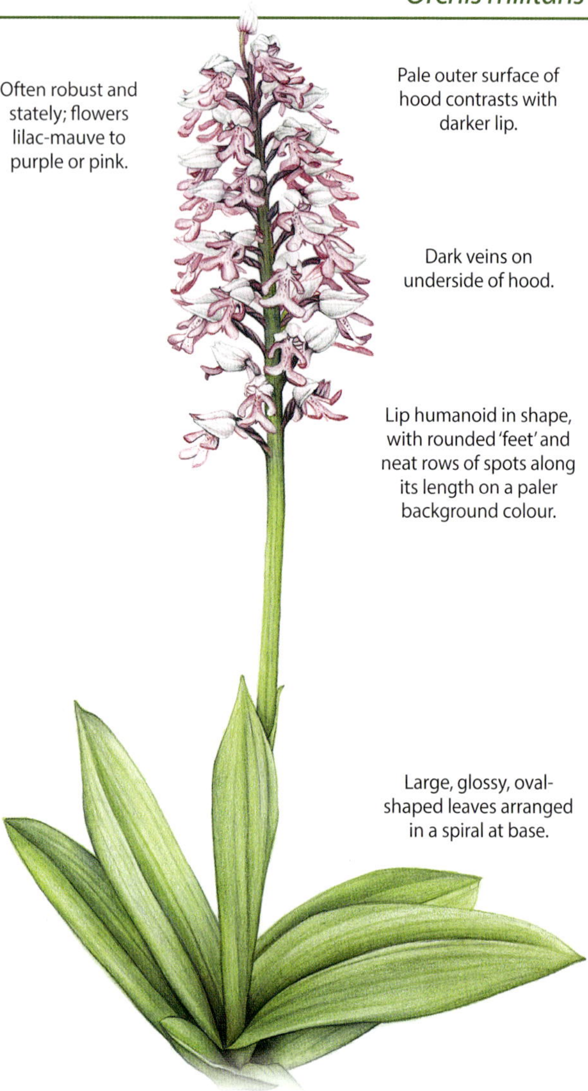

Often robust and stately; flowers lilac-mauve to purple or pink.

Pale outer surface of hood contrasts with darker lip.

Dark veins on underside of hood.

Lip humanoid in shape, with rounded 'feet' and neat rows of spots along its length on a paler background colour.

Large, glossy, oval-shaped leaves arranged in a spiral at base.

HABITAT: Favours sheltered chalk grasslands, scrub and woodland glades, where it can lie dormant for many years should an area become too shaded.

One of Britain's rarest and often most impressive orchids, with its large, pale inflorescence and thick, leathery leaves. The lip is rather humanoid in shape, with characteristic spots along the centre that look like buttons on a soldier's tunic – hence the common name. It is now confined to three nature reserves: two chalk grassland and woodland areas in the Chilterns, and an old chalk pit within a conifer plantation in Suffolk. However, wind-blown seed from continental Europe, where the species is relatively common, could germinate in new locations, as is suspected with a single plant that flowered at a Hertfordshire gravel pit in 2016 and 2019 (but the site was subsequently destroyed). Military Orchid was once relatively common in the Chilterns but declined rapidly during the 19th century.

IN LEAF p. 72
IN FLOWER p. 91
Jan
Feb
Mar
Apr
May
Jun
Jul
Aug
Sep
Oct
Nov
Dec

CONFUSION SPECIES: IN FLOWER **Lady Orchid** (*p. 234*), **Monkey Orchid** (*p. 230*). IN LEAF Monkey Orchid (*p. 72*), Lady Orchid (*p. 73*), Lizard Orchid (*p. 67*), Green-winged Orchid (*p. 66*), Early-purple Orchid (*p. 71*). HYBRIDS × Monkey Orchid (historical) (*p. 249*).

IN BUD *p. 79* | IN HABITAT *p. 46*

VU Lady Orchid *Orchis purpurea*

Local and scarce

up to 100 cm

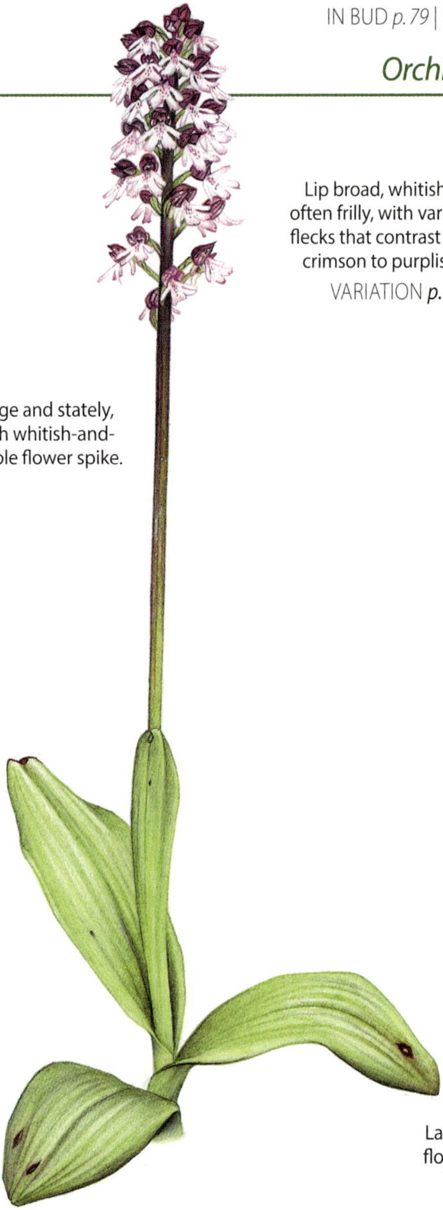

Lip broad, whitish to lilac, often frilly, with variable dark flecks that contrast with dark crimson to purplish hood.

VARIATION *p. 236*.

Large and stately, with whitish-and-purple flower spike.

Large, glossy, floppy leaves.

IN BUD

HABITAT: Principally a species of ancient woodlands on chalk. Thrives best in well-lit glades, coppice, rides and strips of grassland within a woodland complex. Can tolerate quite heavy shade but, conversely, can also grow on open grasslands, although usually never far from trees.

A large and impressive orchid that, although generally rare, is usually obvious at sites where it occurs. Lady Orchid is very variable in appearance, often showing a range of shapes and colours, even within single populations. It could be confused with Military Orchid and Burnt Orchid, but their ranges either do not overlap or their habitat preferences are quite different. Lady Orchid is a speciality of Kent, where there are around 100 sites. Elsewhere it is very rare, with two sites in Oxfordshire (one probably an introduction) and one in Hampshire. A single plant appeared in 2007 at a coastal site in East Sussex, where it still flowers intermittently.

IN LEAF p. 73
IN FLOWER p. 91
Jan
Feb
Mar
Apr
May
Jun
Jul
Aug
Sep
Oct
Nov
Dec

CONFUSION SPECIES: **IN FLOWER** **Burnt Orchid** (although this is much smaller) (*p. 160*).
IN LEAF Monkey Orchid, Military Orchid (both *p. 72*), Lizard Orchid (*p. 67*), Green-winged Orchid (*p. 66*), Early-purple Orchid (*p. 71*). **HYBRIDS** × Man and Monkey Orchids (*p. 270*).

Lady Orchid variation

Lady Orchid is generally unmistakable, being large and stately in appearance, with two-toned purple-and-whitish flowers. It occurs in multiple colour forms, and the lip shape and pattern also vary widely. Some have almost Military or Monkey Orchid-shaped lips, but the spotted pattern and size and structure of the plant always separates this species.

Ophrys orchids

Four species, unique among British and Irish plants, having evolved to mimic the scent, texture and appearance of specific female wasps or bees in order to lure males into attempting to mate with the flower. This causes the pollinia to become 'glued' to the insect, which then transfers it to another flower. **Fly Orchid** is generally scarce; **Early Spider-orchid** has a restricted distribution; and **Late Spider-orchid** is one of Britain's rarest orchids, known from just a handful of sites. However, **Bee Orchid** is self-pollinating and, as a result, is common in many areas.

Shiny silver-blue speculum 'wings', black 'eyes' at base of lip, and thin antennae-like petals.

Fly Orchid
p. 238

Very bee-like flowers: bulbous brownish lip with yellow-edged central pattern, furry 'arms' and hairy greenish or pink petals.

Bee Orchid
p. 242

Flowers have a rounded, furry-edged, brownish lip with silver-blue, 'H'-shaped speculum and lime-green sepals.

Early Spider-orchid
p. 240

Lip deep and roughly square-shaped, reddish-brown with upturned yellow tip.

Late Spider-orchid
p. 244

IN BUD

The two spider-orchid rosettes are identical in appearance, although that of Early Spider-orchid is smaller than that of Late Spider-orchid.

IN LEAF

Typically greyish-green rosettes with a silver 'frosting'; leaves yellow or blackened by flowering time.

IN BUD p. 78 | IN HABITAT p. 50

VU NT Fly Orchid

Ophrys insectifera

Widespread and scarce

up to 50 cm

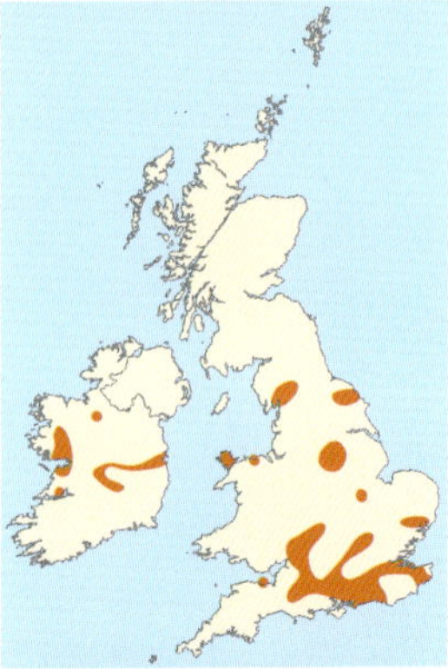

IN BUD

Typically tall, thin green spike, with small, widely spaced dark brown/reddish-lipped flowers and sickly-green sepals.

Very insect-like flowers, with shiny silver-blue speculum 'wings', black 'eyes' at base of lip, and thin antennae-like petals.

Leaves yellowing or blackening by flowering time.

HABITAT: In southern England, Fly Orchid is a specialist of Beech woods and Hazel coppice on chalk and limestone, especially glades and ride edges, but also occurs on open chalk grassland, in quarries and lime pits, and on roadside banks. In western and northern Britain and Ireland, it is more frequent on open limestone grasslands and pavements. It also occurs rarely among rush tussocks in the fens of Anglesey and Ireland.

The long, thin spikes of well-spaced flowers are a challenge to spot. The pale green sepals are typically noticed first, rather than the dark, fly-like petals. When it catches the sun, the shiny blue speculum (which imitates blue sky reflecting on a female wasp's wings) can also be a giveaway. Fly Orchid achieves pollination by luring male Two-girdled *Argogorytes mystaceus* and Farge's *A. fargeii* Digger Wasps to attempt to mate with the flower. Scattered and scarce in Britain, its strongholds are in southern England along the North and South Downs, the Chilterns, Cotswolds and the chalk regions of Hampshire and Wiltshire. Farther north, there are concentrations in the Peak District (Derbyshire), the Morecambe Bay area and Yorkshire as far north as Co. Durham. In Ireland, it is confined to the central and western limestone areas, especially the Burren in Co. Clare.

IN LEAF *p. 75* IN FLOWER *p. 94*

Jan
Feb
Mar
Apr
May
Jun
Jul
Aug
Sep
Oct
Nov
Dec

CONFUSION SPECIES: IN FLOWER **None.** IN LEAF Bee Orchid (*p. 75*), Pyramidal Orchid (*p. 66*).
HYBRIDS × Bee Orchid, Woodcock Orchid (both *p. 272*), Early Spider-orchid (historical) (*p. 249*).

IN BUD p. 78 | IN HABITAT p. 50

LC Early Spider-orchid *Ophrys sphegodes* GB

Locally common

up to 20 (35) cm

IN BUD

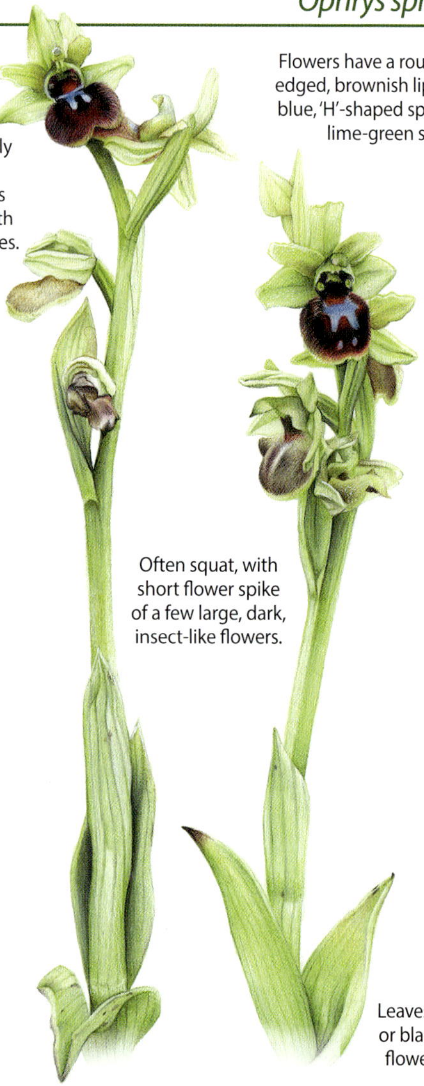
Petals usually greenish (sometimes reddish), with crinkled edges.
Flowers have a rounded, furry-edged, brownish lip with silver-blue, 'H'-shaped speculum and lime-green sepals.
Often squat, with short flower spike of a few large, dark, insect-like flowers.
Leaves yellowing or blackening by flowering time.

HABITAT: A specialist of short turf on chalk and limestone grassland in southern England, especially on the coast. It has been recorded sporadically from quarries, although some of these may be introductions. The species is capable of colonizing newly dumped chalk spoil, one notable example being at Samphire Hoe in East Kent.

Small in stature and surprisingly difficult to spot among the surrounding grass, this orchid is often eventually noticed by its lime-green sepals and blackish lip. It is usually the first orchid to flower in the year, with the earliest plants doing so in late March. Very common in continental Europe but on the edge of its range in England and very rare, although some colonies are large. It is strictly southern and primarily coastal in distribution, with strongholds in Kent, East Sussex and Dorset. There are two colonies on the Isle of Wight and single sites in Surrey (likely an introduction) and Suffolk. It previously occurred in Wiltshire and Gloucestershire, where it was last recorded in 1989 and 1998, respectively.

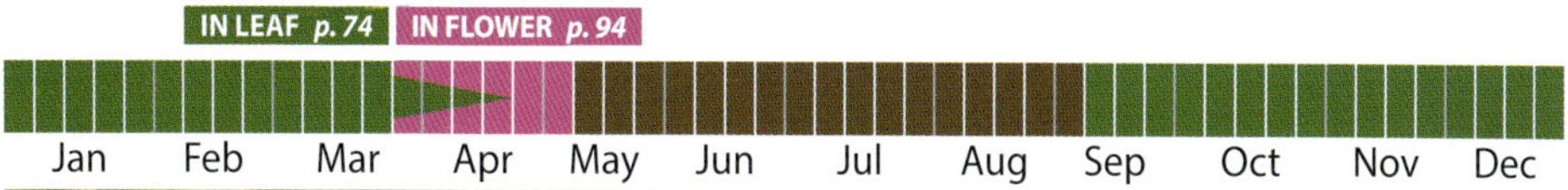
IN LEAF p. 74
IN FLOWER p. 94
Jan
Feb
Mar
Apr
May
Jun
Jul
Aug
Sep
Oct
Nov
Dec

Once pollinated, the flowers turn pale and yellowish; the blue speculum also changes colour.

CONFUSION SPECIES: IN FLOWER **Bee Orchid** (*p. 242*). IN LEAF Bee Orchid, Late Spider-orchid (both *p. 74*), Burnt Orchid (*p. 65*). HYBRIDS × Late Spider-orchid, Fly Orchid (both historical) (*p. 249*).

IN BUD *p. 78* | IN HABITAT *p. 50*

LC LC Bee Orchid *Ophrys apifera* N

Widespread and common

up to 50 cm

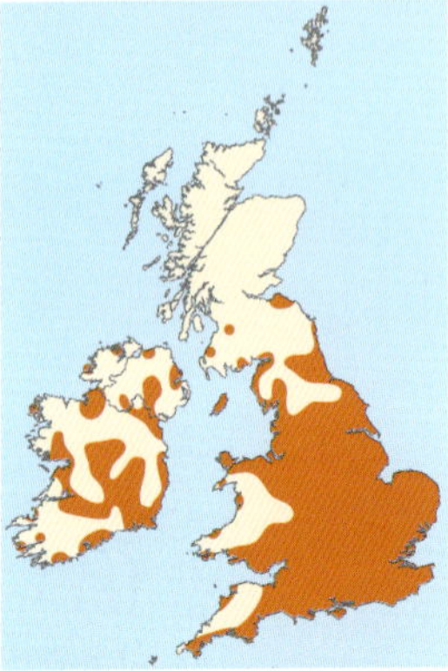

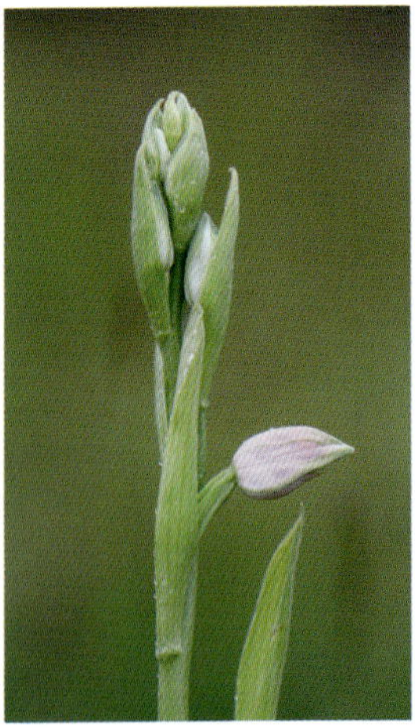

IN BUD

Very bee-like flowers: bulbous brownish lip with yellow-edged central pattern, furry 'arms' and hairy greenish or pink petals.
Yellow appendage under the lip not visible from the front on an open flower.
Often quite tall, with widely spaced, multi-coloured flowers with pink sepals.
Leaves yellowing or blackening by flowering time.

HABITAT: Occurs in a variety of calcareous grasslands – most abundant on wide roadside verges, lawns, sand dunes, landscaped spoil heaps, parks, quarries and gravel pits and, in Ireland, fens. Numbers on chalk and limestone grasslands and in Irish fens tend to be fewer. Bee Orchid, unlike most native orchids, will freely colonize disturbed ground on industrial sites or recently dumped roadside workings.

Truly exotic-looking, yet often occurring in less-than-exotic places, this is the species that often gets people hooked on orchids. The pale to deep pink sepals are usually noticed first. Despite being an insect mimic, in Britain and Ireland Bee Orchid is almost entirely self-pollinated. It is essentially a southern species; most common in southern England and becoming gradually rarer farther north. It is patchily scattered across the whole of Ireland, with most sites in Co. Galway and Co. Clare. It is being increasingly recorded in southern Scotland (where it was first discovered in 2003), reflecting a northward range expansion probably driven by a warming climate.

IN LEAF p. 75
IN FLOWER p. 94
Jan
Feb
Mar
Apr
May
Jun
Jul
Aug
Sep
Oct
Nov
Dec

Side view (RIGHT) showing self-pollination in progress and the backward-pointing yellow appendage not visible from the front (LEFT).

CONFUSION SPECIES: IN FLOWER **Early Spider-orchid** (*p. 240*), **Late Spider-orchid** (*p. 244*).
IN LEAF Early Spider-orchid, Late Spider-orchid (both *p. 74*), Burnt Orchid (*p. 65*).
HYBRIDS × Late Spider-orchid, Fly Orchid (both *p. 272*).

IN BUD *p. 78* | IN HABITAT *p. 50*

VU Late Spider-orchid *Ophrys fuciflora* GB

FORMER NAME: *O. holoserica*

Extremely rare; 6 sites

up to 55 cm

Short flower spike with usually just a few large, multi-coloured 'insect'-like flowers.
Sepals quite rounded, short and pink.
Yellow-edged pattern of varying shape; petals small, triangular and dark pink.
Lip deep and roughly square-shaped, reddish-brown.
Yellow appendage on tip of open flower lip points forwards.
Leaves yellowing or blackening by flowering time.

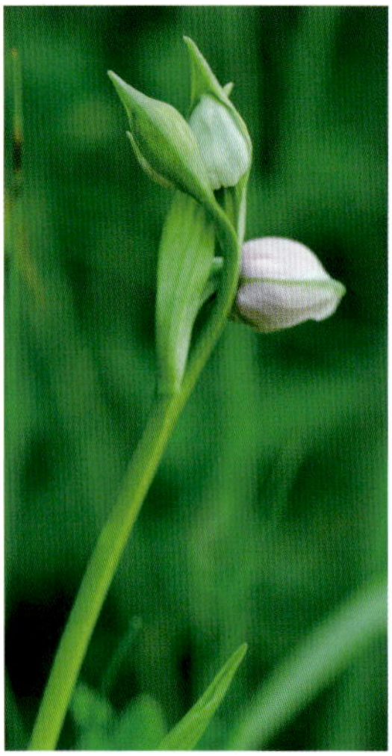

IN BUD

HABITAT: Restricted to botanically-rich, south-facing chalk grasslands.

The rarest of the *Ophrys* species to occur in Britain and Ireland, with only a handful of colonies on the chalk grasslands of Kent. It is on the very edge of its European range in Britain and has always been rare here. The large, often square-shaped lip with small yellow, forward-pointing, appendage at the tip separates it from Bee Orchid, with which it can co-occur. Hybrids with Bee Orchid are regular and can be difficult to separate from 'pure' Late Spider-orchids. To see this species requires a visit to one of its several sites on the downs between Folkestone and Wye in Kent, where plants are often fenced off or caged to protect them from predation and trampling.

IN LEAF p. 74
IN FLOWER p. 94
Jan
Feb
Mar
Apr
May
Jun
Jul
Aug
Sep
Oct
Nov
Dec

CONFUSION SPECIES: IN FLOWER **Bee Orchid** (*p.* *242*). IN LEAF Bee Orchid, Early Spider-orchid (both *p.* *74*), Burnt Orchid (*p.* *65*). HYBRIDS × Bee Orchid (*p.* *272*), Early Spider-orchid (historical) (*p.* *249*).

Ophrys variation

Ophrys are notoriously variable in appearance, particularly in terms of lip shape and pattern. However, misidentification at the species level is only possible in small areas of southern England where Bee Orchid co-occurs with the similar-looking Early Spider- and Late Spider-orchids. In these specific situations, flowering time, lip shape and petal colour can quickly provide a positive identification. Where a plant appears to show characteristics or more than one species, consider the hybrid section (p. *272*).

Bee Orchid formae and variation

Bee Orchid routinely self-pollinates, bringing about genetic mutations in the form of unusual colour patterns and lip shapes that would be much rarer if genes were shared via cross-pollination. These mutations appear to occur at random, usually as a few individuals within a population of the typical form. Four of these forms appear to be especially consistent throughout Britain and Ireland (also continental Europe) and are therefore retained here as formae. Other names, *e.g. 'chlorantha'*, *'flavescens'* and *'fulvofusca'*, are sometimes applied to plants with particular features, but these forms appear to simply represent part of the wide colour spectrum for the species and so are not recognized here (see *Orchid taxonomy pp. 18–20*). One recently named form – *'cambrensis'* (*bottom*) – is not recognized here as the lip pattern differences between it and the nominate form are minor, and intermediates occur. It has been recorded at only three sites and is not recognized by European authorities.

f. *belgarum*

f. *bicolor*

f. *trollii* ('Wasp Orchid')

'sepaloid' form

f. *belgarum* – widespread; lip more oval-shaped than the nominate form with much-reduced side lobes; lip pattern very simple with no speculum and a yellow band meeting across the centre of the lip. The lower half of the lip is often slightly twisted sideways.

f. *bicolor* – rare; lip pattern replaced by a greenish-yellow basal half and reddish-brown lower half.

f. *trollii* – widespread and one of the most common forms; lip very malformed, long and almost triangular, with a variably blotchy yellow-and-brown pattern that lacks a clear speculum. Often confused with a typical Bee Orchid that is not fully open, with the lip yet to unfurl (*right*). NB this form was, for some time, considered as a separate species – 'Wasp Orchid'.

A 'normal' Bee Orchid with its lip not yet fully unfurled can appear to be a variant.

'Sepaloid' forms – rare; forms with large, sepal-like upper petals have been given several names such as *'badensis'*, *'botteronii'* and *'friburgensis'*. The differences between these forms are minor, with slight variations in lip pattern and shape that are not clearly defined; they are therefore referred to collectively in this book.

Bee Orchid variations

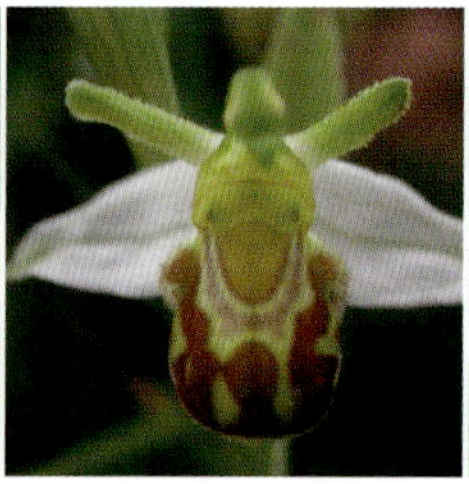

'cambrensis'

Fly Orchid variations
Variants encountered may differ considerably in colour and markings, but the overall form is still distinguishable as a Fly Orchid. Pinkish sepals may indicate a × Bee Orchid hybrid (*p. 272*).

Late Spider-orchid variations
Variable in shape and markings; the forward-pointing appendage at the tip of a squarish (not rounded) lip is diagnostic; the only confusion being hybrids with Bee Orchid.

Early Spider-orchid variations
Variable in lip shape, although the lack of any appendage at the lip tip, usually two-pronged blue speculum and pale green sepals should enable specific identification.

Orchid hybrids

Orchids are well known for hybridizing. Tropical species have been deliberately 'crossed' in cultivation for hundreds of years to create new and unusual forms. However, hybridization is also a natural process and an important driver of evolution that can be common among certain genera (intrageneric hybrids), such as the spotted-orchids and marsh-orchids (*Dactylorhiza*). Members of this group are genetically similar, often grow in mixed-species groups, and also share a wide range of pollinators. This combination of factors hugely increases the chance of cross-fertilization between species, to the extent that hybrids can usually be expected wherever more than one *Dactylorhiza* species occurs together.

Conversely, hybrids between different genera (intergeneric hybrids) are much less common because the wider genetic divergence between them, and a typically much-reduced range of pollinators in common, reduces the chances of successful cross-fertilization significantly. Nonetheless, some intrageneric hybrids have been recorded.

Typically, hybrids are a half-way house between the parent species, sharing characteristics of both. Where the parent species are visually very different, hybrid plants can be easy to spot – for example, the hybrid between Heath Fragrant-orchid and Small-white Orchid (*p. 250*). On the other hand, many *Dactylorhiza* hybrids can be more challenging, especially where the parent species are already visually very similar. In these instances, and without genetic testing to confirm, a 'most likely' approach, based on the surrounding species present, is best applied. For instance, when in a large, mixed colony of Early Marsh-orchids and Southern Marsh-orchids, individuals that show characteristics that are neither one species nor the other, but are intermediate between the two, are most likely to be hybrids.

It must be stressed, however, that in some cases hybrids can be present in colonies where only one of the parents appears to be present. This could be for a number of reasons: wind-blown seed from nearby, one of the parents having died out or simply not being present at the site in that particular season, perhaps due to low numbers.

In this section, the aim has been to show as many hybrid combinations as possible. In some instances, *e.g.* Chalk Fragrant-orchid × Common Spotted-orchid – where parent species are particularly variable and, as a result, the hybrids are similarly variable – several examples are shown.

It is important to note that hybrid combinations will not always look exactly like the ones shown here; those included should instead be used as a guide for spotting intermediate plants that could represent hybrids.

Lady × Monkey Orchid hybrids (*p. 270*)

Historical and dubious records

There are a number of hybrids that have not been recorded in Britain and Ireland for several decades, or even centuries. This is either because the parent species are now very rare and/or no longer occur together, or because the parent species are not closely related – hybridization therefore being an incredibly rare event. For hybrids that are not closely related, misidentification cannot be discounted, particularly where there is a paucity of evidence to support the identification. Nonetheless, all are included here for completeness.

× *Pseudanthera breadalbanensis* [**Small-white Orchid** (*p. 156*) × **Greater Butterfly-orchid** (*p. 172*)]
Recorded in 1980 in Roxburghshire, when four plants were found among a mixed colony of both parent species. The discovery was reported in *Watsonia* (McKean, 1982) and includes two photographs and line drawings. It appears, when compared to examples of plants from Continental Europe, that the plants actually represent mutant examples of Greater Butterfly-orchid. This hybrid combination would be highly unlikely, both morphologically and genetically.

× *Gymnanacamptis anacamptis* [**Chalk Fragrant-orchid** (*p. 176*) × **Pyramidal Orchid** (*p. 218*)]
One record from NW Scotland in 1982.

Dactylorhiza* × *conigerum [**Frog Orchid** (*p. 188*) × **Heath Spotted-orchid** (*p. 192*)]
One recent record from Hampshire in 1999 of this unlikely combination.

× *Anacamptorchis morioides* [**Early-purple Orchid** (*p. 226*) × **Green-winged Orchid** (*p. 220*)]
There are two records of this hybrid, from Cumbria and Anglesey, both in 1974. Neither record has much supporting evidence, although they were confirmed by qualified authorities at the time. However, an image of the Cumbrian plant (which has been seen by the authors) does not seem to show any features suggestive of Green-winged Orchid parentage. Although both species are relatively common and sometimes occur together, it is notable that this hybrid has not been seen more regularly. It is also noteworthy that both records are from a time when Green-winged and Early-purple Orchids were included in the *Orchis* genus. Green-winged Orchid is now known to be only a distant relative of the *Orchis* species. This means that hybridization between the two species is far less likely than previously thought. These records are therefore treated with extreme caution.

Orchis* × *beyrichii [**Military Orchid** (*p. 232*) × **Monkey Orchid** (*p. 230*)]
This hybrid was recorded several times in the Chilterns during the 1800s when both parent species regularly co-occurred. Since then, Military Orchid and Monkey Orchid have become extremely rare and no longer occur together, meaning the reappearance of this hybrid is extremely unlikely.

Ophrys* × *hybrida [**Fly Orchid** (*p. 238*) × **Early Spider-orchid** (*p. 240*)]
Reliably recorded a handful of times on the chalk downlands of East Kent in the early 20th century and last recorded by Francis Rose in 1957. This hybrid could reappear again as both parents occasionally occur together and flower at the same time, even though they typically attract different pollinators. However, this hybrid has been reported widely from across continental Europe.

Ophrys* × *obscura [**Early Spider-orchid** (*p. 240*) × **Late Spider-orchid** (*p. 244*)]
Recorded sporadically during the 19th and 20th centuries from the chalk downlands of East Kent and last recorded in 1984 by Derek Turner Ettlinger. However, it may be that some records of this hybrid could represent forms of Late Spider-orchid, which is notoriously variable in appearance (see *Ophrys variation, p. 246*). Also, the flowering periods of both species barely overlap, and so there is only a very short window for cross-fertilization to take place. Nonetheless, since this hybrid has been reported widely across continental Europe, both species are evidently genetically compatible.

All examples of the unnamed hybrid between Southern and Pugsley's Marsh-orchids are now determined as relating to the Southern Marsh-orchid var. *schoenophila*. Two historical Lesser Butterfly-orchid hybrids (× Heath Fragrant-orchid and × Heath Spotted-orchid) have been re-identified as not being hybrids, but rather abnormal variants, and two reported Frog Orchid hybrids (× Early Marsh-orchid and × Southern Marsh-orchid) have never been confirmed and are excluded.

Cephalanthera helleborine hybrids

Cephalanthera* × *schulzei [**White Helleborine** (*p. 106*) × **Sword-leaved Helleborine** (*p. 108*)]

Description: Often taller than either parent species with **white, widely opening flowers** most like Sword-leaved Helleborine but **with large flower bracts** like those of White Helleborine. The leaves are noticeably broader, stouter and fewer in number than those of Sword-leaved Helleborine, more akin to White Helleborine. **Range and status:** Very rare. Recorded at only three sites: one well-known site in Hampshire and two in West Sussex.

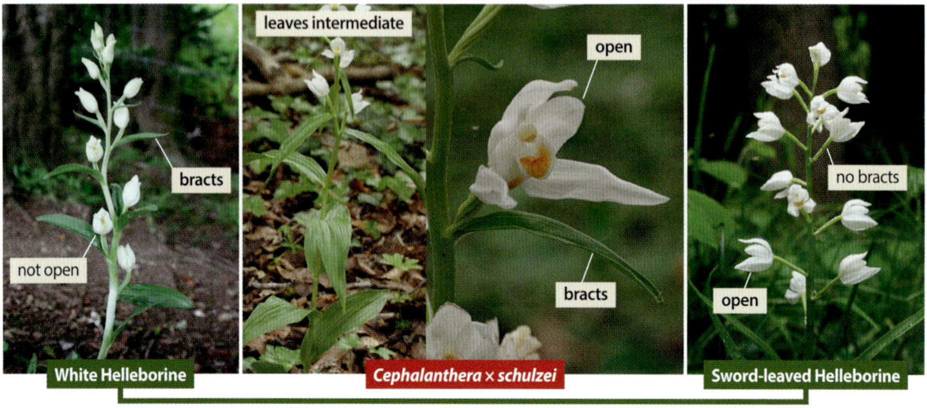
bracts
not open
leaves intermediate
open
bracts
no bracts
open
White Helleborine
Cephalanthera × *schulzei*
Sword-leaved Helleborine

Epipactis helleborine hybrids

Hybrids within the *Epipactis* genus are notoriously difficult to identify. The combination of flower coloration, pollination mechanism and leaf shape, structure and colour are the key elements to consider.

Epipactis* × *schmalhausenii [**Broad-leaved Helleborine** (*p. 126*) × **Dark-red Helleborine** (*p. 122*)]

Description: A difficult hybrid to identify as both parent species can be very variable. Clear hybrids have **broad, oval-shaped leaves that sometimes grow around the stem instead of in two rows, and large leafy bracts** like those of Broad-leaved Helleborine but with **flowers showing clear 'frilly' bosses on the lip** like those of Dark-red Helleborine. The flower colour is often a pale reddish-pink – midway between typical Dark-red Helleborine and Broad-leaved Helleborine. **Range and status:** Very rare. Recorded at a handful of limestone pavement sites in the Morecambe Bay area of Lancashire and Cumbria, where it is most prevalent at Hutton Roof Crags. There is also a single record from Bishop Middleham Quarry in County Durham.

Epipactis* × *schulzei [**Broad-leaved Helleborine** (*p. 126*) × **Violet Helleborine** (*p. 124*)]

Description: Often a difficult hybrid to identify conclusively and is perhaps more variable than previously thought. Clear hybrids have **broad, oval-shaped leaves** like those of Broad-leaved Helleborine, with the **characteristic dull purplish wash to the stem and leaves** of Violet Helleborine. **The flowers are most like Violet Helleborine in shape and structure**, opening widely with (initially) a pale greenish coloration and contrastingly dark green ovaries. However, **the colour influence of Broad-leaved Helleborine is often noticeable** with a dark greenish colouring to the bosses and a gradual increase in pinkish tones in the upper petals as the flowers age – features that are not present in typical Violet Helleborine. **Range and status:** Rare. Recorded at several sites across southern England, including Hampshire, Warwickshire and Somerset, although it is likely to be under-recorded. The authors have seen plants from mixed colonies in Oxfordshire, West Sussex and Worcestershire that represent strong candidates for this hybrid, but these are yet to be confirmed. However, DNA analysis has been undertaken on plants from the Somerset site, confirming their identity as hybrids.

large bracts
oval leaves
Broad-leaved Helleborine

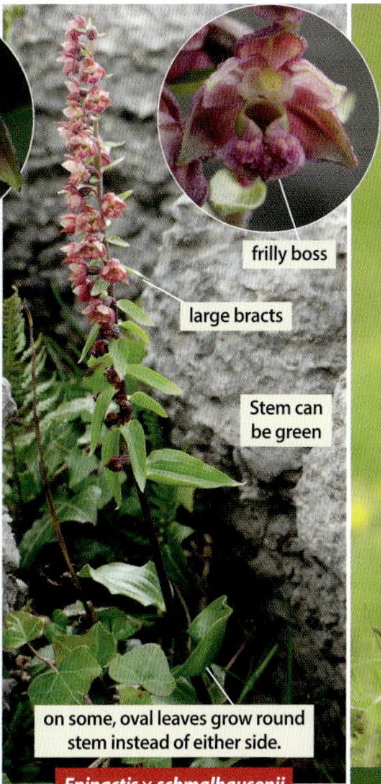
frilly boss
large bracts
Stem can be green
on some, oval leaves grow round stem instead of either side.
Epipactis × schmalhausenii

small bracts
Dark-red Helleborine

pinkish
green
Broad-leaved Helleborine

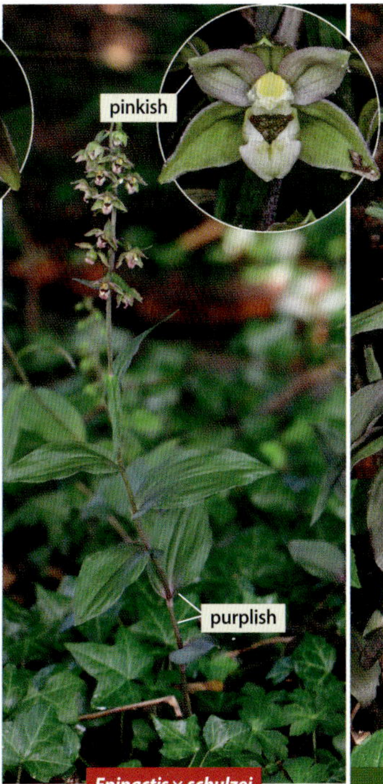
pinkish
purplish
Epipactis × schulzei

green
purplish
Violet Helleborine

UNNAMED [Broad-leaved Helleborine (*p. 126*) **× Dune Helleborine** (*p. 130*)**]**

Description: Intermediate between both parents, for example showing Dune Helleborine-like flowers and Broad-leaved Helleborine leaf structure. Close similarity in appearance makes proving a hybrid difficult without DNA analysis. **Range and status:** No confirmed records although intermediate plants are seen annually within a large mixed colony of both parent species at Alyn Waters Country Park near Wrexham (Flintshire) that almost certainly represent this hybrid (pictured). Based on how frequently Dune Helleborine is misidentified and the broad overlap in distribution of both parent species, this hybrid is probably under-recorded.

Broad-leaved

Broad-leaved × Dune

Dune Helleborine

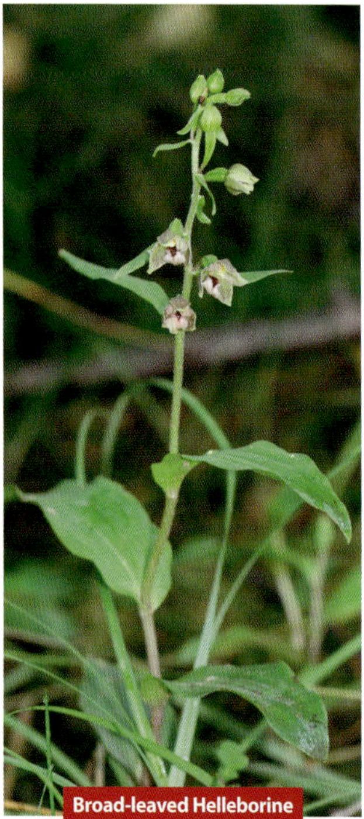
Broad-leaved Helleborine × Dune Helleborine

UNNAMED [Broad-leaved Helleborine (*p. 126*) **× Green-flowered Helleborine** (*p. 136*)**]**

Description: Intermediate between both parents – a very subtle hybrid – but any apparent Green-flowered Helleborine with viscidia ('glue-blobs') and larger-than-usual leaves should be examined closely, especially if both parents are present. Features of the ovaries, such as the presence/absence of 'hairs' and the basal colour, as well as leaf edge characteristics (see *p. 115*), should all be examined. **Range and status:** No confirmed records although a probable single example of this hybrid was found within a mixed colony of both parent species in Hampshire in 2010 (pictured); this had intermediate leaves, drooping green flowers as Green-flowered Helleborine, and pink-tinged sepals and a slightly hairy ovary with a pinkish base as in Broad-leaved Helleborine. Both species regularly occur together, suggesting this hybrid is probably under-recorded.

Broad-leaved

Broad-leaved × Green-flowered

Green-flowered

Broad-leaved Helleborine × Green-flowered Helleborine

Epipactis* × *stephensonii
[Broad-leaved Helleborine (*p. 126*)
× Narrow-lipped Helleborine (*p. 134*)**]**

Description: Superficially most similar to Narrow-lipped Helleborine, being **an entirely greenish plant with alternately ranked leaves** (spiral in Broad-leaved Helleborine) **and a rather lax flower spike, but with flowers that have a clearly functioning 'glue-blob' (viscidium) and a more heart-shaped lip** than typical Narrow-lipped Helleborine. **Range and status:** Very rare. Recorded once from a Beech wood near Marlow (Buckinghamshire) in 1984. However, a much-debated colony of plants from roadside banks near Princes Risborough (Buckinghamshire) where both parent species co-occur would seem to be strong candidates for this hybrid (pictured). These plants show clear characteristics of both species but have long been confused with various European taxa, or anomalous Narrow-lipped Helleborines. Similar plants have also been seen at Warburg NNR in Oxfordshire, suggesting this hybrid is probably under-recorded.

Broad-leaved

Broad-leaved × Narrow-lipped

Narrow-lipped

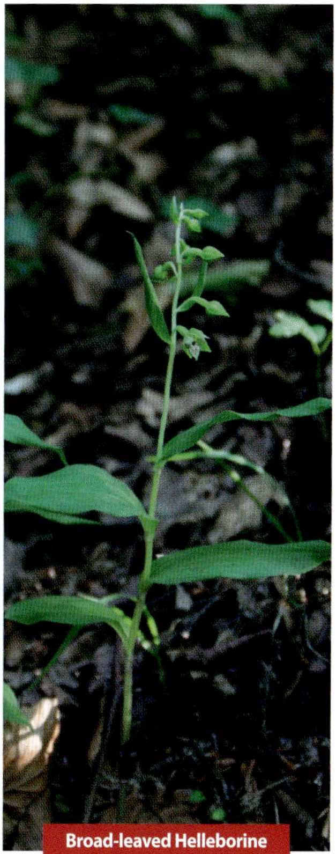

Broad-leaved Helleborine × Narrow-lipped Helleborine

Butterfly-orchid hybrids – see also *p. 248*

Platanthera* × *hybrida **[Greater Butterfly-orchid** (*p. 172*) **× Lesser Butterfly-orchid** (*p. 173*)**]**

Greater Butterfly-orchid | Hybrid butterfly-orchid | Lesser Butterfly-orchid

Description: A subtle intermediate between Greater Butterfly and Lesser Butterfly-orchids with **pollinia that are slightly angled** but not nearly as widely spaced as Greater Butterfly-orchid. **Range and status:** Rare. Recorded widely across England, Wales and Scotland, from Devon to the Isle of Skye, but probably under-recorded. Usually occurs as single plants in mixed colonies; significant populations showing features of this hybrid are known in the Cotswolds (Glos.), but since these usually occur at sites where only one parent is present they pose something of a conundrum.

spaced +
angled

Greater Butterfly-orchid

spaced +
slightly
angled

Platanthera × *hybrida*

little
space +
parallel

Lesser Butterfly-orchid

Intergeneric *Gymnadenia* (fragrant-orchid) hybrids – see also *pp. 249, 260*

The recent recognition of the fragrant-orchids as three species has resulted in some confusion over records of hybrids as, prior to the taxonomic change, records were assigned to the single species and, on occasion, its subspecies/varieties.

Fragrant-orchid × *Dactylorhiza* orchid hybrids

Suspected fragrant-orchid hybrids can be distinguished by the obviously long spur and sweet scent to the flowers, combined with features not present in fragrant-orchids such as leaf and lip markings. Hybrids with spotted-orchids will typically have spotted leaves.

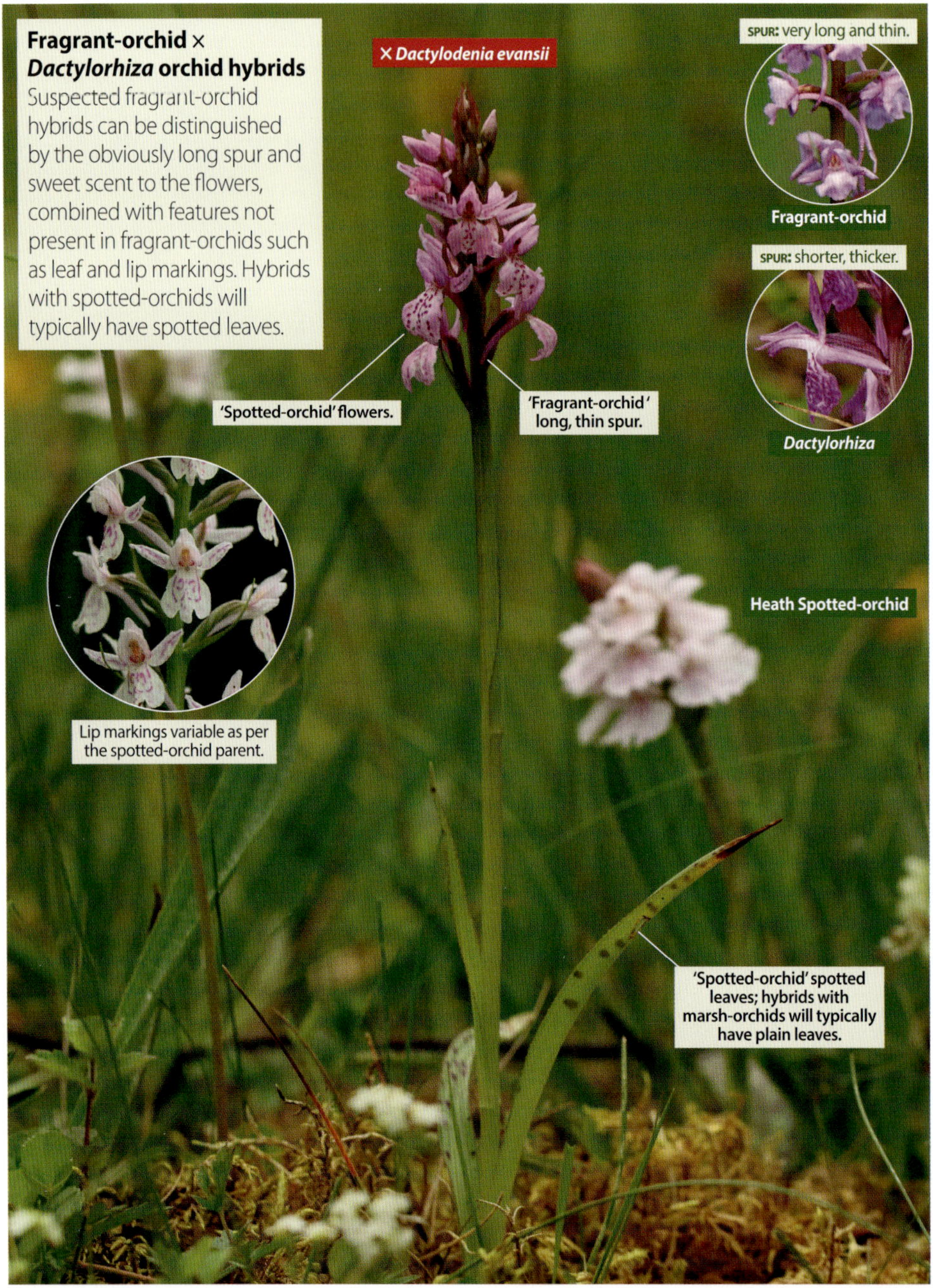

× *Dactylodenia evansii*
SPUR: very long and thin.
Fragrant-orchid
SPUR: shorter, thicker.
Dactylorhiza
'Spotted-orchid' flowers.
'Fragrant-orchid' long, thin spur.
Lip markings variable as per the spotted-orchid parent.
Heath Spotted-orchid
'Spotted-orchid' spotted leaves; hybrids with marsh-orchids will typically have plain leaves.

Heath Fragrant-orchid

× *Dactylodenia evansii*

Heath Spotted-orchid

HYBRIDS WITH SPOTTED-ORCHIDS

Description: Very variable but usually fairly obvious hybrids among mixed colonies of the parent species. Look superficially **like a spotted-orchid but with a narrow spike**. Closer inspection should reveal both a **light, sweet scent and a long spur** inherited from the fragrant-orchid parent.

× *Dactylodenia evansii* [**Heath Spotted-orchid** (*p. 192*) × **Heath Fragrant-orchid** (*p. 176*)]

Range and status: Scarce. Recorded very widely across Britain and Ireland, with a concentration of records in Northern England and Scotland.

× *Dactylodenia legrandiana* [**Heath Spotted-orchid** (*p. 192*) × **Chalk Fragrant-orchid** (*p. 176*)]

NOT ILLUSTRATED

Range and status: No confirmed recent records. Historical hybrid records may involve Chalk Fragrant-orchid, although the vast majority are likely to involve Heath Fragrant-orchid on account of the very different habitat requirements between these two fragrant-orchid species and the fact that Heath Fragrant-orchid is the species that most regularly co-occurs with Heath Spotted-orchid.

× *Dactylodenia st-quintinii* [**Common Spotted-orchid** (*p. 190*) × **Heath Fragrant-orchid** (*p. 176*)]

ILLUSTRATED ON *p. 256*

Range and status: Recorded widely across Britain and Ireland although genuine records are confused because '× *D. st-quintinii*' was the name used when the fragrant-orchids were considered to be a single species. However, it would seem practical to assume that virtually all records from limestone and chalk, wet meadows and fens are highly likely to involve Chalk and Marsh Fragrant-orchids and that most records from Northern England and Scotland are probably of this hybrid.

× *Dactylodenia heinzeliana* [**Common Spotted-orchid** (*p. 190*) × **Chalk Fragrant-orchid** (*p. 176*)]

ILLUSTRATED ON *p. 256*

Range and status: Uncommon. Recorded widely across the Britain and Ireland, with a concentration of records in southern England.

UNNAMED [**Common Spotted-orchid** (*p. 190*) × **Marsh Fragrant-orchid** (*p. 177*)] ILLUSTRATED ON *p. 256*

Range and status: Very rare. There are single records from Nottinghamshire, Denbighshire, Yorkshire, Cumbria, Sutherland and Co. Wicklow, with older records in Hampshire and Suffolk, although it is probably under-recorded. There are almost certainly several records of this hybrid that pre-date the reclassification of fragrant-orchids into three separate species that were labelled as '× *D. st-quintinii*'.

Heath Fragrant-orchid

× *Dactylodenia st-quintinii*

Common Spotted-orchid

Chalk Fragrant-orchid

lip variations

× *Dactylodenia heinzeliana*

Common Spotted-orchid

Marsh Fragrant-orchid

long, thin spur

Common Spotted-orchid × Marsh Fragrant-orchid

Common Spotted-orchid

Marsh Fragrant-orchid | × *Dactylodenia ettlingeriana* | Southern Marsh-orchid

long, thin spur
shorter, thicker spur

Heath Fragrant-orchid | × *Dactylodenia lacerta* | Southern Marsh-orchid

Heath Fragrant-orchid | Early Marsh-orchid × Heath Fragrant-orchid | Early Marsh-orchid

HYBRIDS WITH MARSH-ORCHIDS

Description: Look like a **narrow-spiked, small-flowered marsh-orchid but with a much longer spur**. Closer inspection should reveal both a **light, sweet scent and long spur** inherited from the fragrant-orchid parent.

× *Dactylodenia ettlingeriana* [**Southern Marsh-orchid** (*p. 198*) × **Marsh Fragrant-orchid** (*p. 177*)]

ILLUSTRATED ON *p. 257*

Range and status: Very rare. Regularly occurs at Kenfig Dunes in South Wales, with older records in Hampshire, Somerset and West Sussex.

× *Dactylodenia lacerta* [**Southern Marsh-orchid** (*p. 198*) × **Heath Fragrant-orchid** (*p. 176*)]

ILLUSTRATED ON *p. 257*

Range and status: Recorded once on the Lizard peninsula in Cornwall (2016) but not since. Because their usual habitat preferences are different there are very few locations where both species occur together. In addition, Heath Fragrant-orchid is generally rare throughout the core range of Southern Marsh-orchid.

× *Dactylodenia wintoni* [**Southern Marsh-orchid** (*p. 198*) × **Chalk Fragrant-orchid** (*p. 176*)]

NOT ILLUSTRATED

Range and status: Previously recorded from one or two localities in southern England, but not reliably recorded for several decades. The two parent species rarely co-occur as their habitat preferences are generally very different. However, Southern Marsh-orchid may persist for short periods on chalk grassland, within colonies of Chalk Fragrant-orchid, and therefore hybridization is feasible.

UNNAMED [**Early Marsh-orchid** (*p. 202*) × **Heath Fragrant-orchid** (*p. 176*)] ILLUSTRATED ON *p. 257*

Range and status: Very rare. Known from one site in Cumbria and one on the Isle of Skye, with older records from the Cairngorms and the Lizard peninsula in Cornwall. The purple-flowered variety of Early Marsh-orchid (var. *pulchella*) is one of the parents in all cases.

UNNAMED [**Northern Marsh-orchid** (*p. 196*) × **Marsh Fragrant-orchid** (*p. 177*)]

Range and status: Recorded only twice: in Cumbria (where not seen since 2003); and at Kenfig Dunes in South Wales in 2020. This hybrid is probably under-recorded as both parent species regularly occur together in northern Britain and Ireland.

× *Dactylodenia varia* [**Northern Marsh-orchid** (*p. 196*) × **Heath Fragrant-orchid** (*p. 176*)]

Description: Rare. Recorded widely across northern Britain, with a cluster of records in Cumbria, two in Yorkshire and single records each in Ayrshire, Perthshire and Banffshire. There is a scattering of older records across western Scotland and one near Belfast.

UNNAMED [**Pugsley's Marsh-orchid** (*p. 206*) × **Heath Fragrant-orchid** (*p. 176*)]

Range and status: Very rare. Known from only two sites in Cumbria; probably under-recorded.

HYBRIDS WITH FROG ORCHID

× *Dactylodenia jacksonii* [**Frog Orchid** (*p. 188*) × **Chalk Fragrant-orchid** (*p. 176*)] NOT ILLUSTRATED

Description: Distinctive and fairly obvious in the field among mixed colonies of the parents. The **lip is long** like Frog Orchid but a **much richer pinkish colour with a long spur** inherited from the Chalk Fragrant-orchid parent. **Range and status:** Very rare. Last recorded in 2000 in Hampshire, from where two sites were previously known, with an older record in Wiltshire. Both parents regularly occur together so this hybrid is likely to be under-recorded and should be looked for in suitable locations.

Marsh Fragrant-orchid

long,
thin
spur
Northern Marsh-orchid × Marsh Fragrant-orchid

shorter,
thicker
spur
Northern Marsh-orchid

Heath Fragrant-orchid

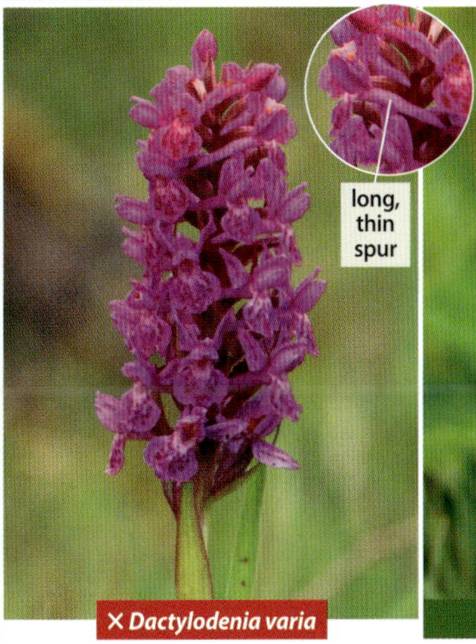
long,
thin
spur
× *Dactylodenia varia*

shorter,
thicker
spur
Northern Marsh-orchid

Heath Fragrant-orchid

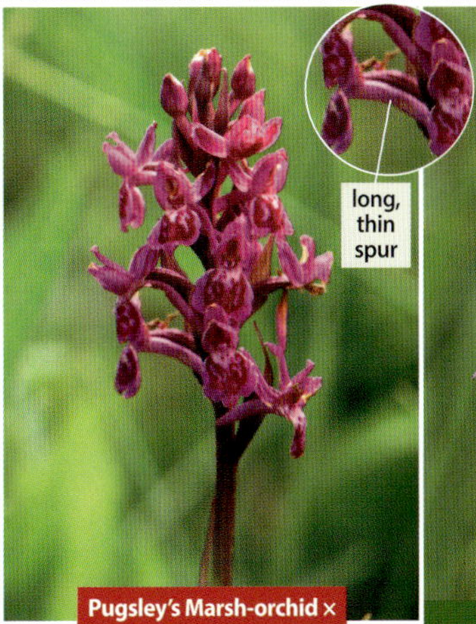
long,
thin
spur
Pugsley's Marsh-orchid × Heath Fragrant-orchid

shorter,
thicker
spur
Pugsley's Marsh-orchid

Small-white Orchid hybrids – see also *p. 249*

UNNAMED [**Small-white Orchid** (*p. 156*) × **Heath Fragrant-orchid** (*p. 176*)]

Description: A distinctive hybrid that is rather delicate, with **small flowers like Small-white Orchid** but with a **characteristic pinkish coloration and greenish hue to the base of the lip**. The **spurs are long and curved like fragrant-orchids** (Small-white Orchid has very short spurs). The flowers are likely to be scented. **Range and status:** Very rare. Single plants have been recorded from Fifeshire, East Inverness-shire and Cumbria, where Heath Fragrant-orchid is the parent in all instances.

short spur

Small-white Orchid

FLOWERS: intermediate
long spur

Small-white Orchid × Heath Fragrant-orchid

long spur

Heath Fragrant-orchid

× *Pseudorhiza bruniana* [**Small-white Orchid** (*p. 156*) × **Heath Spotted-orchid** (*p. 192*)]

Description: Similar in stature to Small-white Orchid but more squat. The **flowers are very small, like Small-white Orchid, but with a larger lip marked with dashes and spots** inherited from the Heath Spotted-orchid parent. **Range and status:** Very rare. Recorded most recently from one site in the Cairngorms (east Inverness-shire), where both parents are abundant, but previously also recorded at single sites on the Orkneys and the Isle of Skye.

unmarked

Small-white Orchid

FLOWERS: intermediate
markings

× *Pseudadenia bruniana*

markings

Heath Spotted-orchid

***Dactylorhiza* hybrids** – see also *pp. 249, 254, 260*

Hybrids between species within the *Dactylorhiza* genus can be difficult to identify, as several of the parent species are already very similar in appearance to each other, and also highly variable. For example, the hybrid between Northern Marsh-orchid and Southern Marsh-orchid is probably fairly common where the two species co-occur but is near impossible to identify. Conversely, hybrids involving Frog Orchid are much more obvious on account of its very different appearance to others in the genus.

Most of the *Dactylorhiza* in Britain and Ireland are closely related genetically, indicating a relatively recent evolutionary history. As a result, they hybridize freely, creating plants that reflect the genetic makeup of two or more parent species. These hybrids are fertile, which means that they are able to '**back-cross**' with each other, or with the original parent species. Over time, successive crossings can then lead to a 'hybrid swarm' that consists of the parent species, hybrids of those, plus hybrids between parent and hybrids, and even plants with two hybrids as their parents! This creates a truly mixed-looking colony that typically contains plants with colours extending to both extremes, and all shades in between, growing together in the same area. Equally, hybrid swarms can stabilize over many years to form populations of similar-looking plants, that, if sufficiently isolated from their original parents, can eventually evolve into new species. 'Hybrid vigour' occurs when two species produce a hybrid that is much larger than either. Size is one clue to a hybrid, but many are the same size as their parents, so this often-quoted feature, while helpful, is of limited use.

It is important to note that because of variability within a single species, such as Heath Spotted-orchid, hybrids are of similarly variable appearance. For hybrids involving one or more highly variable parent, an expanded selection of hybrid forms is included here, but to minimize confusion only first-generation hybrids are shown – *i.e.* those that are the offspring of two pure parent species, rather than 'back-crossed' examples. First-generation hybrids can be obvious where they occur with both parent species, being intermediate in colour, size, flower morphology and markings. However, these features become less obvious in more complex instances over multiple generations involving offspring of pure/hybrid parents.

A *Dactylorhiza* hybrid swarm typically contains a bewildering range of plant colours, sizes and markings that are often subtle and form a continuum between the parent species.

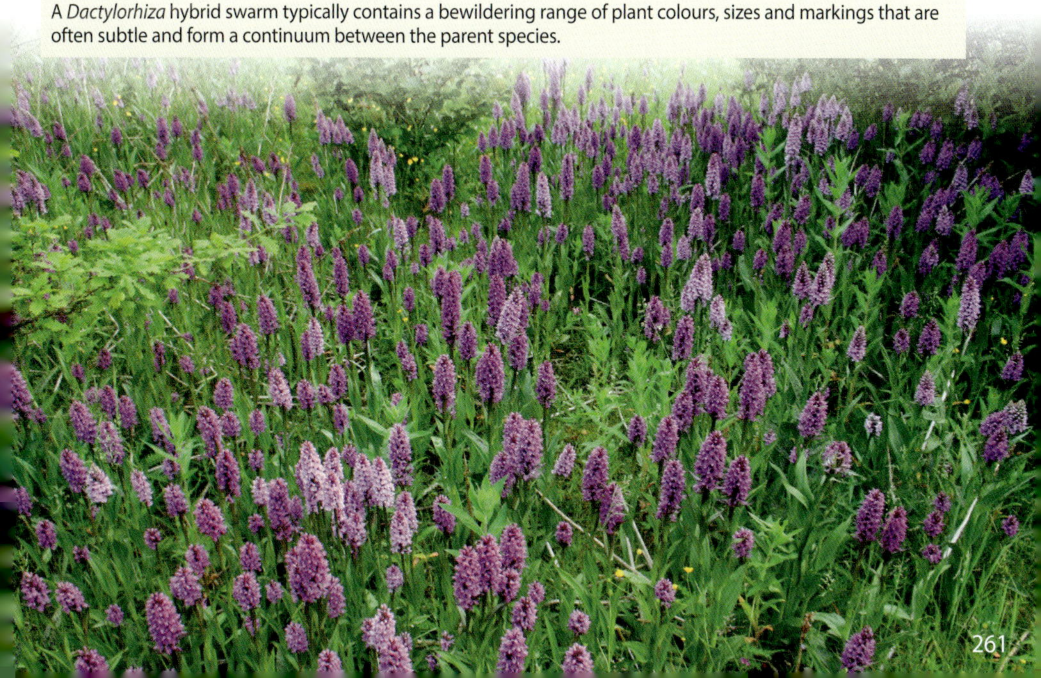

Dactylorhiza × _mixtum_ [**Frog Orchid** (*p. 188*) × **Common Spotted-orchid** (*p. 190*)]

Description: A very variable but distinctive hybrid. Like all hybrids involving Frog Orchid, the **lip is long and straight but is whitish-pink in colour**. **Range and status:** Rare. Recorded very widely across Britain and Ireland with a concentration of records in southern England and the Outer Hebridean machair where both parent species occur together in large numbers. Those occurring in the Outer Hebrides involve var. *hebridensis* of Common Spotted-orchid and are therefore typically a deeper pinkish colour than those occurring elsewhere.

Dactylorhiza × _viridellum_ [**Frog Orchid** (*p. 188*) × **Northern Marsh-orchid** (*p. 196*)]

Description: A very variable but distinctive hybrid. Like all hybrids involving Frog Orchid, **the lip is long and straight but is pink to deep purple in colour**. **Range and status:** Very rare. Recorded in Sutherland, North Uist (Outer Hebrides), Donegal and Cumbria. This hybrid could be confused with *Dactylorhiza* × *mixtum*, particularly in Scotland where the purplish var. *hebridensis* of Common Spotted-orchid is present, resulting in similarly richly coloured hybrids. Differs from *D.* × *mixtum* in adopting the dark purple tones of the Northern Marsh-orchid parent rather than the pale pink of Common Spotted-orchid.

Frog Orchid | *Dactylorhiza* × *mixtum* | Common Spotted-orchid

unmarked
markings

Frog Orchid | *Dactylorhiza* × *viridellum* | Northern Marsh-orchid

Dactylorhiza* × *wintoni [**Southern Marsh-orchid** (*p. 198*) × **Early Marsh-orchid** (*p. 202*)]

Description: A subtle hybrid that looks most **like Southern Marsh-orchid in form but with the characteristic double-loop lip markings** of the Early Marsh-orchid parent and with intermediate flower colour. **Range and status:** Scarce. Scattered across England and Wales with a concentration of records in Lancashire. Probably under-recorded.

Dactylorhiza* × *dufftii [**Early Marsh-orchid** (*p. 202*) × **Pugsley's Marsh-orchid** (*p. 206*)]

Description: A subtle hybrid with intermediate colour and morphology. **Range and status:** Rare. Single records in Yorkshire, Anglesey, Inverness-shire, Donegal, the Isle of Harris and a handful on the Isle of Skye. Almost certainly under-recorded.

Early Marsh-orchid
Dactylorhiza × wintoni
Southern Marsh-orchid

Early Marsh-orchid
Dactylorhiza × dufftii
Pugsley's Marsh-orchid

Early Marsh-orchid var. *coccinea* (RIGHT) with the hybrid between it and Southern Marsh-orchid (LEFT).

Dactylorhiza × venusta

As with other *Dactylorhiza* hybrids, this combination can show 'hybrid vigour' and also a shadowed version of the leaf markings from the Common Spotted-orchid parent.

Common Spotted-orchid
Dactylorhiza × venusta
Northern Marsh-orchid

Dactylorhiza* × *venusta [**Common Spotted-orchid** (*p. 190*) × **Northern Marsh-orchid** (*p. 196*)]

Description: A distinctive and common hybrid within mixed colonies of the parent species, **being intermediate in colour and often larger and more robust than either parent.** **Range and status:** Common. One of the most common orchid hybrids in northern Ireland, northern England and Scotland.

UNNAMED [**Northern Marsh-orchid** (*p. 196*) × **Irish Marsh-orchid** (*p. 204*)] NOT ILLUSTRATED

Description: A subtle hybrid with intermediate colour and morphology. **Range and status:** Very rare. Two records only, in Co. Waterford. Probably under-recorded.

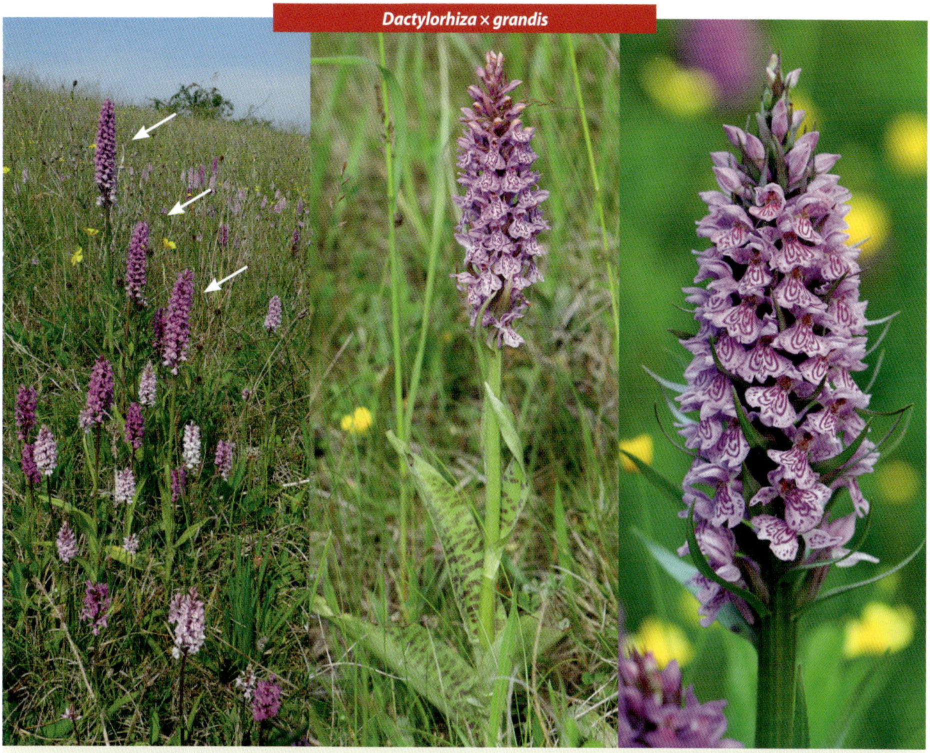
Dactylorhiza × grandis

Hybrids (arrowed) are often quite large compared to either parent, usually showing similar leaf markings to Common Spotted-orchid, but with the general background colour of Southern Marsh-orchid.

Common Spotted-orchid
Dactylorhiza × grandis
Southern Marsh-orchid

Dactylorhiza × grandis [**Common Spotted-orchid** (*p. 190*) × **Southern Marsh-orchid** (*p. 198*)]
Description: A distinctive and common hybrid within mixed colonies of the parent species, being **intermediate in colour and often larger and more robust than either parent**. **Range and status:** Common. One of the most common orchid hybrids in England and Wales, particularly southern and central England. Where both parent species occur together, this hybrid is almost guaranteed to occur.

UNNAMED [**Common Spotted-orchid** (*p. 190*) × **Irish Marsh-orchid** (*p. 204*)] NOT ILLUSTRATED
Description: A subtle hybrid with intermediate colour and morphology. **Range and status:** Rare. Scattered records across Ireland, with several records in Co. Wexford and Co. Limerick and single records in Co. Cork, Co. Mayo and Co. Sligo. Probably under-recorded.

Dactylorhiza* × *latirella **[Northern Marsh-orchid** *(p. 196)* **× Early Marsh-orchid** *(p. 202)***]**

Description: A distinctive hybrid with intermediate colour and morphology. **Range and status:** Scarce. Scattered widely across Britain and Ireland from South Wales to Shetland.

Dactylorhiza* × *insignis/salteri **[Northern Marsh-orchid** *(p. 196)* **× Southern Marsh-orchid** *(p. 198)***]**

Description: An extremely difficult hybrid to identify due to the similar appearance of the parent species. *The examples pictured below represent an intermediate plant from a mixed colony that could be a hybrid.* Intermediate plants like this can be common in mixed colonies of the parent species. **Range and status:** Scarce. Scattered records in the southern half of Wales and northern England. Probably under-recorded.

UNNAMED [Northern Marsh-orchid *(p. 196)* **× Pugsley's Marsh-orchid** *(p. 206)***]**

Description: A subtle hybrid with intermediate colour and morphology. **Range and status:** Very rare. Single records in Anglesey, Yorkshire, Cumbria, Wester Ross and North Uist. Possibly under-recorded.

UNNAMED [Common Spotted-orchid *(p. 190)* **× Pugsley's Marsh-orchid** *(p. 206)***]**

Description: A subtle hybrid with intermediate colour and morphology. **Range and status:** Rare. Scattered records across Yorkshire, Sutherland, the Outer Hebrides (North Uist and Harris) and central Ireland, with older records in North Wales and Anglesey.

Northern Marsh-orchid
Dactylorhiza × latirella
Early Marsh-orchid

Northern Marsh-orchid
Dactylorhiza × insignis/salteri
Southern Marsh-orchid

Northern Marsh-orchid
Northern Marsh-orchid × Pugsley's Marsh-orchid
Pugsley's Marsh-orchid

Common Spotted-orchid
Common Spotted-orchid × Pugsley's Marsh-orchid
Pugsley's Marsh-orchid

Common Spotted-orchid
Dactylorhiza × *transiens*
Heath Spotted-orchid

Common Spotted-orchid
Dactylorhiza × *kernerorum*
Early Marsh-orchid

Dactylorhiza* × *transiens **[Heath Spotted-orchid** (*p. 192*) **× Common Spotted-orchid** (*p. 190*)**]**
Description: An extremely difficult hybrid to identify due to the similar appearance of the parent species. *The examples pictured above represent intermediate plants from a mixed colony that are almost certainly hybrids*. Intermediate plants can be common in mixed colonies of the parent species. **Range and status:** Scarce. Very widely recorded across Britain and Ireland with numerous records. Due to the difficulty of identifying this hybrid, it could be mis-identified in some areas and under-recorded in others.

Dactylorhiza* × *kernerorum **[Common Spotted-orchid** (*p. 190*) **× Early Marsh-orchid** (*p. 202*)**]**
Description: A relatively distinctive hybrid with **characteristic double ring or spot markings surrounded by single or double loop markings near the base of the lip** inherited from the both parents, with **spotted leaves** inherited from the Common Spotted-orchid parent. In all other morphology, the hybrid is intermediate. **Range and status:** Scarce. Widely recorded across England, Wales and Ireland but surprisingly rare in Scotland with only two recent records, on the Outer Hebrides.

UNNAMED **[Heath Spotted-orchid** (*p. 192*) × **Pugsley's Marsh-orchid]** (*p. 206*)]

Description: Because the parents look so different, this is usually quite a distinctive hybrid. However, beware, as some can look like darker examples of Heath Spotted-orchid and a possible hybrid should only be considered where both parent species are nearby. **Range and status:** Rare. A couple of records each in Yorkshire, Cumbria, the Isles of Skye and Harris, Inverness-shire and Donegal, with older records in Caernarvonshire and Anglesey. Almost certainly under-recorded.

Dactylorhiza* × *dinglensis **[Heath Spotted-orchid** (*p. 192*) × **Irish Marsh-orchid** (*p. 204*)]

Description: A distinctive hybrid with intermediate colour and morphology. **Range and status:** Very rare. Single records in Counties Wexford, Waterford, Clare and Cork. Almost certainly greatly under-recorded as neither species is rare in Ireland and they quite regularly occur together.

Dactylorhiza* × *carnea **[Heath Spotted-orchid** (*p. 192*) × **Early Marsh-orchid** (*p. 202*)]

Description: **This hybrid can look rather similar to Northern Marsh-, Irish Marsh- and Pugsley's Marsh-orchids and should only be considered where both parents are present**. Most records involve Early Marsh-orchid var. *pulchella*, which regularly shares habitat with Heath Spotted-orchid. **Range and status:** Scarce. Very widely scattered across Britain and Ireland but probably under-recorded and misidentified.

Dactylorhiza* × *hallii **[Heath Spotted-orchid** (*p. 192*) × **Southern Marsh-orchid** (*p. 198*)]

Description: A distinctive hybrid with intermediate colour and morphology. The shape of the lip is often more similar to Heath Spotted-orchid but is darker purple in colour and often more robust. **Range and status:** Scarce. Restricted to southern England and South Wales, where it can be locally common.

Dactylorhiza* × *formosa **[Heath Spotted-orchid** (*p. 192*) × **Northern Marsh-orchid** (*p. 196*)]

Description: Because the parents look so different, usually quite a distinctive hybrid. **Range and status:** Scarce. Widespread and locally common in Wales, Northern England, the northern half of Ireland and Scotland (particularly the north coast and northern isles).

Heath Spotted-orchid

Heath Spotted-orchid × Pugsley's Marsh-orchid

Pugsley's Marsh-orchid

Heath Spotted-orchid

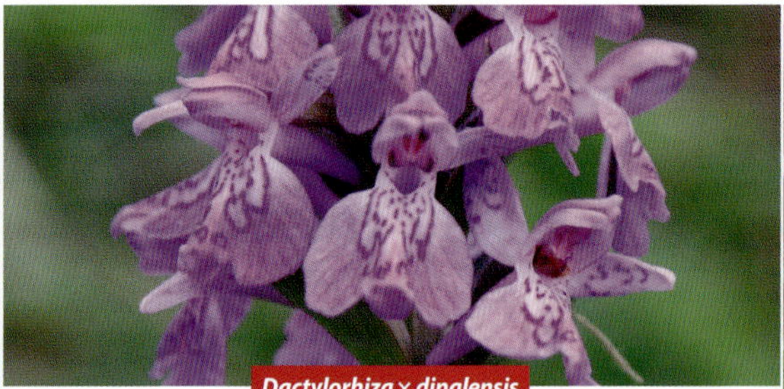
Dactylorhiza × *dinglensis*

Irish Marsh-orchid

Heath Spotted-orchid | ***Dactylorhiza × carnea*** | Early Marsh-orchid

Heath Spotted-orchid | ***Dactylorhiza × hallii*** | Southern Marsh-orchid

Heath Spotted-orchid | ***Dactylorhiza × formosa*** | Northern Marsh-orchid

Orchis hybrids – see also *p. 249*

Due to the rarity of most *Orchis* species, the three recorded hybrids within the genus, although highly distinctive, have only been recorded a handful of times – two are each restricted to a single site.

Orchis × meilsheimeri [Lady Orchid (*p. 234*) × Man Orchid (*p. 228*)]

Description: A rather variable hybrid in appearance but otherwise intermediate between both parents in lip shape and coloration. **Range and status:** Very rare. First recorded in 1998 on private land in Kent where several plants persist.

Orchis × angusticruris [Lady Orchid (*p. 234*) × Monkey Orchid (*p. 230*)]

Description: A large and impressive hybrid; rather variable in appearance but intermediate between both parents in lip shape and coloration. **Range and status:** Very rare. Only known at Hartslock Nature Reserve in Oxfordshire, where a single plant was first recorded in 2006. Since then the number of hybrid plants has expanded greatly to several hundred – outnumbering both parent species. This hybrid was probably rather frequent in the Chilterns where both parents were once common.

Orchis × bergonii [Monkey Orchid (*p. 230*) × Man Orchid (*p. 228*)]

Description: A rather variable hybrid in appearance but otherwise intermediate between both parents in lip shape and coloration. **Range and status:** Very rare. First recorded in Kent in 1988 at a site where both parent species co-occur. This plant persisted until 1992 before disappearing. Another plant was discovered at the same site in 2016 but it has not been seen since. There have been rumours that these plants may have been the product of hand pollination. Similarly, three examples of this hybrid were found alongside a tiny colony of Man Orchids in Hampshire in 2014. No Monkey Orchids are present within 45 miles (70 km) of the site yet DNA analysis of these plants indicated that Monkey Orchid was the pollen parent that, according to European studies, is a much rarer occurrence than Man Orchid being the pollen parent. This fact, combined with the lack of any local Monkey Orchids, suggests these hybrids are highly likely to have been the result of deliberate hand pollination.

Lady Orchid

Orchis × meilsheimeri

Man Orchid

Lady Orchid

Orchis × angusticruris

Monkey Orchid

Monkey Orchid

Orchis × bergonii

Man Orchid

Ophrys hybrids – see also *p. 249*

Hybrids within the *Ophrys* genus are generally very rare with only a handful of occurrences. Pure *Ophrys* can also be very variable in shape and markings – see *p. 246* for a range of examples.

Ophrys* × *pietschii **[Bee Orchid** (*p. 242*) **× Fly Orchid** (*p. 238*)**]** (Name may not be valid)

Description: An often large and impressive hybrid with flowers **intermediate in form and colour between the parent species.** The sepal colour can vary from rhubarb-pink to green. **Range and status:** Very rare. First recorded in 1968 in the Avon Gorge near Bristol. Has since been recorded at several sites across southern England where it persists in Somerset, Dorset and Gloucestershire. This hybrid could appear elsewhere as both parent species regularly occur together.

Ophrys* × *albertiana **[Bee Orchid** (*p. 242*) **× Late Spider-orchid** (*p. 244*)**]**

Description: A rather subtle hybrid of intermediate form. **Range and status:** Very rare. Three of the Kent Late Spider-orchid colonies contain a number of plants intermediate between the parent species, suggesting there may have been repeated instances of hybridization.

Ophrys* × *nelsonii **[Fly Orchid** (*p. 238*) **× Woodcock Orchid** (*p. 276*)**]**

Description: A distinctive hybrid of intermediate form. **Range and status:** Extremely rare. Known from one roadside chalk cutting in Dorset where several plants were first recorded in 2017. The occurrence of this hybrid is inexplicable because Woodcock Orchid *Ophrys scolopax* is a continental European species that has not been recorded growing naturally at the site, nor anywhere else in Britain and Ireland. The site is not easily accessed and had not been the subject of a botanical survey until the date that the hybrids were found, suggesting artificial 'creation' by human intervention is highly unlikely. A mystery!

Bee Orchid | *Ophrys × pietschii* | Fly Orchid

Bee Orchid

Ophrys × *albertiana*

Late Spider-orchid

Fly Orchid

Ophrys × *nelsonii*

Woodcock Orchid

Extinct and adventive species

This section covers the species that have occurred in Britain or Ireland, but which are now extinct, as well as those that occur, but only as known introductions or adventives of uncertain origin. An adventive species is a non-native that has arrived in a new locality, either with or without human assistance and has not (yet) become established.

Testing the provenance of older records can be extremely challenging, and establishing the origin of plants reliably can be problematic, even for recent discoveries. Inevitably, therefore, personal judgement has had to be applied when assessing each species. A number of old records are probably the result of misidentifications: **Mueller's Helleborine** *Epipactis muelleri* was claimed in the days when identification of self-pollinated *Epipactis* had not been refined, and the record of **Short-spurred Fragrant-orchid** *Gymnadenia odoratissima* might well relate to a mutant Small-white Orchid. Without compelling evidence, such species are not considered here.

Determining the likelihood of a species occurring naturally can be fraught with difficulty. By way of illustration, consider **Irish Lady's-tresses** *Spiranthes romanzoffiana* – a species with its origins in North America. Despite the apparently poor odds against wind-borne seeds surviving a transatlantic crossing, it is worth noting how widespread that species is over a broad range of latitudes in the west of Britain and Ireland, having presumably arrived across 4,000 km of open ocean. Given the appearance of **Lady Orchid** on the coast of East Sussex, **Early Spider-orchid** in Suffolk, **Military Orchid** in Suffolk and Hertfordshire, and perhaps even **Tongue-orchid** in Essex, it seems likely that long-distance seed dispersal is perhaps more common than previously thought. However, when a totally new species arrives, or one appears significantly outside its 'normal' range, establishing its probable origin, and therefore the importance of the record, is particularly problematic.

Recent insect colonizers have tended to arrive in – and extend their range from – the south-east of England, which has climatic and habitat conditions most similar to those of the near continent. It seems likely that this is also the part of the country with the highest probability of new orchid species arriving and colonizing naturally.

'Irregular' species – those not recognized as part of the standard British and Irish orchid flora – can usefully be separated into four groups:

1. Former native plants that became extinct during the period of historical records

Summer Lady's-tresses *Spiranthes aestivalis* [PHOTO]

This species once occurred at a few sites confined to a small area to the south-west of Lyndhurst in the New Forest, Hampshire, and on the Channel Islands, but was lost due to habitat change and mass collection for herbaria. The last confirmed record was in the New Forest in 1952. Rumours of reintroductions at former sites have proven unfounded, although some of the sites still appear to be suitable. The species favours acid bogs and was very common at some sites in the past, so is a sad loss from Britain and Ireland's native flora. Summer Lady's-tresses looks similar to Autumn Lady's-tresses (*p. 166*), but has long, thin, pointed leaves, and flowers at least a month earlier, in July.

2. Possibly naturally occurring, and in some cases extant, adventives

Small-flowered Tongue-orchid *Serapias parviflora* [PHOTO]

This species was discovered at Rame Head in Cornwall in 1989, and by 1992 there were five flowering spikes. The colony was later supplemented by transplants that were grown from seed collected from the original plants, and the landowners managed the site appropriately. In 2007 and 2008, two more plants were found flowering in a slightly different location within the area.

Summer Lady's-tresses *Spiranthes aestivalis*

Small-flowered Tongue-orchid *Serapias parviflora*

However, due to accidental mismanagement in the spring of 2009 the site was trampled and disturbed well into the flowering season by grazing cattle, and no plants flowered. The grazing regime then changed and as a consequence the site became unsuitable for this species. Active management to reduce competing vegetation may result in the reappearance of this species, but since it is 'officially' considered to have been an introduction – even though it is perfectly possible that it arrived naturally – there is no intention to do so.

Tongue-orchid *Serapias lingua*

As well as occurrences in the Channel Islands and Essex, this species was found at a site near Kingsbridge in South Devon in 1998, where it persisted and multiplied vegetatively until 2003, by which time it had produced nine flowering spikes. It also occurs at Wakehurst Place in West Sussex among the introduced Loose-flowered Orchids *Anacamptis laxiflora* (see *p. 276*). While the Essex colony is possibly an accidental introduction, it is large and seemingly fully naturalized, so this species is included in the main body of this book (see *p. 216*).

3. Historical adventives of less certain origin

Frivald's Fragrant-orchid *Gymnadenia frivaldii*
Rather like Small-white Orchid in appearance, this fragrant-orchid has pale flowers and an entire, triangular lip. Found on heathland in Dorset in either 1972 or 1973, this species is unlikely to be of natural occurrence, as it is usually confined to a small mountainous area of the southern Balkans.

Dwarf Alpine Orchid *Chamorchis alpina*
Small and very like Frog Orchid, but has thin, grass-like leaves in a rosette around the base. A single plant was found in the New Forest in 1976 and is likely to have been a transplant.

Scarce Tongue-orchid *Serapias neglecta*
Reported to have occurred on the Isle of Wight in 1918, but the specific identity of the plant was never proven.

Heart-flowered Tongue-orchid
Serapias cordigera
Typical tongue-orchid plant shape; flowers are large with a large, almost rounded lip and a large, hairy 'mouth'. Up to three plants flowered in a former chalk quarry in Kent in 1996 and 1997, presumably growing from wind-blown seed originating from a plant growing in a pot outside a nearby house.

Bertoloni's Bee Orchid *Ophrys bertolonii*
Insect mimic: almost black, quite square, furry lip with shiny bluish mirror near the tip, pink petals and sepals. A single plant identified as this species was found in Dorset in 1976, causing much controversy at the time. However, none of the stories surrounding it appear to be confirmed, and neither has the actual identity of the species, due to the poor quality of the original photographs.

Sawfly Orchid *Ophrys tenthredinifera* [PHOTO]
Insect mimic: wide yellow, brown and blue lip, pink petals and pink sepals. In 2014, a flowering plant was discovered in a large colony of Early Spider-orchids in Dorset. It flowered again in 2016, but had died back completely by 2019, having diminished each year after its discovery. This species is native to the Mediterranean region.

4. Known or probable introductions, extant

Loose-flowered Orchid [PHOTO]
Anacamptis laxiflora
Very similar to Early-purple Orchid, but, as its name implies, with flowers widely spaced up a tall stem. The leaves are always unspotted, and there are no dark markings on the lip. This species is naturalized in the gardens at Wakehurst Place in Sussex, as well as being native in the Channel Islands, where it occurs in large colonies in wet meadows.

Ploughshare or **Long-lipped Tongue-orchid**
Serapias vomeracea [PHOTO]
Typical tongue-orchid plant shape; flowers have a very long, narrow, folded-back lip, said to resemble a wizard's long, pointed hood and beard. Occurs on a roadside verge in Somerset alongside Bee (*p. 242*), Pyramidal (*p. 218*) and Woodcock Orchids (*below*); all brought from France by a nearby house owner *c.* 2011 and flowering annually.

Mirror Orchid *Ophrys speculum*
Small insect-mimic orchid with the lip having a shiny blue centre and hairy yellow-and-brown edges, sepals two-toned green with a brown central vein. Discovered in a garden in North Wales in 2019. Due to its urban location and the normal distribution being mainly coastal Mediterranean and sparsely along the west coast of France, this was presumably an escape from cultivation.

Woodcock Orchid *Ophrys scolopax* [PHOTO]
Similar to Late Spider-orchid, but lip bulbous and furry side lobes rounded. Sepals also pink but more oval. Growing in Somerset alongside other introduced species (see **Ploughshare** or **Long-lipped Tongue-orchid** *above*). In addition, a small colony of hybrid Woodcock × Fly Orchid (*p. 272*) was found on a roadside verge in Dorset in 2016, gradually reducing in number in subsequent years. No Woodcock Orchids were present at the site, but it is possible that they had grown there and had died out by the time the hybrids were discovered. However, given that the introduced Woodcock Orchids in Somerset are only 22 km away, there is a possibility that the hybrids originated from seed dispersed by those plants.

Loose-flowered Orchid *Anacamptis laxiflkora*

Ploughshare Tongue-orchid *Serapias vomeracea*

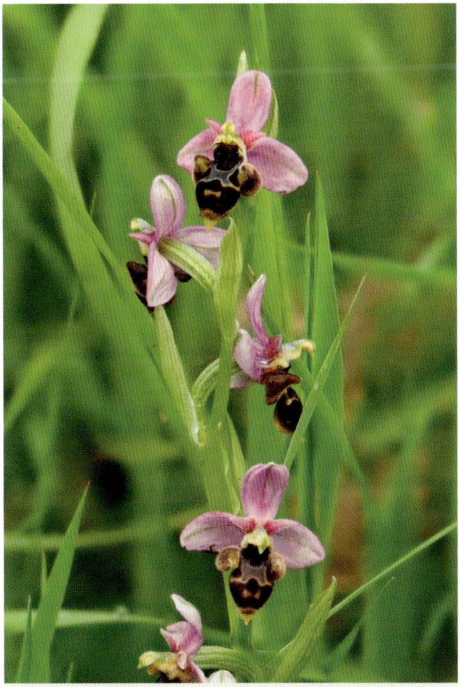

Woodcock Orchid *Ophrys scolopax*

Sawfly Orchid *Ophrys tenthredinifera*

Threats and conservation

Over the last century, many of our once-common orchid species have experienced rapid declines, with some now pushed to the brink of extinction. This decline probably began as early as the 13th century when the Enclosure Acts sought to consolidate common land into larger plots of privately owned land – with the impact fully taking effect during the Tudor period (between 1485 and 1603). This set the scene for further change during the industrial revolution, as the rural working community dwindled, along with traditional land-management techniques. Declines continued into the 20th century, as huge swathes of orchid-rich habitat were wiped out insidiously between the World Wars as a result of land-use changes.

Our orchids now face a whole new suite of threats, some of which can be managed, whereas others may be impossible to avoid.

Habitat destruction and change

The widespread loss of orchids in Britain and Ireland has been almost entirely driven by a mixture of habitat destruction and deterioration – both of which are facets of a shift from traditional subsistence land management to large-scale industrial agriculture, alongside expanding development. The clear-felling of woodlands, ploughing of grasslands and drainage of wetlands spelled instant doom, but perhaps more insidious has been the slow degradation of these habitats with the gradual decline of traditional management practices.

As they are poor competitors, orchids cannot withstand the invasion of fast-growing grasses, shrubs and trees. Traditional management techniques, such as coppicing, hay production, peat cutting (in fens), periodic burning and grazing with a range of livestock, inadvertently helped to ensure that these fragile habitats remained open and light. As these practices began to decline, so did the ecological condition of the woodlands, wetlands and grasslands, which became dark, dry and dense.

The result is that we now have a landscape where only fragments of suitable orchid habitat remain as islands in an inhospitable sea of agriculture and concrete. This poses further problems for orchids, as reproduction and dispersal become increasingly difficult. Meanwhile, the slow leaching of fertilizers and pollution from surrounding areas is gradually altering the soil chemistry, increasing nutrient levels and introducing invisible toxic chemicals – all to the detriment of orchids.

An Early-purple Orchid population being slowly choked by Bramble *Rubus* spp. as a result of lack of management.

The dangers of mowing

Many important orchid populations are now confined to road verges, where ill-timed mowing by local councils is a perennial threat. Organizations such as Plantlife and The Wildlife Trusts have long campaigned to protect important roadside orchid sites, issuing management guidelines or working to designate some as official 'roadside nature reserves'. But every year, horror stories continue to surface where entire orchid populations have been mown when in flower.

Mowing can be a good management technique for orchids, provided it is done outside the flowering period. However, persistent mowing at the wrong time prevents reproduction and will eventually result in the orchid population at that site being eradicated.

A sad sight: Bee Orchids mown down in the middle of the flowering period.

Collecting and trampling

Rampant over-collecting during the Victorian era drove the near extinction of Lady's-slipper, while Summer Lady's-tresses was less fortunate and now mostly resides in the herbaria of London's Natural History Museum. Recent claims that certain orchid colonies have been lost to theft seem alarmist and largely unfounded; it is more likely that a declining population disappeared as the habitat became unsuitable. However, illegal collecting is a continuing threat to some of the more attractive species although, thankfully, proven instances of theft are now relatively rare. Nonetheless, it is sensible to apply a level of caution when sharing orchid site information, and to encourage those wanting to see these plants to join organized orchid walks where possible.

Trampling inflicts annual damage at well-known orchid sites, ironically often by the people who love them the most. When entering a sensitive orchid site, keep to marked paths and make sure to check carefully where you step when walking across the habitat to an obvious plant or colony. Remember that the non-flowering proportion of an orchid population can be five times that of the adult flowering plants and these can easily be missed, often buried in the surrounding vegetation.

Orchids collected by Rev. Adam Buddle (1662–1715) preserved in the Sloane Herbarium, Natural History Museum, London.

Climate breakdown

A new – and potentially devastating – threat to orchids is now beginning to take hold: climate breakdown. Since records began in 1884, Britain's ten hottest years have occurred since 2002, whereas all its ten coldest years occurred before 1963 (Kendon *et al.*, 2019).

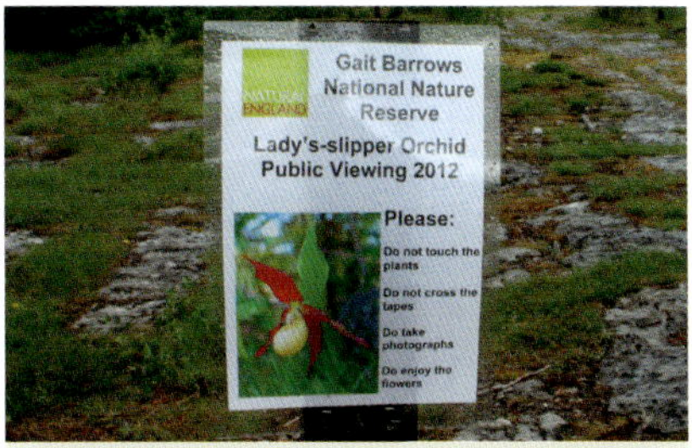
Gait Barrows
National Nature
Reserve
Lady's-slipper Orchid
Public Viewing 2012
Please:
Do not touch the plants
Do not cross the tapes
Do take photographs
Do enjoy the flowers

A specially organized public viewing for the reintroduced Lady's-slipper at Gaitbarrows National Nature Reserve, Lancashire.

Climate winners and losers

Climate breakdown may have already taken its first orchid victim in Britain and Ireland with the demise of the Ghost Orchid, which last appeared at its only regular site in 1987 and has been seen only once since. This is primarily a species of cold mountains and northern forests in other parts of its range, so its future here looks bleak.

Although some boreal and temperate species are expected to decline in response to climate change, others – notably those suited to hot, dry conditions – already appear to be expanding their range. For example, Bee Orchid was first recorded in Scotland in 2003 and has since been found at multiple additional locations. It also seems likely that species from Europe, such as the tongue-orchids, may colonize or become more widely established as conditions in southern England gradually become warmer (see *p. 274*).

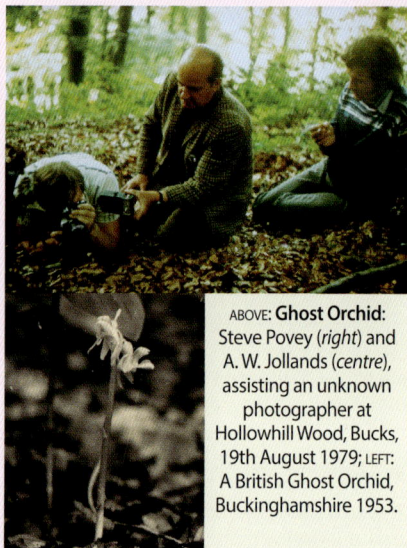

ABOVE: **Ghost Orchid:** Steve Povey (*right*) and A. W. Jollands (*centre*), assisting an unknown photographer at Hollowhill Wood, Bucks, 19th August 1979; LEFT: A British Ghost Orchid, Buckinghamshire 1953.

Climate breakdown poses a multitude of risks for orchids, but extreme heat and drought may present the biggest challenges. Long summer droughts cause significant damage to grasslands, often baking shallow soils to a crisp. Such droughts pose a particular threat to temperate and boreal species, such as Musk and Small-white Orchids, which require cool, damp conditions, reducing population sizes over time by killing off some or all the plants in a colony. As average temperatures increase, many species can be expected to flower earlier, potentially before their pollinators emerge, thus jeopardizing their reproductive success.

Conversely, unpredictable cold snaps and extreme rainfall are likely to put further stress on orchids, especially in wetland areas prone to flooding. Rising sea level, coupled with more intense storms, threaten coastal dune slacks, fens and marshes where many orchids rely on a fragile freshwater hydrology that is easily disrupted by the ingress of saltwater. This is a particular concern for low-lying, high-value orchid areas such as the Norfolk Broads and Scottish machair.

Over time, many habitats are likely to change, as only resilient and adaptable plant species survive or invasive ones move in, competing with orchids for space and light. Increased predation by deer and molluscs in some areas may also become a growing problem as herbivores are forced to alter their browsing patterns.

Threatened species

The International Union for Conservation of Nature (IUCN) has established global criteria for assessing the conservation status of species. These criteria include the rate of decline, population size, area of geographic distribution and degree of population and distribution fragmentation. Based on an analysis of these criteria, species are assigned to one of the following categories: **Extinct** EX, **Critically Endangered** CR, **Endangered** EN, **Vulnerable** VU, **Near Threatened** NT, **Least Concern** LC, **Data Deficient** DD or **Not Evaluated** NE. The latest assessments for British and Irish orchids are included in the ***GB Red List for vascular plants*** (revised Feb 2019) – available online at **bsbi.org/taxon-lists** and the ***Ireland Red List No. 10: Vascular Plants*** (2016) – available online at **biodiversityireland.ie/wordpress/wp-content/uploads/RL10-VascularPlants.pdf**.

In Great Britain, 20 orchid taxa are categorized as threatened: four as Critically Endangered, four as Endangered and 12 as Vulnerable; in addition, four are Near Threatened, three are considered

Data Deficient (due to a lack of sufficient data to undertake an assessment) and one has yet to be assessed. In Ireland, four species are categorized as threatened: one as Endangered and three as Vulnerable; in addition, six are Near Threatened and two are 'Wait Listed' pending an assessment. The GB and Irish Red List status for each species is indicated in the relevant species account and included in the *List of British and Irish orchids* on *p. 282*.

Legal protection

As environmental awareness slowly began to grow from the 1950s onwards, the British and Irish Governments, pressured by an increasingly vocal conservation sector and passionate public, began to listen – ushering in a new era of environmentalism.

Along with most other wild plants, orchids were afforded legal protection in the UK through the Wildlife and Countryside Act 1981 (as amended), making it illegal to uproot them without prior consent from the landowner. However, a number of Britain's rarest orchids – those listed in Schedule 8 of the Act – are afforded much stricter protection. For these species (listed below) it is illegal for anyone to pick, uproot or destroy any part of the plant, or to sell or advertise for sale any part of the plant, whether dead or alive.

Lady's-slipper	**Military Orchid**
Red Helleborine	**'Lapland Marsh-orchid'** (now reclassified as a spotted-leaved form of Pugsley's Marsh-orchid)
'Young's Helleborine' (now reclassified as a form of Broad-leaved Helleborine)	**Lizard Orchid**
Ghost Orchid	**Late Spider-orchid**
Fen Orchid	**Early Spider-orchid**
Monkey Orchid	

In Northern Ireland, Schedule 8 of the Wildlife (Northern Ireland) Order 1985 (as amended), provides similar protection to the following species:

Bird's-nest Orchid	**Small-white Orchid**
Marsh Helleborine	**Pugsley's Marsh-orchid**
Green-flowered Helleborine	**Green-winged Orchid**
Bog Orchid	**Dense-flowered Orchid**
Irish Lady's-tresses	**Bee Orchid**

In the Republic of Ireland, the Flora (Protection) Order 2015 lists the following species that are protected by the Wildlife Acts 1976 and 2000:

Sword-leaved Helleborine	**Irish Lady's-tresses**
Bog Orchid	**Small-white Orchid**

A summary of the legal protection afforded to the British and Irish orchids that are recognized in this book is included in the table that appears on *p. 282*.

In addition, many of the most important orchid sites in Great Britain are designated as Sites of Special Scientific Interest (SSSI) and some have been declared as National Nature Reserves (NNR); in Northern Ireland, important sites are designated as Areas of Special Scientific Interest (ASSI), and in the Republic of Ireland as Natural Heritage Areas (NHA). The most important of these sites also lie within a European-designated Special Area of Conservation (SAC) or Special Protection Area (SPA), or a Ramsar site (designated under the Ramsar Convention on Wetlands of International Importance), which gives them an additional layer of statutory legal protection. For these sites there is a legal duty on the land manager to maintain the special habitats and species present.

List of British and Irish orchids

The following is a taxonomic list of all the species, subspecies and varieties that are recognized in this book, together with details of their conservation status and a summary of the legal protection they are afforded in Great Britain (GB), Northern Ireland (NI) and the Republic of Ireland (Ir).

Key: CR Critically Endangered; EN Endangered; VU Vulnerable; NT Near Threatened;
LC Least Concern; DD Data Deficient; WL Wait Listed (Ireland only); NE Not Evaluated.

GB Red List status following ***GB Red List for vascular plants*** (revised Feb 2019) online at **bsbi.org/taxon-lists**.
Ir Red List status following Nelson, B. & Marnell, F. (Eds). 2016. ***Ireland Red List No. 10: Vascular Plants***.

* 'Young's Helleborine' (now reclassified as a form of Broad-leaved Helleborine)
** 'Lapland Marsh-orchid' (now reclassified as a spotted-leaved form of Pugsley's Marsh-orchid)

✓	Red List		ENGLISH NAME	SCIENTIFIC NAME	Special protection			Page
	GB	Ir			GB	NI	Ir	
	CR		**Lady's-slipper**	*Cypripedium calceolus*	✓			102
	VU		**White Helleborine**	*Cephalanthera damasonium*				106
	VU	VU	**Sword-leaved Helleborine**	*Cephalanthera longifolia*			✓	108
	CR		**Red Helleborine**	*Cephalanthera rubra*	✓			110
	LC	LC	**Marsh Helleborine**	*Epipactis palustris*		✓		120
	LC	LC	**Dark-red Helleborine**	*Epipactis atrorubens*				122
	LC		**Violet Helleborine**	*Epipactis purpurata*				124
	LC	LC	**Broad-leaved Helleborine**	*Epipactis helleborine*	[✓]*			126
			'Dutch Helleborine'	ssp. *neerlandica*				130
	DD	WL	**Narrow-lipped Helleborine**	*Epipactis leptochila*				134
	DD	NE	**Dune Helleborine**	*Epipactis dunensis*				130
	EN		'Lindisfarne Helleborine'	ssp. *sancta*				132
			'Tyne Helleborine'	var. *tynensis*				133
	LC	EN	**Green-flowered Helleborine**	*Epipactis phyllanthes*		✓		136
	LC	LC	**Common Twayblade**	*Neottia ovata*				140
	LC	LC	**Lesser Twayblade**	*Neottia cordata*				142
	NT	LC	**Bird's-nest Orchid**	*Neottia nidus-avis*		✓		144
	CR		**Ghost Orchid**	*Epipogium aphyllum*	✓			146
	EN		**Fen Orchid**	*Liparis loeselii*	✓			150
	LC	NT	**Bog Orchid**	*Hammarbya paludosa*		✓	✓	152
	VU		**Coralroot Orchid**	*Corallorhiza trifida*				148
	NT	NT	**Autumn Lady's-tresses**	*Spiranthes spiralis*				166
	LC	NT	**Irish Lady's-tresses**	*Spiranthes romanzoffiana*		✓	✓	168
	LC		**Creeping Lady's-tresses**	*Goodyera repens*				164
	VU		**Musk Orchid**	*Herminium monorchis*				154

✓	Red List GB	Red List Ir	ENGLISH NAME	SCIENTIFIC NAME	Special protection GB	Special protection NI	Special protection Ir	Page
	NT	LC	**Greater Butterfly-orchid**	*Platanthera chlorantha*				172
	VU	LC	**Lesser Butterfly-orchid**	*Platanthera bifolia*				173
	VU	VU	**Small-white Orchid**	*Pseudorchis albida*		✓	✓	156
	LC	LC	**Chalk Fragrant-orchid**	*Gymnadenia conopsea*				176
	LC	LC	**Marsh Fragrant-orchid**	*Gymnadenia densiflora*				177
	LC	LC	**Heath Fragrant-orchid**	*Gymnadenia borealis*				176
	VU	NT	**Frog Orchid**	*Dactylorhiza viridis*				188
	LC	LC	**Common Spotted-orchid**	*Dactylorhiza fuchsii*				190
		WL		var. *hebridensis*				210
	LC	LC	**Heath Spotted-orchid**	*Dactylorhiza maculata*				192
	LC	LC	**Early Marsh-orchid**	*Dactylorhiza incarnata*				202
	CR			var. *ochroleuca*				213
	LC	LC		var. *coccinea*				213
				var. *pulchella*				212
				var. *cruenta*				212
	LC	NE	**Southern Marsh-orchid**	*Dactylorhiza praetermissa*				198
				var. *schoenophila*				211
	LC	LC	**Northern Marsh-orchid**	*Dactylorhiza purpurella*				196
	LC	LC	**Pugsley's Marsh-orchid**	*Dactylorhiza traunsteinerioides*	[✓]**	✓		206
	DD	LC	**Irish Marsh-orchid**	*Dactylorhiza kerryensis*				204
	LC	LC	**Early-purple Orchid**	*Orchis mascula*				226
	VU		**Lady Orchid**	*Orchis purpurea*				234
	VU		**Military Orchid**	*Orchis militaris*	✓			232
	VU		**Monkey Orchid**	*Orchis simia*	✓			230
	EN		**Man Orchid**	*Orchis anthropophora*				228
	EN		**Burnt Orchid**	*Neotinea ustulata*				160
				var. *aestivalis*				162
		NT	**Dense-flowered Orchid**	*Neotinea maculata*		✓		158
	LC	LC	**Pyramidal Orchid**	*Anacamptis pyramidalis*				218
	NT	VU	**Green-winged Orchid**	*Anacamptis morio*		✓		220
	LC		**Lizard Orchid**	*Himantoglossum hircinum*	✓			214
	NE		**Tongue-orchid**	*Serapias lingua*				216
	VU	NT	**Fly Orchid**	*Ophrys insectifera*				238
	LC		**Early Spider-orchid**	*Ophrys sphegodes*	✓			240
	LC	LC	**Bee Orchid**	*Ophrys apifera*		✓		242
				f. *bicolor*				246
				f. *belgarum*				246
			'Wasp Orchid'	f. *trollii*				246
	VU		**Late Spider-orchid**	*Ophrys fuciflora*	✓			244

Artwork and photographic credits

The production of this book would not have been possible without the help and co-operation of the photographers whose images have been reproduced. The plates are one of the key features of the book and we would like to acknowledge the skill and patience of the photographers listed below who kindly allowed us to use their work. Although the majority of the 1,199 images in this book were taken by the authors, all the other photographs are specifically credited below. Sixty other photographers have contributed images and they are listed here in alphabetical order by surname (the initials in square brackets are those used in the individual photo credits that follow):

Prof. Richard Bateman [RB]; **Mihai Bobocea** [MB]; **John Bowler** [JB]; **Jean Claessens** [JC]; **Mark Curley** [MC]; **Clare Dell** [CD]; **John Devries** [JD]; **David Farrell** [DF] and **Frances Farrell** [FF] "www.wildwest.ie"; **John Fennell** [JF]; **Alan Gendle** [AG]; **Chris Gibson** [CGi]; **Chris Gladman** [CGl]; **Rex Graham** [RG]; **Pauline Greenhalgh** [PG]; **Jonathan Greenwood** [JG]; **Mark Gurney** [MG]; **Ian Hadingham** [IHad]; **Isabel Hardman** [IHar]; **Simon Harrap** [SH]; **Jeff Hodgson** [JHod]; **Jeremy Holden** [JHol]; **Mark Joy** [MJ]; **Gareth Knass** [GK]; **Brian Laney** [BL]; **Jim and Dawn Langiewicz** [J&DL]; **Iain Leach** [IL]; **Steff Leese** [SL]; **Les Lewis** [LL]; **Durwyn Liley** [DL]; **Mark Lynes** [ML]; **Paul Masters** [PM]; **Simon Melville** [SM]; **Rich Mielcarek** [RM]; **Prof. Attila Molnár** [AM]; **Lara Pearson** [LP]; **Roger Powley** [RP]; **Chris Raper** [CR]; **Su Reed** [SR]; **Martin Roome** [MR]; **Gus Routledge** [GR]; **Patrick Sabonnadiere (Alamy Stock Photo)** [PS/Alamy]; **Chris Scaife** [CS]; **Alan Smith** [AS]; **David Steere** [DS]; **Robert Still** [RS]; **Terry Swainbank** [TS]; **Andy and Gill Swash** [A&GS]; **Barry Tattersall** [BaT]; **Bill Tattersall** [BiT]; **Robert Thompson** [RT]; **Paddy Tobin** [PT]; **Derek Turner Ettlinger** [DTE]; **Richard Upton** [RU]; **Kevin Walker** [KWa]; **Alan Watson Featherstone** [AWF]; **Keith Wilson** [KWi] and **Richard Would** [RW].

In all cases, the position on the page of the relevant image is coded as follows:
T = top; M = middle; B = bottom; L = left; C = centre; R = right; C/L = centre left; C/R = centre right.

p. 14: (T) [RS]. **p. 15:** (BL) [J&DL]. **p. 16:** (MR) [KWi], (BR) [KWi]. **p. 22:** (BC) [PG], (BR) [J&DL]. **p. 27:** (B) [JB]. **p. 28:** (B) [DL]. **p. 30:** (L) [ML]. **p. 33:** (L) [IHar]. **p. 45:** (TR) [KWa].**p. 50:** (TR) [BL]. **p. 54:** (MC) [RM], (BC) [DF]. **p. 55:** (ROW 2 R) [JG]. **p. 61:** (TL) [J&DL]. **p. 64:** (TR) [RW], (BR) [JC]. **p. 65:** (BR) [JG]. **p. 68:** (TL) [CGi], (TR) [DF]. **p. 72:** (TL) [CR], (BL) [CR]. **p. 74:** (BL) [IHad], (BR) [DS]. **p. 80:** (TR) [RS], (MR) [RS]. **p. 96:** (ROW 3 L) [AS]. **p. 97:** (BL) [SL]. **p. 103:** (TL) [SL]. **p. 107:** (BL) [JHol]. **p. 111:** (TC) [SL], (TR) [CD], (BL) [ML], (BR) [AM]. **p. 118:** (BL) [AS]. **p. 119:** (BL) [ML], (BL INSET) [ML], (BC/L) [ML], (BC/R) [J&DL]. **p. 125:** (TC) [J&DL]. **p. 128:** (ALL(3)) [SM]. **p. 131:** (TC) [ML], (TR) [PM], (BR) [AM]. **p. 133:** (TL) [JHod], (BL) [JHod], (R) [ML]. **p. 138:** (ROW 2 L) [SM], (BC) [AS], (BR) [AS]. **p. 139:** (ROW 2 R) [JHod]. **p. 147:** (TR) [A&GS], (BL) [DTE], (BR) [MB]. **p. 153:** (BR) [AM]. **p. 161:** (BR) [JCo]. **p. 165:** (TR) [JHod], (BL) [MR]. **p. 178:** (TR) [JHod]. **p. 183:** (BR) [SH]. **p. 187:** (TR) [JD], (BR) [JD]. **p. 189:** (ML) [JHod], (MC) [JHod]. **p. 197:** (BR) [GR]. **p. 199:** (TC) [RP]. **p. 203:** (BL) [SR]. **p. 205:** (BR) [PT]. **p. 207:** (TL) [GK], (BR) [CS]. **p. 208:** (TR) [GK], (MR) [AWF], (BR) [RS]. **p. 209:** (TC) [LP], (TR) [FF], (ROW 2 R) [RU], (ROW 3 C) [JHod], (BR) [GK]. **p. 210:** (B) [RT], (BC) [SH].**p. 211:** (TC) [RP], (BC) [SH]. **p. 212:** (TR) [JD], (BR) [DF]. **p. 214:** (L) [JHod]. **p. 215:** (TR) [MC]. **p. 216:** (L) [JG]. **p. 229:** (BR) [BL]. **p. 231:** (BR) [AM]. **p. 235:** (BR) [IHad]. **p. 236:** (TC) [IHad], (TR) [IHad]. **p. 239:** (BR) [JHod]. **p. 241:** (BR) [AM]. **p. 244:** (L) [PS/Alamy]. **p. 245:** (BR) [AM]. **p. 246:** (BC/R) [RU]. **p. 247:** (ROW 2 C/L) [CGl]. **p. 250:** (C/L) [JHod], (C/R) [JHod]. **p. 251:** (TC + INSET) [JHod], (TR) [IL], (BC INSET) [J&DL]. **p. 252:** (BR + INSET) [GK], (BC/L) [GK]. **p. 253:** (TC) [ML], (MC/L) [ML]. **p. 256:** (TC) [RM], (BL) [JHod]. **p. 257:** (TL) [JHod], (TC) [LL], (MC) [BaT], (BC) [TS]. **p. 259:** (TL) [JHod], (TC) [AG]. **p. 260:** (TC + INSET) [AG]. **p. 263:** (ROW 2 C/L, C, C/R & R) [MG]. **p. 50:** (TR) [BL]. **p. 264:** (TL) [AG]. **p. 267:** (TC) [RB], (ROW 2 C/L, C & C/R) [RM], (ROW 3 C/L) [JF]. **p. 269:** (BC) [JF]. **p. 273:** (TC) [SM], (BC) [MJ]. **p. 275:** (R) [GK]. **p. 280:** (T) [BiT], (B) [RG].

All the artwork in the book – a total of 98 watercolour pencil illustrations – was prepared by Sarah Stribbling and we would like to reiterate our thanks to her for producing such beautiful and accurate illustrations. We would also like to thank photographers who provided images that we used as reference for the plates and descriptions, namely: Mike Clark, Simon Close, Jules Cox, Gerry Davies, James Lowen, Roger Newman and Gerry Trask.

References

Bateman, R.M. (2020). Implications of next-generation sequencing for the systematics and evolution of the terrestrial orchid genus *Epipactis*, with particular reference to the British Isles. *Kew Bulletin*, **25(4)**.

Bateman, R.M. & Denholm, I. (2012). Taxonomic reassessment of the British and Irish tetraploid marsh-orchids. *New Journal of Botany*, **2(1)**: 37–55.

Bateman, R.M. & Denholm, I. (2019). Mapping the near-cryptic fragrant orchids of Britain and Ireland. *BSBI News*, **140**: 6-12.

Brandrud, M.K., Baar, J., Lorenzo, M.T., Alexander Athanasiadis, A., Bateman, R.M., Chase, M.W., Hedrén, M. & Paun, O. (2019). Phylogenomic relationships of diploids and the origins of allotetraploids in *Dactylorhiza* (Orchidaceae). *Systematic Biology*, **69(1)**: 91–109.

Campbell, V.V., Rowe, G., Beebee, T.J.C. & Hutchings, M.J. (2007). Genetic differentiation among fragrant orchids (*Gymnadenia conopsea* s.l.) in the British Isles. *Botanical Journal of The Linnean Society*, **155**: 349–360.

Cole, S.R. (2014). History and status of the Ghost Orchid (*Epipogium aphyllum*, Orchidaceae). England *New Journal of Botany*, **4**: 13-24.

Hedren, M., Paun, O. & Sayers, B. (2011). The polymorphic early marsh orchids, *Dactylorhiza incarnata* s.l. (Orchidaceae), at Lough Gealain, Ireland. *New Journal of Botany*, **1(1)**: 16–23.

Hollingsworth, P.M., Squirrell, J., Hollingsworth, M.L., Richards, A.J. & Bateman, R.M. (2006). Taxonomic complexity, conservation and recurrent origins of self-pollination in *Epipactis* (Orchidaceae). In J. Bailey & R. G. Ellis (Eds), *Current taxonomic research on The British & European flora*. pp. 27–44. BSBI. London.

Jacquemyn, H., de Kort, H., Vanden Broeck, A. & Brys, R. (2018). Immigrant and extrinsic hybrid seed inviability contribute to reproductive isolation between forest and dune ecotypes of *Epipactis helleborine* (Orchidaceae). *Oikos*, **127**: 73–84.

Johnson, D. (2019). *Wild Orchids of Kent*. Kent Field Club.

Kreutz, C.A.J. & Lewis, L. (2015). Neotypification and distribution of *Gymnadenia conopsea* (L.) R. Brown var. *friesica* Schlechter. *J. Eur. Orch.*, **47(1)**: 239–249.

Mckean, D.R. (1982). × *Pseudanthera breadalbanensis* Mckean: A new intergeneric hybrid from Scotland. *Watsonia*, **14**: 129–131.

Paulus, H.F. (2018). Pollinators as isolation mechanisms: field observations and field experiments regarding specificity of pollinator attraction in the genus *Ophrys* (Orchidaceae und Insecta, Hymenoptera, Apoidea). *Entomologia Generalis*, **37(3–4)**: 261–316.

Quina, F.H., Moreira Jr., P.F., Vautier-Giongo, C., Rettori, D., Rodrigues, R.F., Freitas, A.A., Silva, P.F. & Maçanita, A.L. (2009). Photochemistry of anthocyanins and their biological role in plant tissues. *Pure Appl. Chem.*, **81(9)**: 1687–1694.

Richards, A.J. & Porter, A.F. (1982). On the identity of a Northumberland *Epipactis*. *Watsonia*, **14**: 121–128.

Rose, F. (1998). A new orchid hybrid for Britain – × *Orchiaceras melsheimeri* (*Aceras anthropophora* × *Orchis purpurea*). *BSBI News*, **79(19)**.

Squirrell, J., Hollingsworth, P.M., Bateman, R.M., Tebbitt, M.C & Hollingsworth, M.L. (2002). Taxonomic complexity and breeding system transitions: conservation genetics of the *Epipactis leptochila* complex (Orchidaceae). *Molecular Ecology*, **11**: 1957–1964.

Stace, C.A., Preston, C.D., Pearman, D.A. (2015). *Hybrid Flora Of The British Isles*. BSBI. Bristol.

Stace, C.A. (2019). *New Flora of the British Isles*. Fourth Edition. C&M Floristics. Suffolk.

Stark, C., Michalski, S.G., Babik, W., Winterfeld, G. & Durka, W. (2011). Strong genetic differentiation between *Gymnadenia conopsea* and *G. densiflora* despite morphological similarity. *Plant Syst. Evol.*, **293**: 213–226.

Święczkowska, E. & Kowalkowska, A.K. (2015). Floral nectary anatomy and ultrastructure in mycoheterotrophic plant, *Epipogium aphyllum* Sw. (Orchidaceae). *The Scientific World Journal*, **2015**: 201702. doi:10.1155/2015/201702.

Taylor, L. & Roberts, D.L. (2011). Biological flora of the British Isles: *Epipogium aphyllum* Sw. *Journal of Ecology*, **99**: 878–890.

Turner Ettlinger, D.M. (1998). A new variety of *Ophrys apifera* Hudson (Orchidaceae). *Watsonia*, **22**: 105–107.

Wróblewska, A., Szczepaniak, L., Bajguz, A., Jędrzejczyk, I., Tałałaj, I., Ostrowiecka, B., Brzosko, E., Jermakowicz, E. & Mirski, P. (2019). Deceptive strategy in *Dactylorhiza* orchids: multidirectional evolution of floral chemistry. *Annals of Botany*, **123**: 1005–1016.

Young, D.P. (1952). Studies in the British *Epipactis*. *Watsonia*, **2**: 253–276.

Sources of further information

BOOKS

Brooke, J. (1950). ***The Wild Orchids of Britain.*** The Bodley Head.

Claessens, J. & Kleynen, J. (2011). ***The flower of the European orchid – form and function.*** Self-published.

[*An amazing account of the biology, and especially pollination, of orchids, with incredible photos.*]

Foley, M. & Clarke, S. (2005). ***Orchids of the British Isles.*** The Griffin Press.

Harrap, A. & Harrap, S. (2009). ***Orchids of Britain and Ireland – A Field and Site Guide.*** Bloomsbury Publishing.

Harrap, S. (2016). ***A Pocket Guide to the Orchids of Britain and Ireland.*** Bloomsbury Publishing.

Kuhn, R., Pedersen, H. & Cribb, P. (2019). ***Field Guide to the Orchids of Europe and the Mediterranean.*** Royal Botanic Gardens, Kew.

[*The most recent pan-European guide, illustrated with many photos to show variation within the species.*]

Lang, D. (2004). ***Britain's Orchids.*** WILD*Guides*.

Summerhayes, V.S. 1968 (2009). ***Wild Orchids of Britain.*** HarperCollins.

Turner Ettlinger, D.M. (1997). ***Notes on British and Irish Orchids.*** Rayment Printers.

Turner Ettlinger, D.M. (1998). ***Illustrations of British and Irish Orchids.*** Rayment Printers.

Additionally, there are many local orchid books covering specific counties or regions that can be particularly useful when planning trips. Similarly, local floras can often provide a valuable resource of detailed information about the occurrence of orchids within a given county.

ORGANIZATIONS AND SOCIETIES

Botanical Society of British and Ireland (BSBI) **bsbi.org**

The 'official' and oldest recording organization for botany, with a network of county recorders and referees feeding information into an invaluable database on which conservation decisions can be based. The BSBI produces two publications triannually – the ***New Journal of Botany*** and ***BSBI News*** – and also holds an annual exhibition meeting and arranges field trips and courses on plant identification.

Hardy Orchid Society **hardyorchidsociety.org.uk**

Plantlife **plantlife.org.uk**

Index

This index includes the English and *scientific* (in *italics*) names of all the orchids mentioned in this book.

The 'types' of orchid are in UPPER CASE; all regularly occurring species are in **bold text** (scientific names in ***bold italics***); former names are shown in *red italics*; introduced species in regular black text. English names of subspecies or varieties are indicated using single quotes.

Bold black figures highlight the main species accounts and introductions to the 'types' of orchid.
Italicized figures are used for other images/illustrations (*e.g.* comparative plates).
Brown figures indicate the section *Orchids in their habitats* (*page 40*).
Green figures refer to the *Guide to British and Irish orchids in leaf when mature* (*page 54*).
Maroon figures relate to hybrids (**bold** if illustrated).
Regular black text indicates where other useful information may be found.